D1807410

Human Rights Law and Regulating Freedom of Expression in New Media

The Nordic countries are well known globally for their high human rights standards and, at the same time, high degree of internet freedom. This edited collection reveals how the Nordic countries have succeeded in the task of protecting freedom of expression in the new media. It contains an overview of public policy choices and best practices of domestic online companies, which have the aspiration of finding global acceptance.

Reviewing the topic of freedom of expression in new media within Nordic and Baltic countries, this book incorporates both general themes and interesting country-specific themes that will provide wider knowledge on the development of freedom of expression and media law in the online media era. A comprehensive analysis of regulation of online media, both at the level of legislation and application of law in courts and other authorities, are included. This book will contribute to the ongoing discussion as to whether there is a need to modify prevailing interpretation of freedom of expression.

Human Rights Law and Regulating Freedom of Expression in New Media focuses on the multi-layered and complicated relationship between internet and human rights law. It contributes to the ongoing discussion regarding the protection of freedom of expression on the internet in the context of various doctrines of constitutional law, including the proliferation of constitutional adjudication. It will be of interest to researchers, academics, policymakers, and students in the fields of human rights law, internet law, political science, sociology, cultural studies, media and communications studies and technology.

Mart Susi is Professor of Human Rights Law and Head of Legal Studies at Tallinn University. He has been leading several international research and development projects (EU Commission-funded Horizon 2020 project "Hurmur" and Nordic Council of Ministers-funded project "Law and Media Network"). He has authored several monographs and more than 50 articles. Currently, he is editing several books on the topics of new media, and human rights and the digital society. Susi has recently introduced and is developing the concept of the Internet Balancing Formula.

Jukka Viljanen is Professor of Public Law, Adjunct Professor of Human Rights Law and University Lecturer at the University of Tampere. He is an author of several international articles on the European Court of Human Rights and its doctrines. Viljanen has been leading several important research projects, e.g. ALL-YOUTH (Strategic Research Council, 2018–2020), Law and Media (Finnish sub-group) (Nordplus, 2015–2017), evaluation of Finnish Human Rights National Action Plan (Ministry of Justice, 2013–2014) and Finnish environmental constitutional right (Ministry of Environment, 2014).

Eiríkur Jónsson graduated as Cand. Juris from the University of Iceland (Faculty of Law) in 2002, LL.M. from Harvard Law School in 2006 and Ph.D. from the University of Iceland in 2011. Among other positions he has served as the chairman of the Icelandic Media Commission, chairman of the Icelandic Appeals Committee of Consumer Affairs, appointed judge at the District Court of Reykjavík and as an alternate judge at the Supreme Court of Iceland. He has written several books on Icelandic law, among other things on media law.

Artūrs Kučs is a judge of the Constitutional Court of Latvia and professor of the Faculty of Law of the University of Latvia. His research areas include comparative human rights law and media law, especially analysis on privacy, defamation and hate speech laws. Artūrs Kučs has been Fulbright Visiting Scholar at the University of Connecticut and DAAD Visiting Scholar at Max Planck Institute for Comparative Public Law and International Law in Heidelberg.

Routledge Research in Human Rights Law

https://www.routledge.com/Routledge-Research-in-Human-Rights-Law/book-series/HUMRIGHTSLAW

Human Rights Law and Regulating Freedom of Expression in New Media

Lessons from Nordic Approaches

Edited by
Mart Susi, Jukka Viljanen,
Eiríkur Jónsson, and Artūrs Kučs

Routledge
Taylor & Francis Group

LONDON AND NEW YORK

First published 2018
by Routledge
2 Park Square, Milton Park, Abingdon, Oxon OX14 4RN

and by Routledge
711 Third Avenue, New York, NY 10017

*Routledge is an imprint of the Taylor & Francis Group, an informa
business*

© 2018 selection and editorial matter, Mart Susi, Jukka Viljanen, Eiríkur
Jónsson and Artūrs Kučs; individual chapters, the contributors

The right of Mart Susi, Jukka Viljanen, Eiríkur Jónsson and Artūrs Kučs
to be identified as the authors of the editorial material, and of the authors
for their individual chapters, has been asserted in accordance with
sections 77 and 78 of the Copyright, Designs and Patents Act 1988.

All rights reserved. No part of this book may be reprinted or reproduced
or utilised in any form or by any electronic, mechanical, or other means,
now known or hereafter invented, including photocopying and recording,
or in any information storage or retrieval system, without permission in
writing from the publishers.

Trademark notice: Product or corporate names may be trademarks
or registered trademarks, and are used only for identification and
explanation without intent to infringe.

British Library Cataloguing-in-Publication Data
A catalogue record for this book is available from the British Library

Library of Congress Cataloging-in-Publication Data
Names: Susi, Mart, 1965–, author.
Title: Human rights law and regulating freedom of expression in new
media: lessons from Nordic approaches / edited by Mart Susi,
Jukka Viljanen, Eiríkur Jónsson and Artūrs Kučs.
Description: New York, NY: Routledge, 2018. | Series: Routledge
research in human rights law | Includes bibliographical references and
index.
Identifiers: LCCN 2017059110
Subjects: LCSH: Mass media—Law and legislation—Europe. | Digital
media—Law and legislation—Europe. | Online journalism—Law
and legislation—Europe. | Human rights—Europe | Freedom of
expression—Europe.
Classification: LCC KJC6947.H86 2018 | DDC 342.4808/53—dc23
LC record available at https://lccn.loc.gov/2017059110

ISBN: 978-1-138-49789-4 (hbk)
ISBN: 978-1-351-01759-6 (ebk)

Typeset in Galliard
by codeMantra

Contents

Notes on contributors

Lolita Bērziņa Researcher in Latvian NGO "Baltic Human Rights Society".

Linda Bīriņa Attorney at law and senior associate at law firm "COBALT".

Victoria Enkvist Researcher at the faculty of Law at Uppsala University.

Mikko Hoikka CEO of Finnish Periodical Publishers' Association.

Laura Jambuševa Legal adviser of the Legal bureau of the Parliament of the Republic of Latvia.

Eiríkur Jónsson Professor and Vice Dean of the Faculty of Law at the University of Iceland.

Artūrs Kučs Judge at the Constitutional Court of Latvia and professor of the Faculty of Law of the University of Latvia.

Ellen Lexerød Hovlid Associate Professor at Volda University College, the Faculty of Media and Journalism.

Vygantė Milašiūtė Associate Professor at Vilnius University.

Riku Neuvonen Adjunct Professor of Media Law at University of Tampere.

Tiina Pajuste Lecturer at Tallinn University.

Sten Schaumburg-Müller Professor at the Law Department, University of Southern Denmark.

Sverker Scheutz Senior lecturer in Public Law at Uppsala University.

Robert Spano Judge and President of the 2nd Section of the European Court of Human Rights.

Mart Susi Professor of Human Rights Law at Tallinn University.

Rain Veetõusme PhD Candidate at Tallinn University.

Jukka Viljanen Professor of Public Law at University of Tampere.

1 Introduction

Mart Susi, Jukka Viljanen, Eiríkur Jónsson,
and Artūrs Kučs

In the new media landscape, the prevailing doctrines concerning freedom of expression are under review. Contemporary democratic societies are facing an unprecedented challenge to balance freedom of expression against the right to privacy in the new media environment. The rapid development of the internet has led the international legal communities, media enterprises and the civil society to question the adequacy of traditional methods of regulating the freedom of speech vis-à-vis the right to privacy. A new paradigm is emerging, whereby the task of achieving effective realisation of both these significant rights is moving away from the vertical power structures towards horizontal accountability of media enterprises in relation to new media users.

In the aftermath of the European Court of Human Rights' (ECtHR) Grand Chamber judgment in *Delfi AS v. Estonia* (16 June 2015),[1] there has been a strong need for a scholarly contribution to the discussion about the new media. The Nordic Council provided NORDPLUS funding for our Law and Media network at just the right moment. Our network was founded as a co-operation between Tallinn University (Estonia), University of Iceland, University of Latvia and University of Tampere (Finland). Nordic and Baltic countries are the avant-garde of new media applications. In addition, they are well-known for their good records on freedom of expression. Four Nordic states (Norway, Sweden, Finland and Denmark) are topping the recent World Press Freedom Index according to Reporters Without Borders.[2]

This book shows Nordic and Baltic practices in the new media era and the articles that follow combine the different levels of protection, national, regional and global, under the same theme. The European Convention on Human Rights (ECHR) is often described by the Strasbourg Court as a "living instrument", which means that it should be interpreted in light of present day conditions. The book illustrates the similarities, but also the divergence of practices. The national traditions are embedded in the legal culture and this is also relevant in the field of media. Celebrating 250 years of freedom of the press in Sweden and

---

1 *Delfi AS v. Estonia*, Grand Chamber, 64569/09, 16.6.2015.
2 Reporters without borders. World Press Freedom Index https://rsf.org/en/ranking

Finland (2 December 1766) perfectly demonstrates the long Nordic and Baltic tradition.

The ECtHR itself acknowledged both the benefits and dangers of the internet. The Court noted at the outset that user-generated expressive activity on the internet provides an unprecedented platform for the exercise of freedom of expression. Dangers are related to the dissemination of "defamatory and other types of clearly unlawful speech, including hate speech and speech inciting violence". This might happen in a manner like "never before, worldwide, in a matter of seconds, and sometimes remain persistently available online".

This book contributes to the existing debate and reflects on the dialogue between national courts and legislators and the ECtHR in Strasbourg. It also answers questions that are related to cross-fertilisation. New practices are emerging in a dynamic setting, often via self-regulation, but new practical changes that happen in the new media also require vigilance at all levels. As the Strasbourg Court often mentions, national courts and authorities have a certain margin of appreciation, but it goes hand in hand with European supervision, embracing both the legislation and the decisions applying it, even those given by an independent court. The Court is, therefore, empowered to give the final ruling on whether a "restriction" is reconcilable with freedom of expression as protected by Article 10 of the ECHR. However, the introduction of a "strong reasons" approach means that if national courts have found a fair balance in conformity with the criteria laid down in the Strasbourg case law, there must be strong reasons for the Court to substitute its own view for that of the domestic courts.

In the opening article, Judge Robert Spano (ECtHR) discusses *Intermediary liability for online user comments under the European Convention on Human Rights*. According to his interpretation, the Court has chosen a middle ground between two opposing viewpoints on the regulation of the internet: one advocating for an environment free from regulation of online conduct and the other campaigning for a regulated internet, where the same legal principles apply both online and offline. It seems that dramatic forecasts made by critical scholars have not revolutionised the practice after the *Delfi* judgment. However, it is clear from the concluding article by Artūrs Kučs and Jukka Viljanen, contributing to the doctrinal discussion between human rights supervisory bodies, what further guidance from the Strasbourg Court would be required. They conclude that the Court should address concepts of media neutrality, online media as a democratic platform, expansion of the definition of journalists, the chilling effect and censorship in new media.

In Chapters 3–10 there is provided in-depth country by country analysis on the freedom of expression in Nordic and Baltic countries and in the specific context of new media. These chapters are written by experts of the national freedom of expression doctrines. Chapters introduce media landscape, institutional setting, relevant national legislation, case-law and practices including the dialogue with the European Court of Human Rights. In their article, Mart Susi and Eiríkur Jónsson conclude that the Nordic countries exhibit restraint in incorporating the new principle of horizontal governance and the authority of private online portals to assess user content into national human rights regulation.

In sum, several difficult questions are raised in the book: How does the chancing concept of a journalist in the new media influence the outcome of the protection? Why does the concept of horizontal governance remain in a state of contestation and is not yet a generally accepted principle in the European and global human rights landscape?

The underlying message of this book is that developing freedom of expression doctrines should be in accordance with the 2016 United Nations Human Rights Council resolution on the promotion, protection and enjoyment of human rights on the internet,[3] which affirms that "the same rights that people have offline must also be protected online".

---

3 A/HRC/32/L 20 The promotion, protection and enjoyment of human rights on the Internet, HRC Adopted as orally revised 1.7.2016.

2 Intermediary liability for online user comments under the European Convention on Human Rights

Robert Spano[1*]

Preliminary remarks

The Internet has transformed modern society, including the law. In almost all fields of law the Internet's influence on the development of existing principles and rules is currently being analysed and examined, including in the field of human rights law. Due to the advent of the Internet, numerous conceptual and practical problems have arisen in connection with the right to privacy, freedom of expression and the right to property. In this article,[2] I will discuss the recent case-law of the European Court of Human Rights (hereinafter 'the Court' or 'the Strasbourg Court') dealing with freedom of expression when contracting States are faced with questions relating to the imposition of liability for unlawful[3] user comments which are posted anonymously online or under a pseudonym. The Strasbourg Court has recently delivered judgments in two cases, including in a Grand Chamber case, where the Court, for the first time, has had

---

1[*] Judge and President of Section, European Court of Human Rights (ECtHR).

2 This book chapter is based an article published by the author in the *Human Rights Law Review*, 2017, Vol 17, No 4, 665–679. The article was in part based on a series of five public lectures I have recently given on the case-law of the ECtHR dealing with the Internet and the right to privacy and freedom of expression under Articles 8 and 10 of the European Convention on Human Rights respectively (ECHR). The first lecture was in Tallinn, Estonia, as part of the seminar: 'Human Rights in Cyberspace – Scoping, Protecting, Regulating International Human Rights Law and Tackling Future Aspects of Cyber Norms', 1–2 October 2015. I then took part in a panel discussion during a conference organised by the Council of Europe on 13–14 October 2015 in Strasbourg, entitled: 'Freedom of Expression: Still A Precondition for Democracy?' Thereafter I discussed the topic during a seminar organised by the George C. Marshall European Center for Security Studies as part of the 'Program on Cyber Studies' in Garmisch Partenkirchen, Germany, on 2–17 December 2015. Subsequently I gave a lecture on 18 January 2016 in the Human Rights Building in Strasbourg, entitled: 'The Internet and the ECHR – A Paradigm Shift?' Finally, I took part in a high-level panel discussion during a conference organised by the Council of Europe on 9 September 2016 in Strasbourg, entitled: 'Freedom of Expression – A Constant Factor for Democratic Security in Europe'. The analysis presented in this article reflects my personal viewpoint and should not in any way be understood as reflecting the views of the ECtHR or other sitting judges.

3 'Unlawful' comments are in this context those that are defamatory or that constitute hate speech or speech that incites violence.

to formulate the general principles to be applied when an assessment is made of the latitude that contracting States have under Article 10 of the European Convention on Human Rights (hereinafter 'the Convention') to impose liability on online intermediaries for unlawful comments posted on their websites by anonymous users.

The 'unprecedented' nature of the Internet – opposing viewpoints on its regulation

It is axiomatic that the Internet has had a dramatic impact on the form, scope, and patterns of human communications. Unlimited and rapid access to vast amounts of information, whether through smartphones, tablets or other Internet communication devices, has reshaped modern societies around the world. It is thus not surprising that the Strasbourg Court has held that 'user-generated expressive activity on the Internet provides an unprecedented platform for the exercise of freedom of expression'.[4] The Court has, however, been mindful that such positive developments may harbour some negative side effects. Hence, the Court has declared that alongside the Internet's benefits

> certain dangers may also arise. Defamatory and other types of clearly unlawful speech, including hate speech and speech inciting violence, can be disseminated like never before, worldwide, in a matter of seconds, and sometimes remain persistently available online.[5]

In other words, difficult tensions arise on the Internet between freedom of expression on the one hand, and the right to privacy and personality rights on the other.

There are two diametrically opposing views within the ongoing debate on whether and to what extent the Internet should be regulated. On the one hand, it has been argued that the *sui generis* nature of the Internet and its impact on human relations require that governments (and even private stakeholders such as large online social media and communication networks)[6] refrain from imposing regulatory measures of any kind. The Internet should be a wholly free environment where users are granted unlimited discretion. On the other hand,

---

4 *Delfi AS v Estonia*, Application No. 64569/09, Merits and Just Satisfaction, 16 June 2015 at para 110.
5 Ibid.
6 For example, the principle of net neutrality is directed first and foremost at Internet service providers and provides that as a general rule they should 'treat Internet traffic equally and without discrimination on the basis of sender, receiver, content, application, service or device': see Article 2.2.3 of *Recommendation CM/REC(2016)5 of the Committee of Ministers of the Council of Europe to member States on Internet freedom*, adopted on 13 April 2016 at the 1253rd meeting of the Ministers' Deputies. On net neutrality, see also the judgment of the United States Circuit Court of Appeals for the District of Columbia Circuit, 14 June 2016, in case no. 15-1063, *United States Telecom Association et al. v Federal Communications Commission and United States of America*.

a contrary viewpoint has been elaborated. Under this view, the same legal principles should apply offline and online. Although the Internet may require the reformulation and adaptation of some classical legal principles, due to its special nature and impact, the Internet cannot become a legal vacuum where no rules exist.

As I will discuss below, the Strasbourg Court's first judgments in this field suggest that the Court is attempting to find a middle ground between these opposing viewpoints so as to secure the beneficial effects of the Internet, in particular as regards freedom of expression, while at the same time safeguarding other fundamental rights, in particular the right to reputation and the right to privacy.

Differing forms of liability for anonymous and defamatory comments on the Internet

The advent of Web 2.0 technologies and applications have enabled everyday Internet users, who were previously mere consumers of online content, to publish their own content on various websites, such as blogs, consumer-evaluation platforms (such as Amazon, eBay, and TripAdvisor), news websites (through reader comments), social networking services (such as Facebook, Twitter, and LinkedIn), media-sharing websites (such as Instagram and YouTube), and collaborative-writing projects (such as Wikipedia).[7]

It is to be expected, then, that online user contributions may sometimes take the form of content that is unlawful. One of the most complex and intriguing legal questions in this context is who should be liable for defamatory statements made online by anonymous (or pseudonymous) users. Recently, it has convincingly been argued by Professors Perry and Zarsky that the legal response to online anonymous defamation should be viewed and analysed as a combination of two components. The first is the ability (or inability) to bring an action against the content provider, namely the platform displaying the unlawful statement. Such an action may require modification of substantive law through the recognition of some sort of indirect liability. The second component is the ability (or inability) to bring an action against the speaker, that is, the anonymous user. Such an action does not usually require the modification of substantive defamation law, but does entail an adaptation of procedural law such as to establish a de-anonymisation process.[8]

Because this framework provides two potential defendants, each of whom can be either liable or non-liable, there seems at first glance, according to Professors Perry and Zarsky, to be four possible liability regimes. In the first, neither the

---

7 Perry, R. and Zarsky, T., 'Who Should be Liable for Online Anonymous Defamation?' (2015) 82 *University of Chicago Law Review Dialogue* at 162. See also by the same authors, 'Liability for Online Anonymous Speech: Comparative and Economic Analyses' (2014) 5 *Journal of European Tort Law* at 205.

8 Perry, R. and Zarsky, T. (2015), supra n 6 at 162–163.

speaker nor the content provider is liable. This option does not seem to exist in any jurisdiction, and for good reason: forgoing liability undermines the delicate balance that has developed in defamation law between the right to reputation and freedom of speech. In the second, only the speaker is liable (*exclusive direct liability*). This is in substance the framework adopted in the United States under Section 230 of the Communications Decency Act of 1996. In the third, only the content provider is liable (*exclusive indirect liability*),[9] or, in the fourth, both may be liable. The latter framework has a basis in the EU E-Commerce Directive 2000/31/EC.[10]

Professors Perry and Zarsky reject the above-mentioned options. In their view, the most efficient solution to the problem of anonymous unlawful speech online lies beyond these four classical categories and involves an innovative combination of direct and indirect liability. In a legal regime they call it *residual indirect liability*,[11] the speaker is exclusively liable, but where he or she is not reasonably reachable, the content provider becomes liable. They observe that a version of this framework has been adopted in the Defamation Act 2013 in the United Kingdom.[12]

It is important to stress at the outset that Article 10 of the Convention does not, as such, mandate any particular form of intermediary liability. However, the question of whether States are under a positive obligation to have such a regime in place to safeguard rights under Article 8 of the Convention has not, as yet, been determined by the Strasbourg Court.[13] Like other Convention provisions,

---

9 See Perry, R. and Zarsky, T. (2015), supra n 6 at 167, which notes the existence of such a system in Israel.

10 Directive 2001/29/EC of the European Parliament and of the Council of 22 May 2001 on the harmonisation of certain aspects of copyright and related rights in the information society, OJ L 167, 22.06.2001, pp. 10–19. See also *Delfi AS*, supra n 3 at paras 50–57.

11 Perry, R. and Zarsky, T. (2015), supra n 6 at 172–175.

12 Ibid. at 172–173.

13 See, however, the case of *K.U. v Finland*, Application No. 2872/02, Merits and Just Satisfaction, 2 December 2008 at para 49, concerning an offence of 'malicious misrepresentation' of a sexual nature against a minor (an advertisement which was characterised as being particularly reprehensible) where the Court found that

> [a]lthough freedom of expression and confidentiality of communications are primary considerations and users of telecommunications and Internet services must have a guarantee that their own privacy and freedom of expression will be respected, such guarantee cannot be absolute and must yield on occasion to other legitimate imperatives, such as the prevention of disorder or crime or the protection of the rights and freedoms of others. As noted in *Delfi AS*, supra n 3 at para 149, the Court in *K.U. v Finland* rejected the Government's argument that the applicant had had the possibility of obtaining damages from the service provider, finding that this was not sufficient in the circumstances of the case, having regard to both the public interest and the protection of the interests of victims of crime. It held that there had to be a remedy enabling the actual offender to be identified and brought to justice, whereas at the relevant time the regulatory framework of the respondent State had not provided for the possibility of ordering the Internet service provider to divulge the information required for that purpose (ibid., paras 47 and 49). Although *K.U. v Finland* concerned a criminal breach entailing a more sweeping intrusion into the victim's private

Article 10 only provides for *minimum rights* in the field of freedom of expression, cf. Article 53 of the Convention. However, in leaving open the choice of different potential liability regimes, Article 10 sets certain boundaries so as to safeguard against excessive restrictions on speech rights to an extent not corresponding to a pressing social need in a democratic society.[14] On this basis, it is useful to analyse the Court's existing case-law to determine whether the Court has formulated certain general principles which contracting States are required to bear in mind when choosing between the different potential liability regimes aimed at regulating unlawful user content online.

The case-law of the European Court of Human Rights

The Grand Chamber judgment in Delfi AS v Estonia

In *Delfi AS v Estonia*, the online intermediary had published an article about a ferry company on its webpage, discussing a particular decision taken by the company to change its ferry routes, which had delayed the construction of cheaper and faster connections to certain islands. Below the article, many offensive and threatening comments were left, directed at the ferry operator and its owner. About six weeks after their publication, *Delfi AS* removed the offensive comments immediately at the request of the ferry company owner's lawyers.

The domestic courts considered the comments to be defamatory, found *Delfi AS* to be responsible for them and awarded the owner of the ferry company 5,000 kroons in damages (around 320 euros). An appeal by *Delfi AS* was dismissed by Estonia's Supreme Court, which rejected the portal's argument that, under the EU E-Commerce Directive 2000/31/EC, its role as an information society service provider or storage host was merely technical, passive and neutral, finding that the portal exercised control over the publication of comments. It did recognise that there was a difference between a portal operator and a traditional publisher of printed media, pointing out that the former could not reasonably be required to edit comments before publishing them in the same manner as the latter. However, both had an economic interest in the publication of comments and should therefore both be considered 'publishers/disclosers'.[15] The Supreme Court therefore held *Delfi AS* liable under the relevant domestic law, finding that the portal had not only failed to prevent the publication of comments which degraded human dignity, contained threats and were thus clearly unlawful, but also failed to remove the comments from its portal on its own initiative.

Delfi AS complained before the Strasbourg Court that the Estonian civil courts' finding of liability against it in respect of comments written by its readers constituted a violation of Article 10 (freedom of expression).

---

life than the facts presented by *Delfi AS*, the requirement to balance the value of anonymity on the Internet against other Convention rights and interests persists (ibid., para 149).

14 As provided for by Article 10(2) of the Convention.

15 *Delfi AS*, supra n 3 at para 31.

In its Chamber judgment, the Court held, unanimously, that there had been no violation of Article 10, finding that the imposition of liability by the Estonian courts had been a justified and proportionate restriction on the portal's right to freedom of expression. *Delfi AS*'s request for the case to be referred to the Grand Chamber in accordance with Article 43 of the Convention was accepted.

In the Grand Chamber judgment, an overwhelming majority of judges (15 out of 17) first noted the conflicting realities between the benefits of the Internet, notably the unprecedented platform it provides for freedom of expression, and its dangers, namely the possibility of hate speech and speech inciting violence being disseminated worldwide in a matter of seconds and sometimes remaining available online indefinitely, in violation of personality rights.[16] As this was the first case in which the Court had been called upon to examine such a complaint in an evolving field of technological innovation, it decided to narrow the scope of its inquiry to that concerning both the nature of the applicant company as well as of the speech in question.[17]

As concerning the nature of *Delfi AS*, the Grand Chamber saw no reason to call into question the distinction made by the Supreme Court between a portal operator and a traditional publisher of printed media and considered that their duties and responsibilities might differ. Next, the Grand Chamber noted the Supreme Court's characterisation of the comments posted on *Delfi AS*'s portal as unlawful. Since this assessment was based on the fact that the comments were tantamount to hate speech and incitement to violence, the remarks, established as manifestly unlawful, did not require any linguistic or legal analysis.[18] Consequently, the case concerned the duties and responsibilities under Article 10, § 2 of the Convention of Internet news portals providing, on a commercial basis, a platform for user-generated comments on previously published content where some users, whether identified or anonymous, engage in clearly unlawful speech, which infringes the personality rights of others and amounts to hate speech and incitement to violence against them. The case did not, on the other hand, concern:

> other fora on the Internet where third-party comments could be disseminated, for example an Internet discussion forum or a bulletin board where users can freely set out their ideas on any topics without the discussion being channelled by any input from the forum's manager; or a social media platform where the platform provider does not offer any content and where the content provider might be a private person running the website or a blog as a hobby.[19]

16 Ibid. at para 110.
17 Ibid. at paras 112–117.
18 Ibid. at para 117.
19 Ibid. at para 116.

It was not in dispute that the national courts' decisions had constituted an interference with *Delfi AS*'s right to freedom of expression and that that restriction had pursued the legitimate aim of protecting the reputation and rights of others.

The parties' opinions differed, however, as regards the law to be applied. *Delfi AS* argued in particular that the national courts had erred in applying the general provisions of the domestic law as they should have relied upon the domestic and European legislation on Internet service providers. Notably, the domestic courts, in interpreting and applying the relevant provisions of the domestic law, considered that *Delfi AS* was a 'publisher/discloser'[20] and could be held liable for the uploading of clearly unlawful comments on its news portal. The domestic courts chose to apply those norms, having found that the special regulation contained in the Information Society Services Act transposing the EU E-Commerce Directive 2000/31/EC into Estonian law had not applied to *Delfi AS*'s case since the Directive related to activities of a merely technical, automatic, and passive nature, unlike *Delfi AS*'s activities, which went beyond merely providing an intermediary service.[21]

However, the Grand Chamber found that it was for the national courts to resolve issues of interpretation and application of domestic law. Thus, it did not address the issue under EU law and limited itself to the question of whether the Supreme Court's application of the domestic law to *Delfi AS*'s situation had been foreseeable. Indeed, as a professional publisher running one of the largest Internet news portals in Estonia for an economic purpose, *Delfi AS* should have been familiar with the relevant legislation and case-law, and could also have sought legal advice on the matter. Moreover, public concern had already been expressed in respect of comments posted on the portal, prior to the publication of the comments in question, and the Minister of Justice had made it clear that the victims of insults could bring a suit against *Delfi AS* and claim damages.[22] Thus, the Grand Chamber considered that *Delfi AS* had been in a position to assess the risks related to its activities, therefore concluding that the interference with *Delfi AS*'s freedom of expression had been 'prescribed by law'.[23]

The Grand Chamber considered that the offensive comments posted on *Delfi AS*'s news portal, amounting to hate speech or incitement to violence, did not enjoy the protection of Article 10 and thus the freedom of expression of the authors of the comments was not at issue. The question before the Grand Chamber was rather whether the national courts' decisions, holding *Delfi AS* liable for comments posted by third parties, were in breach of its freedom to impart information as guaranteed by Article 10 of the Convention.

The Grand Chamber went on to examine whether that finding of liability by the domestic courts, notably the Supreme Court, had been based on relevant and sufficient grounds. The Grand Chamber agreed with the Chamber's

---

20 Ibid. at para 31.
21 Ibid. at para 128.
22 Ibid. at para 129.
23 Ibid. at para 129.

assessment of the question which had identified four key aspects: the context of the comments; the liability of the actual authors of the comments as an alternative to *Delfi AS* being held liable; the steps taken by *Delfi AS* to prevent or remove the defamatory comments; and the consequences of the proceedings before the national courts for *Delfi AS*.

First, as regards the context, the Grand Chamber attached particular weight to the extreme nature of the comments and the fact that *Delfi AS* was a professionally managed Internet news portal run on a commercial basis which sought to attract a large number of comments on news articles published by it.[24] Moreover, as the Supreme Court had pointed out, *Delfi AS* had an economic interest in the posting of the comments. The actual authors of the comments could not modify or delete their comments once they were posted. The Grand Chamber therefore agreed with the Chamber and the Supreme Court that, although *Delfi AS* had not been the actual writer of the comments, that did not mean that it had no control over the comment environment, and its involvement in making the comments on its news articles public had gone beyond that of a passive, purely technical service provider.[25]

Second, *Delfi AS* had not ensured a realistic prospect of the authors of the comments being held liable, since it allowed readers to make comments without registering their names, and the measures to establish the identity of the authors were uncertain.[26] Nor had *Delfi AS* put in place any instruments to identify the authors of the comments in order to provide to the victims of hate speech the possibility of bringing a claim.

Third, the steps taken by *Delfi AS* to prevent or remove without delay the defamatory comments once published had been insufficient. *Delfi AS* did have certain mechanisms for filtering hate speech or speech inciting violence, namely a disclaimer (stating that authors of comments were liable for their content, and that threatening or insulting comments were not allowed), an automatic system of deletion of comments containing a series of vulgar words and a notice-and-take-down system (whereby users could notify the portal's administrators about offensive comments by clicking a single button). Nevertheless, both the automatic word-based filter and the notice-and-take-down system had failed to filter out the manifest expressions of hatred and blatant threats directed at the owner of the ferry company by *Delfi AS*'s readers, thereby limiting the portal's ability to remove offending comments in good time. As a consequence, the comments had remained online for six weeks. The Grand Chamber considered that it was not disproportionate for *Delfi AS* to have been obliged to remove from its website, without delay, clearly unlawful comments, even without notice from the alleged victims or from third parties whose ability to monitor the Internet was obviously more limited than that of a large commercial Internet news portal such as *Delfi AS*.[27]

24 Ibid. at para 144.
25 Ibid. at para 146.
26 Ibid. at para 151.
27 Ibid. at para 158.

Finally, the Grand Chamber agreed with the Chamber that the consequences of *Delfi AS* having been held liable were small. The 320 euro fine was by no means excessive for one of the largest Internet portals in Estonia, and its popularity with those posting comments had not been affected in any way; the number of comments posted had, in fact, increased.[28]

Based on a concrete assessment of the above aspects and taking into account the reasoning of the Supreme Court in the present case, the Grand Chamber found that the Estonian courts' finding of liability in respect to *Delfi AS* had been a justified and proportionate restriction on the portal's freedom of expression. Accordingly, there had been no violation of Article 10 of the Convention.

The Chamber judgment in Magyar T.E. & Index.hu Zrt v Hungary

In the case of *Magyar T.E. and Index.hu Zrt v Hungary*,[29] the applicants 'MTE' and 'Index', had allowed users to comment on publications appearing on their portals. MTE published an opinion criticising the business practice of two real estate websites, while Index subsequently wrote about the opinion, publishing the full text on its website. The opinion attracted offensive and vulgar comments on both applicants' portals.

The company operating the real estate websites brought a civil action against the applicants, complaining that the opinion and subsequent comments had damaged its reputation. On learning of the court action, the applicants immediately removed the comments in question. In their counterclaims they argued that, as intermediary publishers, they were not liable for user comments, and that, in any event, their criticism was justified given the numerous consumer complaints and proceedings which had been brought against the real estate websites' business practices.

The national courts subsequently found that the comments had gone beyond the acceptable limits of freedom of expression, stressing that the applicants, by enabling readers to make comments on their websites, had assumed liability for readers' injurious or unlawful comments.[30] The *Kúria* (the highest judicial body in Hungary) thus imposed 75,000 Hungarian forints (approximately 250 euros) on each applicant in costs. The applicants' constitutional complaint was dismissed.

Relying on Article 10, the applicants complained about the Hungarian courts' rulings against them, which they claimed had effectively obliged them to moderate the contents of comments made by readers on their websites, arguing that that had gone against the very essence of free expression on the Internet.

It was not in dispute between the parties that the Hungarian courts' rulings had interfered with the applicants' freedom of expression and the Court saw

---

28 Ibid. at para 161.
29 *Magyar T.E. and Index.hu Zrt v Hungary*, Application No. 22947/13, Merits, 2 February 2016.
30 Ibid. at para 22.

no reason to hold otherwise. Nonetheless, the Court was satisfied that a media publisher running a large Internet news portal for an economic purpose and a self-regulatory body of Internet content providers would have been in a position to assess the risks related to their activities and should have been able to foresee that they could be held liable under domestic law for the unlawful comments of third parties. The Court therefore found that the interference at issue had been 'prescribed by law' and accepted that that interference had pursued the legitimate aim of protecting the rights of others.[31]

However, the Court considered that the Hungarian courts had not carried out a proper balancing exercise between the competing rights involved, namely between the applicants' right to freedom of expression and the right of the company operating the real estate websites to respect in terms of its commercial reputation. Notably, the Hungarian authorities accepted at face value that the comments had been unlawful as being injurious to the latter company's reputation.[32] The Court reiterated that

> in cases where third-party user comments take the form of hate speech and direct threats to the physical integrity of individuals, the rights and interests of others and of the society as a whole might entitle Contracting States to impose liability on Internet news portals if they failed to take measures to remove clearly unlawful comments without delay, even without notice from the alleged victim or from third parties.[33]

For those reasons in particular, in *Delfi AS*, the Court had held that, in view of the 'duties and responsibilities' of a large, professionally managed Internet news portal, the finding of liability of such portals for the comments of users who engage in clearly unlawful speech which infringes the personality rights of others and amounts to hate speech and incitement to violence against them, is not contrary to the Convention.[34]

The impugned comments in *Magyar* were, however, devoid of the pivotal elements of hate speech and incitement to violence. Although offensive and vulgar, the comments had not constituted clearly unlawful speech. Moreover, while Index is the owner of a large media outlet which must be regarded as having economic interests, MTE is a non-profit, self-regulatory association of Internet service providers, with no such known interests.

The Court applied the relevant criteria developed in its established case-law for the assessment of the proportionality of the interference in situations not involving hate speech or calls to violence. Namely, it considered: the context and content of the comments; the liability of the authors of the comments; the steps

---

31 Ibid. at paras 51–52.
32 Ibid. at para 65.
33 Ibid. at para 91.
34 *Delfi AS*, supra n 3 at para 162.

taken by the applicants; the conduct of the injured party; and the consequences of the comments.[35]

First, as regards the context and contents of the comments, the Court noted that the comments concerned a matter of public interest (a misleading business practice), which had already generated numerous complaints to the consumer protection services and had prompted various procedures against the company concerned. The content, although offensive and even outright vulgar, was not a defamatory factual assertion but a value judgement or opinion protected under Article 10 of the Convention, and the expressions used were common in communications on many Internet portals.[36]

Second, the Court noted that the national courts had found against the applicants because they had enabled readers to make comments on their websites.[37] At no point did the authorities weigh up the liability of the actual authors of the comments against that of the applicants.

Third, the Court explained that the Hungarian courts had imposed liability on the applicants without examining the conduct of either the applicants or the real estate websites, and despite the fact that the applicants had taken certain general measures – such as a disclaimer and a notice-and-take-down system – to prevent defamatory comments on their portals, or to remove them.

Fourth, the Court reiterated that what was at stake in this case was the commercial reputation of a private company, which does not have the same moral dimension as the right to reputation of an individual. In that context, the consequences of the comments had to be put into perspective. Since there were already ongoing inquiries into the real estate websites' business conduct, the Court was not convinced that the comments had any additional or significant negative impact on the attitude of the consumers concerned.[38] On the other hand, holding the applicants liable could have had negative consequences on their comment environment, perhaps even impelling them to close the space altogether. Indeed, the Hungarian courts were hardly concerned with what had been at stake for the applicants as protagonists of the free electronic media and had failed to carry out any balancing at all between the interests of freedom of expression on the Internet and the right to its commercial reputation of the plaintiff company.

Last, the Court, referring to *Delfi AS*, found that, if accompanied by effective procedures allowing for a rapid response, the notice-and-take-down system could function in many cases as an appropriate tool for balancing the rights and interests of all those involved. The Court saw no reason to hold that such a system, in place on both applicants' websites, could not have provided a viable

---

35 *Magyar T.E.*, supra n 28 at paras 69–71.
36 Ibid. at paras 75–77.
37 Ibid. at para 80.
38 Ibid. at para 85.

avenue to protect the commercial reputation of the company operating the real estate websites.[39]

The foregoing considerations were therefore sufficient for the Court to conclude that there had been a violation of Article 10. It should be noted that the Hungarian Government requested that the Chamber judgment be referred to the Grand Chamber in accordance with Article 43 of the Convention. The Grand Chamber Panel rejected the request and the judgment thus became final on 2 May 2016.

Analysis

It flows from Article 43 of the ECHR that the Grand Chamber judgment in *Delfi AS v Estonia* has, in principle, greater precedential value than *Magyar T.E. v Hungary* in respect of the weight to be ascribed to the general principles formulated by the Court in the examination of liability for online user comments. However, it is clear that the Court's Chamber judgment in the case of *Magyar* contributes useful added elements to the holistic assessment of the situation as it stands, as the judgment further develops the boundaries between those situations where contracting States are free to impose liability on news portals for online user comments, and those where such liability transgresses the limits of Article 10.

On this basis, I will proceed in two brief parts. First, I will provide some further reflections on the precedential scope of the Grand Chamber judgment in *Delfi AS*, taking into account parts of the reasoning in *Magyar* as well as the general doctrinal elements presented above. Second, I will very briefly comment on some criticism levied at the judgment in *Delfi AS*, to the extent possible in light of my position as a serving judge of the Strasbourg Court.

The precedential value of Delfi AS

When assessing the precedential value of the Grand Chamber judgment in *Delfi AS*, it is important at the outset to bear in mind that the case was the first of its kind decided at Strasbourg. It is, I submit, self-evident that when it comes to complex legal problems in the field of Internet law, judges, whether national or international, will tread carefully as uncertainty still exists as to how the Internet will develop. Exhaustive empirical and academic studies on the sociological and cultural effects of this transformative technological innovation have yet to be finalised. The most popular social media platforms are relatively novel and new applications are constantly being introduced. It follows that, although the Court's judgment in *Delfi AS* was in the form of a Grand Chamber judgment, the case is to some extent unique and unsuitable as a basis for broad interpretive

---

39　Ibid. at para 91.

conclusions over and above the facts presented by the case. As was explained above, the Grand Chamber thus in fact circumscribed the scope of the case as follows.

The nature and structure of the news portal on which the comments were uploaded

In *Delfi AS*, the news portal in question was one of the largest in Estonia and was run on a commercial basis. The portal published its own content which was then open to user comments. The commenting environment was thus an integral part of its commercial activity. In this regard, it is possible to distinguish the facts in *Delfi AS* somewhat from the facts in *Magyar*, where at least the first applicant was a non-profit, self-regulatory body of Hungarian Internet content providers. This important distinguishing element conforms to the reasoning in *Delfi AS* where the Grand Chamber explicitly stated that that case did not concern other fora on the Internet where user comments could be disseminated.[40]

   This limitation of the holding in *Delfi AS* may perhaps be understood to mean that it is, as things stand, an open question how the Court will resolve a complaint by an online intermediary that is not run on a commercial basis, although some indications may be drawn from the Fourth Section's judgment in *Magyar*, at least as regards the first applicant. In other words, it may be argued that it will be considerably more difficult for contracting States to claim that a pressing social need in a democratic society existed to justify the imposition of liability on an online intermediary, managed on a non-profit basis, for anonymous and unlawful user comments posted on its website, than on big and powerful news portals like *Delfi AS*. It is, of course, a different question whether this conceptual difference is, in substance, based on sound arguments but an assessment of the status of the intermediary in question will certainly be made on a case-by-case basis.

The content and context of user comments

In *Delfi AS*, the user comments in question were considered, both by the domestic and the Strasbourg courts, to be clearly unlawful as they constituted hate speech and speech that incited violence against a particular individual.[41] The content of the comments was therefore such as to circumscribe entirely any protection afforded to the authors themselves under Article 10 of the Convention.[42] Had Estonia been able to provide for the effective imposition of liability on the authors at the national level, an element which the Court considered crucial in its evaluation of the proportionality of the interference in question,[43] it seems more

40 *Delfi AS*, supra n 3 at para 116.
41 Ibid. at para 140.
42 Ibid. at para 140.
43 Ibid. at paras 142–143.

likely that the complaint lodged at Strasbourg by the authors would have been dismissed as manifestly ill-founded (or even as *incompatible ratione materiae* with the Convention, if Article 10 would not have been considered applicable in light of Article 17).[44] On the other hand, it is an entirely different matter if user comments are 'merely defamatory', in which case a balancing exercise invariably needs to be performed between free speech interests as protected by Article 10 and reputational interests as protected by Article 8.[45]

It seems a persuasive proposition to interpret the judgment in *Delfi AS* as placing great emphasis on the gravity of the comments in question. An argument could thus be made that this element constituted the decisive factor in the Court's decision to afford the Estonian Government quite a substantial margin of appreciation. If this is correct, contracting States cannot necessarily rely on *Delfi AS* as a basis for the conclusion that they would have the same latitude to impose liability on intermediaries in other situations where the user comments in question do not attain the level of hate speech or speech that incites violence, but only constitute unlawful speech on the basis of traditional national defamation laws. This understanding seems to conform to the reasoning in *Magyar*, where the Court explicitly noted that the impugned comments were not of the same gravity as the ones examined in *Delfi AS*. Thus in *Magyar*, the margin of deference afforded to the Government was considerably narrower than that granted in *Delfi AS*.

In the section on differing forms of liability, I described the different potential liability regimes, as formulated by Professors Perry and Zarsky, which are applicable to unlawful user comments posted online either anonymously or pseudonymously. The Grand Chamber in *Delfi AS* has formulated certain general principles that may have an impact on the contracting States' choice between these liability regimes. It may be deduced from the Court's reasoning that it was assumed that the most appropriate form of liability under Article 10 should be direct liability of the authors themselves. However, it cannot be precluded that contracting States can be justified under the Convention in imposing liability on intermediaries when user comments are clearly unlawful and have been posted anonymously or under a pseudonym, at least where no domestic mechanisms are in place to afford the injured party a real and effective opportunity to pursue the actual authors. In other words, the judgment in *Delfi AS* may be understood as the Court accepting that, in principle, a form of residual indirect liability may, on the particular facts, conform to Article 10 of the Convention. However, the judgment in *Magyar* seems to suggest that such a regime of intermediary liability should be subject to clear limitations when the comments in question do not attain the severity of those examined in *Delfi AS*.

---

44 See, in this respect, the Court's analysis of the liability of the authors of the comments in *Delfi AS*, ibid. at paras 150–151.

45 Brunner, L., 'The Liability of on Online Intermediary for Third Party Content – The Watchdog Becomes the Monitor: Intermediary Liability after *Delfi v Estonia*' (2016) 16 *Human Rights Law Review* at 163–173.

Reflections on the criticism directed at Delfi AS

The Grand Chamber judgment in *Delfi AS* has been criticised by academics and other free speech commentators.[46] In particular, it has been argued that the judgment restricts free speech on the Internet by allowing the imposition of liability on intermediaries, which afford individuals the opportunity to participate freely online and disseminate content, and that these intermediaries are now obliged to institute monitoring mechanisms akin to private censorship.[47] The Strasbourg Court in this regard has been criticised for not accepting that the so-called notice-and-take-down system, which *Delfi AS* had in place, and which facilitates the immediate removal of the comments in question upon notice by the injured party, constituted a sufficient safeguard by adequately balancing the conflicting interests at stake.[48]

I am not in a position to comment directly on each and every element of the criticism levied at the Court in this regard. However, it goes without saying that some critical remarks certainly have merit whilst others are perhaps based on an overly broad evaluation of the precedential scope of the findings in *Delfi AS*. In this context, I will restrict myself to the following remarks.

As correctly noted in the Chamber judgment in *Magyar*, the Grand Chamber in *Delfi AS* explicitly observed that if accompanied by effective procedures allowing for a rapid response, the special notice-and-take-down system set in place by the applicants in the latter case can 'function in many cases as an appropriate tool for balancing the rights and interests of all those involved'.[49] However, in cases such as *Delfi AS*, where user comments take the form of hate speech and direct threats to the physical integrity of individuals, the rights and interests of

---

46 See, for example, ibid.; Cox, N., 'Delfi v. Estonia: Privacy protection and chilling effect', *Verf-Blog*, 19 June 2015, available at: www.verfassungsblog.de/delfi-v-estonia-privacy-protection-and-chilling-effect/ [last accessed 30 January 2018]; Woods, L., 'Delfi v Estonia: Curtailing online freedom of expression', *EU Law Analysis*, 18 June 2015, available at: www.eulawanalysis.blogspot.fr/2015/06/delfi-v-estonia-curtailing-online.html [last accessed 30 January 2018]; Gstrein, O., 'The difficulties of information management for intermediaries', *Jean-Monnet-Saar/Europarecht online*, 30 July 2015, available at: www.jean-monnet-saar.eu/?p=881 [last accessed 30 January 2018]; Voorhoof, D., '*Delfi AS* v. Estonia: Grand Chamber confirms liability of online news portal for offensive comments posted by its readers', *Strasbourg Observers*, 18 June 2015, available at: www.strasbourgobservers.com/2015/06/18/delfi-as-v-estonia-grand-chamber-confirms-liability-of-online-news-portal-for-offensive-comments-posted-by-its-readers/ [last accessed 30 January 2018]. Article 19, 'Europe: European court confirms Delfi decision in blow to online freedom', *Article 19*, 16 June 2015, available at: /www.article19.org/resources/europe-european-court-confirms-delfi-decision-blow-online-freedom/ [last accessed 30 January 2018].

47 Woods, L., ibid. This is also addressed comprehensively in the dissenting opinion in *Delfi AS* of my colleagues Judges Sajó and Tsotsoria, see *Delfi AS,* supra n 3 at paras 1–2 and 33–38.

48 Brunner, L., supra n 44 at 171; Woods, L., supra n 45; for a more optimistic view of this finding, see Bodrogi, B., 'The European Court of Human Rights rules again on liability for third party comments', *LSE Media Policy Project Blog*, 19 February 2016, available at: http://blogs.lse.ac.uk/mediapolicyproject/2016/02/19/the-european-court-of-human-rights-rules-again-on-liability-for-third-party-comments/ [accessed 30 January 2018].

49 *Magyar T.E.*, supra n 28 at para 91, citing *Delfi AS*, supra n 3 at para 159.

others and of society as a whole may entitle contracting States to impose liability on Internet news portals if they fail to take measures to remove clearly unlawful comments without delay, even without notice from the alleged victim or from third parties.[50]

On the basis of this reasoning, it may be argued that the Strasbourg Court was in some sense encouraging contracting States to consider the beneficial value of the notice-and-take-down system as a suitable mechanism for balancing the implicated interests, although States are not precluded from adopting more stringent forms of intermediary liability when confronted with the gravest forms of negative online comment. I appreciate that this 'middle-ground' approach of the Court may not satisfy those that argue that the Internet should not be regulated at all, nor does it satisfy the opposite camp, campaigning for robust online regulation. However, the Court's approach in this respect should come as no surprise, considering that, historically, the Strasbourg Court has taken great pains to maintain a fair equilibrium between Article 10 free speech interests on the one hand, and Article 8 privacy and reputational interests on the other.

Conclusions

In this article, I have discussed the most recent case-law of the ECHR dealing with freedom of expression when contracting States are faced with questions concerning the imposition of intermediary liability for unlawful user comments posted online anonymously or under a pseudonym. The discussion has centred on two cases, one of them a Grand Chamber case, where the Court, for the first time, formulated the general principles to be applied when an assessment is made of the latitude that contracting States have under Article 10 to impose such liability on online intermediaries.

My conclusions are thus as follows.

First, in its Grand Chamber judgment in *Delfi AS v Estonia*, the Court, in the first case of its kind, trod carefully in the light of prevailing uncertainties as to the future development of the Internet. Although *Delfi AS* is a Grand Chamber judgment, the case is to some extent unique and unsuitable as a basis for broad interpretive conclusions over and above the facts presented by the case, as set out in the preceding analysis section. The Court in *Delfi AS* did however formulate certain general principles under Article 10 of the Convention that may have an impact on the contracting States' choice between different liability regimes. The Court assumed that the most appropriate form of liability under Article 10 would be direct liability of the authors of the comments themselves. However, it could not preclude that contracting States can be justified under the Convention in imposing liability on intermediaries when user comments are clearly unlawful and have been posted anonymously or under a pseudonym, at least where no

---

50 *Delfi AS*, supra n 3 at para 159.

domestic mechanisms are in place to afford the injured party a real and effective opportunity to pursue the actual authors.

Second, it may be argued that in *Delfi AS*, by in some sense encouraging contracting States to consider the beneficial value of the notice-and-take-down *system* as a suitable mechanism for balancing the relevant conflicting interests, the Court adopted a *middle ground* between two diametrically opposing viewpoints on the regulation of the Internet, one advocating for an environment free from regulation of online conduct and the other campaigning for a regulated Internet where the same legal principles apply both online and offline.

3 Freedom of speech and online media in Denmark

Sten Schaumburg-Müller

Online media in Denmark

Danes are online and so are the media. Ninety one per cent of the Danish population is connected to the internet, 85 per cent use the internet on a daily basis and 67 per cent have a Facebook account.[1] Every traditional media, newspaper and broadcasting company has an online version, and a range of media is online only. This ranges from professional media to blogs of varying quality and social media, to more obscure fora. Most of these various types of media have direct commenting capabilities without intervention by an editor or a moderator. Most, of course, are subsequently edited with the option to delete comments and features that may be unlawful, against the ethics of journalism, against the policy of the media outlet in question or against the inclinations of the moderator.

As a point of departure, the law applies to online media as well. However, there are some important modifications and exceptions:

Importantly, the implementation of the law in regards to online media seems to be lacking. In my assessment, various factors contribute to this relatively poor implementation.

First, knowledge of the law is poor. Many participants are non-professionals without a basic knowledge of the law. Whereas professional journalists have some knowledge of the law and of the ethics of journalism, including editorial and ethical considerations, the general public does not have this background knowledge. In addition, it is likely that many online contributors perceive the internet to be a kind of private space, a continuation of a gathering of friends, where the language used is relaxed and the exchange of private information abounds. The problem, of course, is that the internet is not private at all. The Danish public may also have the impression that freedom of speech has no limits and that everybody has the right to voice whatever they want. This misunderstanding was common in the political discourse of the 2000s. For instance, the Danish Prime Minister at the time, Anders Fogh Rasmussen, repeatedly stated that freedom of speech is absolute, which legally speaking is nonsense. Politically, however, it was

---

1 Danmarks Statistik, "It-anvendelse i befolkningen 2016" [Statistics Denmark, "The use of IT 2016"], pp. 8, 11 and 31.

highly convenient when dealing with the cartoon crisis. In addition, the fact that the large players, including Facebook, Instagram and Google, are all US corporations may add to the idea that freedom of speech prevails when weighed against private life considerations.

In summary, knowledge of the law is lacking, even among members of the executive and legislative bodies, and although the law may be complicated, information on key principles could easily be disseminated. In Danish schools, pupils receive basic tuition concerning traffic law, and the present author is in favour of rolling out similar teaching of online "traffic law" in primary or secondary schools.

Second, the poor implementation of unlawful online expressions is linked to prosecution problems. In many cases, prosecution is left to the offended parties, and as noted above, they may not even know that the infringements are against the law, and even if they do, they may not have the means to initiate proceedings. In cases of public prosecution, it is slow and often only reluctantly carried out, e.g. in cases concerning the unlawful distribution of nude pictures. More recently, some improvements appear to have been made.[2] The professional media has taken an interest in the problems of online dissemination and the police have acknowledged the need for proper prosecution of criminal online acts, etc.

Third, when dealing with mainly US-owned social media, such as Facebook, it is difficult to gain a reasonably clear picture of prevailing law, involving complicated elements of private international law, contract law, competition law involving at least two national jurisdictions, EU law and human rights law. The uncertain state of the prevailing law makes it easier for social media providers to make the decisions themselves without too much consideration for the law.

In summary, implementation of the law with regard to online violations is relatively poor, however there is some indication that things may be slowly improving.

In addition to the practical issue of implementing the law regarding unlawful online expressions, two pieces of Danish legislation explicitly distinguish between traditional media, i.e. printed or broadcasted media, and "other media" which covers online media.

According to the Media Liability Act of 1990 (MLA), online media outlets may choose whether to fall under the Act or not. In contrast, traditional media (Danish newspapers, magazines and broadcasting) do not have a choice and must abide by the MLA and the ensuing rights and obligations. Falling under the MLA implies that there is an obligation to adhere to the ethics of journalism and to accept the authority of the Press Council, which decides on issues relating to the ethics of journalism. Importantly, the MLA ensures that civil and criminal liability is limited to very few actors, excluding distributors and other related

---

2   As of 21 February 2018, 1,004 youngsters have been charged with child pornography for having shared a video depicting a 15-year-old couple having sex. In four test cases, the culprits have received suspended prison sentences from 10 to 40 days prison. The test cases are presently on appeal to the High Courts.

individuals, and, on the other hand, ensuring that someone is always held liable, even for anonymous publications, which is most often the editor in chief. There are other legal implications associated with falling under the rights and obligations of the MLA (for further details, see below). In summary, online media outlets can choose whether they wish to abide by the obligations of the MLA or not.

In 1994, when the internet was still in its infancy, the Media Database Act (MDA) was set up. The Act regulated databases that also functioned as media, and this Act now covers most, if not all, online media. The MDA has some harsh provisions, such as requiring the media database (the online media) to delete all personal information after three years if public interest does not override the interest of the private persons. In practice, this is not achievable, and currently no media outlets covered by the MDA consider whether information that is three years old should be deleted.

The Constitution

The Danish Constitution, the first version of which was enacted in 1849, provides limited protection of freedom of speech. It outlaws censorship and requires freedom of speech cases to be decided by the courts and not by administrative or other bodies. However, the constitution does not prevent the legislator from implementing restrictions according to political will. In practice, however – apart from two problematic periods in Danish history[3] – the legislator has been reasonably protective of freedom of speech. For example, in the 2000s the *Folketing* debated a proposal to criminalise the burning of the Danish flag. The majority clearly dissociated themselves from this kind of expression, while at the same time rejecting its criminalisation. Also, the courts have generally, although not consistently, protected freedom of speech. In the 1930s, a high court judgment dismissed a libel charge initiated by the Minister of Justice, based on the argument that in politics a liberal language prevails;[4] and from the late 1970s the courts embarked on a more explicit reference to the importance of free debate on issues of public interest (but with no reference to the constitutional provision). This coincided with the emerging case law of the European Court of Human Rights (ECtHR),[5] but without any direct inspiration as Danish lawyers at the time did not bother with international conventions.

In summary, protection of freedom of speech has been somewhat unprincipled, but successful nevertheless. The legislator has been protective of freedom of speech, except for the periods when legislative power was partly out of control. This rather persistent freedom of speech-friendly attitude of the legislator – a relatively unique feature of European history – has influenced the more unprincipled

---

3 A constitutional crisis in the late 19th century and the Nazi-German occupation 1940–1945.
4 UfR 1938.576V [UfR = Ugeskrift for Retsvæsen = Weekly Law Journal. The "'V'" indicates the Western High Court].
5 *Sunday Times v UK [GC]*, no. 6538/74, ECtHR 1979; *Lingens v Austria*, no. 9815/82, ECtHR 1986.

judicial approach. There is a certain pragmatism to the approach: solving problems as they arise, no adherence to a strict and principled line of thought, but rather seeking logical and practical answers. This tradition may be traced back at least to A.S. Ørsted (1778–1860), who rejected the school of natural law as well as strict legal positivism.[6] On the positive side, the main focus is on practicality rather than adherence to neatly worked out principles, whereas on the negative side there is an overly flexible approach with a focus on accepting whatever is less cumbersome in the present situation.

European landmark cases

Denmark has lost very few cases in the ECtHR. Moreover, in freedom of speech cases only one has been lost – the *Jersild* case from 23 September 1994.[7] As is probably well known, Jens Olav Jersild was (and still is) a Danish journalist, and in the mid-1980s, when the national Danish Broadcasting Corporation for which he worked enjoyed a monopoly, Jersild interviewed some back street youngsters, "green jackets", who willingly voiced their opinions on immigrants, black people, etc., and their racist remarks easily fell under the scope of section 266b of the Danish Criminal Code (CC), the Danish "hate speech" clause (see below section "Group defamation"). Jersild had taken his case before the Danish court system, and the Supreme Court upheld his conviction with a reference to CC section 23 on complicity: Jersild had actively sought out the green jackets, provided them with beer and selected a few remarks from several hours of recordings, and broadcast their opinions on Sunday night prime time on the only TV station available at the time. Still, the Supreme Court was not unanimous, and one judge argued that as a media reporter, Jersild ought not to be convicted for reporting publicly relevant opinions that had been voiced by others.[8] In a 12–7 judgment, the ECtHR held that Denmark had violated Article 10 of the European Convention on Human Rights (ECHR), pointing out that the media has a responsibility, and hence a special protection, for disseminating information of public interest. As it was clear that Jersild did not propagate racist views, but exposed them, a conviction for the dissemination was a violation of Article 10.

Although there was special protection for media reporting in Danish law even before *Jersild*,[9] the case had several repercussions. The courts as well as the

---

6 See Sverre Blandhol, *Nordisk rettspragmatisme. Savigny, Ørsted og Schweigaard om vitenskap og metode* [Nordic legal pragmatism; Savigny, Ørsted and Schweigaard on legal science and method], Jurist- og Økonomforbundets Forlag, Copenhagen 2005; Sten Schaumburg-Müller, "On Danish legal method", in Ingvill Helland and Sören Koch (eds.), *Nordic and Germanic legal methods*, Mohr Siebek, Tübingen 2014, pp. 141–164.

7 *Jersild v Denmark [GC]*, no. 15890/89, ECtHR 1994.

8 UfR 1989.399H [the "H" indicates the Supreme Court].

9 In UfR 1980.1075V an editor was acquitted for violation of CC section 266b as he was initiating a combined interview with an obvious hate speech orator and his opponent.

legislature (see below for information on media source protection) tended to give more weight to journalistic reporting after this judgment. In 1994, a few months after *Jersild* was tried, the Supreme Court had to decide whether trespassing was also unlawful for a journalist and a photographer who followed demonstrators in order to cover a story which was of public interest. In the late 1980s, the Supreme Court had convicted journalists in two similar cases (by votes of 4–1 and 3–2, respectively),[10] but after *Jersild*, the Court unanimously acquitted the news reporters.[11] *Jersild* definitely played its part, but it was not the only reason for the acquittal. As previously mentioned, the Danish Court already gave some weight to reporting and contributions to issues of public interest, and in addition, the first voting judge in the 1994 case happened to be the same defence lawyer as in the 1987 cases.[12] In addition, in 1988, the legal scholar Preben Stuer Lauridsen performed a thorough analysis,[13] arguing that there was too little protection of the press *and* too little protection of private life. In a series of cases, the courts weighed the protection of news reporting as an important factor.

In other cases involving freedom of speech, the courts quickly adapted to the ECtHR jurisprudence – which was not beyond criticism and not without questionable judgments, but on the whole an accommodating approach. The courts are loyal to the judgments and decisions of the ECtHR, and the idea is that it is not for the courts to reject the jurisprudence of an international court. Rejecting an international legal obligation is a political question and, consequently, it is for the politically elected legislature and government to decide.

As for the EU, Denmark has not been involved in European Court of Justice cases relating to freedom of speech. Obviously, judgments like *Google Spain* (which we will explore below) have repercussions.

Legislation

The 1930 Criminal Code and defamation in the spirit of logical positivism

In 1930, Denmark implemented a new Criminal Code. Preparations for this began around the turn of the century, and the Code was set in force on 1 January 1933. The sections dealing with defamation have undergone few cosmetic changes, and the basic ideas and general line of thought dates back to the beginning of the 20th century. Section 267 (unaltered since 1930) is as follows:

> Any person who defames the character of another person by *offensive expressions* or acts or by making or propagating *allegations* of acts suited to reduce

---

10 UfR 1989.934H and UfR 1989.937H.
11 UfR 1994.988H.
12 Due to a scandal in the Ministry of Justice, the recruitment of judges had changed.
13 *Pressefrihed og personlighedsret* [Freedom of the press and protection of private life], Gyldendal, Copenhagen 1988.

the esteem in which such person is held by his fellow citizens is sentenced to a fine or imprisonment for a term not exceeding four months.

(Italics added by the author)[14]

The Danish terms are "ringeagtsytring" (offensive expression) and "sigtelse" (allegation), respectively. The distinction between the two is of utmost importance. An "allegation" makes claims about real life phenomena, hence they can be proved to be true or not. "X is a murderer" is an allegation, which may be true if Mr. X has committed murder, whereas it is false if Mr. X did not commit such an act. The basic idea in the sections on defamation is that defamatory allegations may be presented if and only if they are true. Section 269 modifies the rigidity of this idea, but the focus is still on truth and proof.

In contrast, offensive words do not refer to any real life phenomena, and by definition they can be neither true nor false. Therefore, if defamatory, offensive words are criminal.

There are two problems with this distinction:

First, it does not work. Words cannot be divided into two neat categories, which either refer to real phenomena or not. Logical positivism, the prevailing philosophy of the time, is easily recognisable, and the problem is that as a philosophy logical positivism has to a large extent been defeated, whereas we still have the Criminal Code. Danish courts are, therefore, faced with the difficult, in fact impossible, task of making linguistic distinctions. For example, if an expression was degrading, but acceptable in the circumstances, they had to: (1) categorise it as an allegation because offensive words were automatically criminal if sufficiently offensive; and (2) claim truth or something similar, otherwise the allegation was criminal according to the statute. This is, of course, stupid, and the courts had their ways of going about the problem. For example, in the late 1980s, during political discussions in relation to a referendum on EU issues, the Minister of Foreign Affairs – who had been a journalist and had a knack for catchy language – stated that a political opponent was engaged in "dingy mole activity". The Court agreed that the words were degrading, and then, in order to acquit the speaker, had to categorise the expression as an allegation that was proven to be true. Logically speaking, this is nonsense. What are "dingy mole activities", and how can the truth of the charges be proven or rejected? Legally, it made a lot of sense. The words appeared in a political discussion, and the speaker referred to activities, carried out by the opponent, which he then characterised as "dingy mole activities". According to the terms of the ECtHR, this would be categorised as a "value judgement" with some factual basis, contained in a political discussion. However, back then – before *Jersild* – neither the Danish courts, nor any other Danish lawyer for that matter, took any notice of the ECHR. Hence, the Supreme Court had to categorise the words as an allegation

---

14 Translated by Anette Nørgaard Jappe and Karen Wolf-Frederiksen, Karnov Publishers.

proven to be true. This was a wise solution but it was not in accordance with the wording of the statute.

Second, the distinction between "sigtelse" and "ringeagtsytring" does not fit with the ECtHR's distinction between "value judgements" and "allegations of fact". The categories are somewhat similar, but they do not cover the areas, and besides, the ECtHR does not consider that value judgement with some factual basis in relation to an issue of public interest can be sanctioned, whereas the Danish provision requires that a "ringeagtsytring" must be sanctioned, as it cannot be proven to be true.

After *Jersild*, and with some transitory vacillation, the courts now briefly state that the sections in the Criminal Code dealing with defamation must be read and interpreted "in light of" the ECHR, and Danish case law fits nicely with that of the ECtHR: harsh, defamatory allegations with no factual basis are crim-inalised – in some cases even with prison sentences[15] – and greater levels of public interest, together with a more factual basis of the case, are associated with a lower likelihood of a criminal conviction. Sometimes, of course, the balance is difficult. In 2015, the Supreme Court convicted a historian and public debater for calling a journalist and debater a "KGB agent". The Eastern High Court ac-quitted the historian, arguing *that* it was of public interest, *that* there was some factual basis – the journalist had connections with the KGB, which he readily admitted, adding that the connections were for journalistic purposes – and *that* the journalist was a public figure himself who was also voicing political opinions. The Supreme Court, however, in a 5–2 majority judgment, convicted the his-torian with the argument – convincingly, I believe – that the historian must let the journalist answer his case. The historian had access to secret files, which he claimed proved that the journalist was a proper agent, but he did not give the journalist access to the documents. Hence, the journalist had no chance of de-fending himself, and the historian received a fine of DKK 100,000 (€13,500) and costs of DKK 500,000 (€67,000).[16]

As a point of departure, defamation charges under section 267 come under private criminal prosecution. This is a rare occurrence in Danish law, and only criminal prosecution of many copyright violations, vigilantism and defamation cases can be carried out by the injured party. This implies that in order to run a defamation case, one has to consider the costs, in contrast to public prosecution where the authority runs the show, including carrying out investigations and bearing the costs. There are two situations in which public prosecution is an op-tion: *one*, civil servants have a right to public prosecution. Consequently, a public servant who is accused of being corrupt has the right of public prosecution, whereas a person who has her own company or is privately employed must bear the costs and the inconvenience of investigating the case. *Two*, if the accusation

---

15 UfR 2004.690Ø [the "Ø" indicates the Eastern High Court].
16 UfR 2015.3106H.

of defamation is reported by an anonymous party, the offender may ask the public prosecutor to intervene. In reality, this never happens, and according to informal inquiries the police refuse to receive any report concerning anonymous defamation.[17]

As a consequence, online defamations against private persons are rarely prosecuted. As for defamation of public servants, including ministers and members of Parliament, there seems to be a tendency to report gross online defamation and for the offenders to be prosecuted and receive sentences.

In 2017, the Criminal Code Commission issued a report on defamation and the protection of private life,[18] including in-depth considerations as to the impact of the internet. The Commission suggests the following:

- A public prosecution, when reported by the offended, in cases of grossly unlawful charges ("sigtelser", see above), i.e. not only for public servants.
- An increase in the maximum penalty from 4 to 12 months' imprisonment, reserved for gross defamation widely distributed on the internet.
- An update to the wording of the provisions in order to be more in line with prevailing law, including European human rights law.

It is likely that these suggestions will be implemented by legislation although not necessarily exactly as suggested.

Threats and approval of criminal behaviour

The professional media do not usually engage in direct threats towards individuals, and neither do professional journalists regularly approve of criminal behaviour. Journalists and editors may, of course, discuss the relevance and appropriateness of prevailing law, which may be criticised, even heavily. The latter clearly falls within freedom of speech, and the media are responsible for raising awareness of information and assessing publicly relevant issues, such as the question of whether the prevailing law is acceptable.

However, to approve of illegal behaviour is another matter, and to incite people to engage in illegal activities may be criminal in itself. In addition, of course, threatening people, including announcing that politicians ought to be shot or female politicians ought to have an iron pole up theirs, is normally not published in edited media due to the existence of the editing process. But online media abounds with this kind of language, and a brief on the relevant rules is needed.

According to CC section 266, *threats* are criminalised. Recently, a young lady, who probably did not even know how to handle a gun, received a suspended sentence for the following statement published on an open Facebook chatroom: "Let me shoot this disgusting, wrinkle faced bitch once and for all", which was directed towards a member of Parliament and a leader of a political party.[19] It

---

17 Private conversation with a police director and a police investigator.
18 Betænkning 1563/2017 om freds- og æreskrænkelser.
19 UfR 2010.2085Ø.

may be difficult to distinguish between political statements and threats, but taking into consideration that the politician in question had previously been physically attacked and that she is regularly, if not constantly, protected by security guards, the conviction appears well-founded.

Promoting terrorist activities is also criminalised (section 114e), together with a range of other activities relating to terror. In a spectacular case, the Kurdish ROJ TV, which broadcasts from Denmark, was given a fine of DKK 4 million (more than half a million euro), and its broadcasting license was withdrawn.[20]

For a long time, the provision criminalising *public incitement* to criminal activity (section 136(1)) was rarely in use. There was one published conviction in the 1930s – amidst a rather violent political atmosphere – and another after 2001. Apparently, the prosecutor only considers cases when the expressions are forwarded in connection with violent acts, such as "kill a fascist" after an incident of torching the private car of the Minister of the Interior,[21] or linking to a violent ISIS video with the remark "Message to all Muslims in the West, especially Denmark", were both punished with prison sentences.

In a more questionable provision, section 136(2), *public approval* of certain criminal acts is criminalised. The mere approval, perhaps even a "like" on Facebook is criminal, at least in principle. To date there have been no published cases from the upper level courts that have convicted solely according to section 136(2). However, it appeared that the prosecutor was more proactive following "likes" of the attacks on Charlie Hebdo and other terrorist or violent attacks, and recently a young woman received a prison sentence for stating that "Omar is a hero", after Omar shot two people in Copenhagen in what certainly looked like a terrorist attack.

As of 1 January 2017, section 136 was amended, rendering it criminal for religious preachers to approve of a range of criminal acts including bigamy. In addition to the questionable interference in freedom of speech – mere approval is criminalised – the relationship to discrimination may cause a problem as the restrictions only relate to *religious* preachers, cf. ECHR Article 9 (freedom of religion) and 14 (no discrimination in relation to convention rights). At any rate, online priests now risk prison sentences of up to three years for approving of a specified range of criminal acts.

Protection of private life

In 1971, the legislator amended the provisions for the protection of private life, based on considerations for new technologies. The prevailing rules can be summarised as follows:

- For taking photographs (and films), it is relevant whether the person being captured is located on private or public land. If the location is private, taking photos is forbidden, and if public it is not.

---

20 UfR 2014.1540H.
21 TfK 2007.774Ø [TfK = Tidsskrift for Kriminalret = Journal of Criminal Law].

- For an audio recording, it is decisive whether the person recording is a part of the gathering or the conversation. Therefore, bugging is criminal, whereas an interviewer's recording of the interview is not, no matter whether the interviewee is informed of the recording or not.
- The dissemination of private information and private pictures is forbidden. "Private" is defined as intimate situations, such as sexual relations, holidays, illnesses, etc. Pictures taken in public places are as a point of departure *not* private. In exceptional cases, the dissemination of pictures taken in public places may be deemed unacceptable, and persons depicted may have a civil claim if the picture is mainly private with no public interest involved.[22] Nude pictures are private, and forwarding nude pictures of girlfriends – apparently a popular pastime – is criminal even if the girl herself sent the picture to the boyfriend. It is still private, and there is no implicit consent to any further dissemination. It is one thing to be nude, appealing and pretty with your intimate friend(s), but quite another to be exposed to the entire online world, including masturbating sites,[23] porn revenge web pages or just ordinary web pages.[24]

Importantly, three elements must be taken into consideration when dealing with possible infringements of private life:

- *First*, and obviously, consent decriminalises, including tacit consent. In real life, there is a lot of consenting going on when it comes to taking photos and disseminating photos and information. Legally, consent is specific in the sense that consenting to, e.g. sharing private information or pictures with somebody, does *not* imply consent to wider dissemination, including wider online dissemination.
- *Second*, and closely related to consent, information including pictures that have been made public by the relevant person are no longer private. Thus, a person who has told her story to media A must accept that the story is also available to media B. (This, of course, does not apply to copyright issues, only to protection of private life.)
- *Third*, there may be other reasons for rendering the act legal, especially journalists passing on publicly relevant information. In 1989, the Supreme Court accepted a news feature from a psychiatric hospital. Most of the

---

22 UfR 1991.549H: The case concerned a photograph of a woman on a beach looking for her husband who had just drowned. It was taken in a public place, but the photo plus text was held to be a violation of private life. UfR 2010.2448H: The case concerned a photograph of a highly pregnant celebrity bathing topless on a deserted, yet public beach, with the picture printed in a weekly magazine. Not criminal, but tort.

23 UfR 2015.2561H: A young man received a six month prison sentence and had to pay DKK 40,000 (€5,300) for manipulating the Facebook profile picture of a young woman and publishing it on a pornographic site, with directions for use.

24 UfR 1999.177V: A prison sentence was given to man who had uploaded some explicit pictures of his ex-partner with grossly degrading remarks.

photos had been taken of people in private locations. The photos and associated information was related to illness, hence it was private, and the patients could not give any legally valid consent due to their mental state. Nevertheless, the Court accepted the reports as lawful, arguing *that* the reporting had public interest (how we treat our mentally ill people), and *that* the report was written in close collaboration with medical personnel, patients and the patients' relatives. The only party that was not involved was the authority running the hospital, whose interest the Supreme Court set aside. In summary, there was no infringement of private life.[25]

The above mentioned Criminal Code Commission has declared that, in general, the prevailing provisions function well and there is no need for a renewed definition of private life. However, the Commission does suggest that the maximum penalty for gross violations of private life, such as the unconsented dissemination of nude pictures online, should be two years, compared to the present maximum of six months. It is likely that the legislature will follow this proposal.

Group defamation[26]

In the late 1930s, in order to avoid "German conditions", the legislator passed an amendment to the Criminal Code criminalising certain defamatory words and deeds against groups. In 1971, the section was updated following Denmark's ratification of the Convention on the Elimination of Racial Discrimination. The present section 266b, is basically the same, with some later amendments to include "sexual orientation" among the relevant group affiliation, and to emphasise that "propaganda" is an aggravating element. This section has been much debated and heavily criticised. According to the present author, overall the section functions well, even though one may, of course, criticise particular judgments for not having struck the right balance.

When drafting the bill, freedom of speech was indeed a major concern, and the end result can be summarised as follows:

- Only public remarks are criminalised. In UfR 2012.2361H, the Supreme Court acquitted a person for expressions that clearly fell within the scope of section 266b, emphasising that the person had expressed himself in a private situation and that he may not have known that the interviewer intended to publish the remarks.
- Protected groups are based on: race, colour, national or ethnic origin, religious belief or sexual orientation. Thus, defamatory remarks against women, blondes or law professors do not fall within the criminal scope. It is

---

25 UfR 1989.726H.

26 In international discourse, this is often referred to as "hate speech", which is misleading for the Danish CC section 266b, according to which hate is immaterial.

immaterial whether the group is a minority, and it is immaterial whether the individual giving his/her views belongs to the particular group or not.

- According to the preparatory works, scientifically based expressions are not criminalised, and the same goes for remarks made in a serious debate. In addition, the words have to reach a certain level of rudeness.
- The normal sanction is a fee, but in at least one case a prison sentence was imposed for distributing pamphlets with the call to "kill them wherever you see them", relating to a religious group.

Group defamation is also criminal when published online, and publishing on a web page is usually categorised as "propaganda" and consequently regarded as an aggravating factor. The problem here seems to be of the "buddy syndrome" kind. You voice your opinion on the internet as if it were around the regulars' table at the local pub. For group defamation to be criminal, it must be made public, and therefore the harsh language, which is perfectly legal in non-public gatherings, suddenly renders the speakers criminals. Some knowledge of the law is needed, and perhaps a less politicised one is appropriate. Group defamation has for the past 10–15 years been under attack from various political stakeholders who argue – correctly – that it interferes with freedom of speech, and – incorrectly – that it hinders debate and criticism of immigration.

Criminal jurisdiction

In 2008, a new jurisdiction clause was added, section 9a of the Criminal Code:

> An offence relating to text, sound or image data, etc., made generally available in Denmark through the Internet or a similar system for dissemination of information by acts committed abroad is deemed to have been committed within the Danish state if the data is related specifically to Denmark, and hereafter any activity in relation to text, sound and visual material which has a particular relation to Denmark.[27]

This provision is obviously relevant for online offences. It is immaterial where a defamatory statement, a disclosure of private information or a threat is uploaded. The crucial requirement is whether the material has a "particular relationship to Denmark", which will be the case if the material is in Danish and if the material relates to persons living in Denmark.

The Media Liability Act

Before 1991, only traditional printed media, i.e. newspapers, etc., were covered by special media liability and rights of protection of sources, etc. In 1991, a new

---

27 Translated by Anette Nørgaard Jappe and Karen Wolf-Frederiksen, Karnov Publishers.

Media Liability Act was passed, and during the 1990s various alignments were made in order to include seizure, confiscation, etc., in the source protection. Prevailing law functions well with a coherent set of rules regarding liability and protection of sources, and a good protection of journalists' rights. However, there are some problems in relation to who has rights as journalists, and also in relation to media databases.

As regards *scope*, the MLA divides the media into three groups: media covered by the MLA (and the ensuing legislative provisions), media that cannot fall under the MLA, and media that can choose whether to fall under the MLA or not. Traditional Danish media, such as newspapers and magazines edited in Denmark and Danish broadcasting corporations, automatically fall under the MLA. On the contrary, newspapers and magazines that are not edited in Denmark and broadcasters from abroad *cannot* fall under the MLA. This applies even if the content is directed at a Danish audience, which is the case with some TV stations broadcasting from London, which they do mainly in order to avoid the Danish regulation on advertising. As a side effect, they forfeit the privileges (and obligations) under the MLA. Books and media without a mix of edited content cannot fall under MLA, either. As a consequence, a journalist writing a book rather than articles for a newspaper is not covered by the MLA and, therefore, has none of the rights and privileges associated with the MLA. The same applies to online media, blogs, single issue websites and other sites without an edited mix of content that cannot fall under the MLA. Only online media with an edited mix of various content, which include all online versions of traditional media, have an option to stay out or stay in, the latter of which is easily done by registering with the Press Council. Currently, as of 21 February 2018, 871 media outlets have registered.[28]

As the title indicates, the MLA regulates *media liability*. When under the MLA, liability is roughly restricted to editors, journalists and authors of expressions. Other actors, including technical providers, are excluded from legal liability. In return, the MLA prescribes strict liability for the editor. If no one else can be held liable, the editor must bear the costs or face criminal sanctions. This is particularly relevant in relation to anonymously published content, including headlines and contents bills. The MLA liability is intentionally different from the general liability system, according to which any accomplice may be (co) liable. The idea is that the editor is in charge, it is her decision whether to publish a feature and whether to publish it anonymously, and it is considered to be a way to protect freedom of speech. The editorial content is not decided by external stakeholders such as publishing companies, paperboys, kiosk owners or internet service providers.

The MLA provisions are numerous and perhaps too detailed, but the overall idea, restricting media liability to the people professionally involved, functions

---

28 Figures available from the Press Council's website www.pressenaevnet.dk (last accessed 1 February 2018).

well. In particular, there is no publisher's liability – except in cases where the editor has gone mad (sic!), has emigrated permanently or has gone bankrupt – and unprofessional participants, giving interviews, can only be held liable for their expressions if they have willingly accepted that their expressions are disseminated and their identity revealed. If not, the liability lies with the editor, or in some cases, the journalist involved.

Since many online media outlets are not covered by the MLA, mainly because they do not fulfil the requirement of a mixed editorial content and in a few cases because they have not registered, the general liability rules apply, involving considerations of complicity.

The MLA also requires the covered media outlet to act in accordance with *ethics of journalism*. The Act states that a *Press Council* must deal with complaints – free of charge and with swift procedures, at least when compared to courts. The Council consists of one appointed judge as the chair, one member from the editors' side, one from the journalists' side, and one appointed by relevant non-governmental organisations. The media sector has agreed on Guiding Rules for Ethics of Journalism (latest update 2013),[29] which are in principle not binding but, nevertheless, mainly followed by the Press Council. This results in a comparatively strange set-up in the sense that the state is involved in professional media ethics. However, it is a rather smooth system, and the Press Council can only (1) voice its criticism; and (2) require the media to publish its critique. It has no authority whatsoever to deal with issues of criminal law or the paying of damages.

The Press Council deals with roughly 100 cases per year, and its decisions generally seem to be followed by the professional media. In relation to this, it is important to note that many online websites are not covered by the MLA, therefore they have no formal obligation according to the ethics of journalism and cannot be brought before the Press Council. However, the majority of professional media outlets, purely online or with additional online editions, are registered and thus fall under the authority of the Press Council.

For issues especially related to online media including subsequent deletion, de-indexing and anonymisation, see the section below.[30]

In special cases, persons have a *right of reply*, i.e. the media must publish a small statement from the relevant person, *if* the media has published incorrect information, and *if* that information may be damaging to that person.

In *addition to the MLA*, there is a range of provisions in the Administration of Justice Act (AJA) linked to the MLA. In other words, it is a package. If a media outlet is subject to the conditions of the MLA, it – and its journalists – are also covered by a range of other rights. If the media outlet is not subject to the MLA, either because it is inherently a non-MLA medium, such as foreign broadcasting stations and newspapers, or because the online media outlet has chosen not to

---

29 www.pressenaevnet.dk/press-ethical-rules/
30 Section "Online media's special obligation according to the ethics of journalism".

sign up, the range of other provisions does not apply either. This is to some extent logical, but it is not without problems.

The relevant provisions provide roughly for the following:

- Protection of sources, including the right not to have possessions seized, if the seizure can reveal journalistic sources, and not to be required to hand over material to the court if that material may reveal sources. The right is not absolute. In gross cases, journalists may be required to give evidence, but only if it is the only way to reveal important information and only if the interest of the investigating police outweighs the interests of the media and the public in source protection. In cases of breach of confidentiality, a journalist can never be required to reveal her source if the journalist or the source intended to reveal information of public interest. According to court practice, there is a strong protection of sources.
- Protection of non-sources is another matter. In a TV series relating to paedophilia, the TV station anonymised individuals recorded by hidden camera. The police wanted the unedited recordings in order to be able to investigate a serious crime. The Court decided that the parts of the recordings where proper sources were revealed should not be handed over, whereas the sections only revealing the ones secretly recorded were not covered by the source protection.[31] The ECtHR accepted this decision.[32]
- Throughout the 1990s, access to court material was increased. Previously, it was difficult even to access judgments. Presently, it is much easier, and the media have certain additional rights, such as the right to browse through the previous month's judgments and decisions (at the court registrar) and to access supplementary material during court sessions.
- In cases where the courts consider excluding the public from the hearings, journalists have a right to be heard and a right to appeal the decision by the court.

These rights are closely connected to the MLA. Only journalists working for media that is subject to the MLA have the right to source protection, the right to access additional material at the courts, and the right to be heard and appeal decisions in camera. In a way, this is well-founded: there is a close connection between the special media liability and the protection of sources; if an editor or journalist decides to publish information without disclosing the source, they must be liable for any unlawfulness. In UfR 2003.624H, a tabloid newspaper ran a headline that read, "She killed 6", referring to a much published case involving a social worker at a nursing home. Apparently, the newspaper had sources within the police, and not wanting to disclose the source, the editor had to face the damages required, which amounted to DKK 100,000, (approximately €13,500), a large amount by Danish standards.

---

31 UfR 2002.2503H.
32 *Nordisk Film v Denmark (decision)*, no. 40485/02, ECtHR 2002.

On the other hand, the connection implies that according to the Danish statutes, a foreign journalist, a journalist writing a book or a journalist working for a non-registered online media outlet cannot claim protection under the AJA. This is not in line with ECHR Article 10, nor is it in accordance with the judgments by the ECtHR, such as *Goodwin v UK*.[33]

There is *no* option of *cherry picking* from the various components of the MLA and the ensuing rights according to the AJA. The media outlets that are automatically covered are covered by all provisions, and the media outlets that have a right to opt in must opt for the full package. There is no such thing as accepting the special liability but not the competence of the Press Council.

Personal data and media databases

Obviously, the regulation governing how personal data is processed is highly important for online media, which contains personal data of all kinds. According to the present Article 9 of the Data Protection Directive 95/46/EC,[34] as well as Article 85(1) of the General Data Protection Regulation (GDPR),[35] the Member States shall provide suitable legislation for journalistic activities, balancing the right to the protection of personal data with the right to freedom of expression.[36]

Presently, this is regulated in the Danish Personal Data Act (PDA), and the relevant sections are merely copied into a draft GDPR Supplementing Act (GDPR-SA). At the time of final editing of this article in February 2018, it is still unknown whether the bill will pass unaltered, and the following description follows the current version of the PDA.[37]

For processing personal data on online media, the PDA has the following sections which may not conform with the Directive or the GDPR.

First, section 2, § 2 of the PDA states that the Act does not apply if it would imply a violation of ECHR Article 10. Obviously, the PDA must be understood and interpreted in a way that does not result in a violation of ECHR Article 10. However, the way the provision is worded simply renders the PDA inapplicable if there is a conflict between the protection of personal data and freedom of expression. In practice, this provision has resulted in some remarkable decisions by the

33 *Goodwin v UK* [GC], no. 17488/90, ECtHR 1996.
34 Directive 95/46/EC of the European Parliament and of the Council of 24 October 1995 on the protection of individuals with regard to the processing of personal data and on the free movement of such data.
35 Regulation (EU) 2016/679 of the European Parliament and of the Council of 27 April 2016 on the protection of natural persons with regard to the processing of personal data and on the free movement of such data, and repealing Directive 95/46/EC (General Data Protection Regulation).
36 The wording of the respective articles is slightly different, which is of little interest to the present analysis of Danish law.
37 It is most likely that the provisions of the draft relating to media will pass unaltered. In the new act, section 3 restate the rules, albeit with different sub-numbering.

Data Protection Board, e.g. accepting gross defamation of civil servants merely doing their job, including uploading names, addresses, and telephone numbers of the civil servants. Quite clearly, official authorities including civil servants must accept some criticism, but totally unfounded and gross allegations against identified civil servants are not acceptable. This is not in line with case law from the ECtHR, nor is it in line with the Directive (or the GDPR for that matter), and luckily it is not in line with case law from Danish courts, either.[38] Still, the Data Protection Agency persists.

Second, three exemptions from the PDA are explicitly mentioned in section 2, §§ 6–8, relating to media databases. (For a description of the types of media databases, see below.) This implies that various media databases are not covered by the PDA if they fulfil certain criteria including notification to the Press Council and/or the Data Protection Agency. So far, so good. Nowadays, media agencies have all sorts of internal or public databases that they cannot function without, and the media outlet cannot function if it must fulfil all the rules and requirements set up by the PDA, including, for example, deletion, informing the registered parties, etc.

However, the only media outlets exempted from the strict rules of the PDA are the ones governed by the MLA. As a consequence, only Danish media outlets are exempt, and as for Danish online media, only those who have registered under the MLA and whose registration is valid are included. Foreign media, unregistered media, or media without mixed content must follow the PDA – which, in fact, is impossible to do. For foreign EU-based media, this is not in line with EU law, as the favourable rules only apply to national media.

Third, any other activities carried out for journalistic purposes are exempt from the PDA, except for a few provisions including security measures and the requirement to have a person responsible for the handling of personal data.[39] This exemption is *not* dependent on the journalists being affiliated with MLA-governed media, and it seems to function well in relation to professional media. Furthermore, the Data Protection Agency dismisses complaints in relation to professional journalistic activities. However, there is no indication as to when the processing of personal data has a journalistic purpose and when it does not. In addition, the fact that the professional media (except for the very few, purely online professional media outlets that have *not* registered) have obligations according to the MLA should be taken into consideration: the requirement to act in accordance with the ethics of journalism, to accept the decisions by the Press Council and, last but not least, strict liability for anonymous content. The result of this legal incoherence seems to be that amateur online media has the double advantage of having to bother neither with the PDA, nor with the MLA. This

---

38 City Court of Holbæk, judgment of 6 January 2014 (BS 6-769/2013): The punishment in this case was 20 daily fines (or 20 days' imprisonment), and DKK 100,000 (€13,500) in damages to each of the civil servants involved.

39 In the proposal for a new Act, there is a reference to the GDPR Art.s 28 and 32, the only provisions in the Regulation to applied in cases involving journalistic purposes.

result does not appear to be convincingly in line with the requirement to balance the rights of freedom of expression and the requirement of the press on the one hand and the protection of private life and personal data on the other.

In addition to the PDA, a statute on media databases (MDA) was enacted in 1994,[40] i.e. before the Data Protection Directive and before the advent of the internet. The Act was well thought out in 1994, but with the advent of online media and the EU regulation of personal data there have been some problems with it.

The Act distinguishes between three types of media databases:

- Unaltered, full text databases. This type of media database is rather uninteresting as it merely gathers information from the media under the MLA. This type neither falls within the PDA or the MDA.
- Internal or editorial databases. For journalistic purposes, it is possible to run databases with personal information without applying the PDA on the condition *that* the database is registered with the Press Council and the Data Protection Agency, and *that* only journalists have access to the information. One media company merely needs to register in order for all its internal databases to be included. This is a smooth solution, making it possible for media outlets to work with databases in a closed circuit. The problem is that the protection only applies to media outlets under the MLA, i.e. Danish media. Journalists working in Denmark for foreign (online) media do not fall under the MDA and, accordingly, must fall under the PDA, which is unacceptable according to EU regulation, be it the Directive or the GDPR.
- Media outlets that are also databases. This was a rare occurrence in 1994, whereas today all online media also function as databases. Such media/ media databases are exempted from the PDA if they register under the Press Council and the Data Protection Agency. Without registration, they may fall under the PDA, under whose rules it is impossible to run a proper media outlet. Please note again that foreign media cannot register. Furthermore, even with the registration, the media/databases are required to delete sensitive and private data such as information on political affiliation, sexual orientation (and activities), criminal records, etc., if that information is not required under freedom of speech. This is highly problematic, *first*, as it is cumbersome and not obviously relevant for media to continuously overhaul all stored information more than three years old and make an assessment of each and every piece of information including pictures. *Second*, there is only the option of deleting, whereas de-indexing (as required in the *Google* judgment)[41] or anonymising is not an option according to the MDA. In summary, this particular regulation is both outdated and out of touch with EU law.

40 As mentioned in the introductory section of this article.
41 C-131/12 *Google Spain SL and others v Agencia Española de Protección de Datos*, 13 May 2014.

Online media's special obligation according to the ethics of journalism

As mentioned above, the media organisations have agreed on a set of Guiding Rules for Ethics of Journalism which, by law, are compulsory for media covered by the MLA.

In 2013, the rules were updated, and two amendments are of special interest for online media outlets.

First, the introductory section of the Guiding Rules state that "if unedited discussion items are brought, visible and clear guidelines on such items should be published and an effective procedure for handling complaints of such items should be set up by the relevant medium."[42] This implies, on the one hand, that the unedited content, including anonymous remarks, etc., are not directly included under the Guiding Rules. On the other hand, the Guiding Rules require the media to have effective internal complaints procedures in place in relation to unedited comments. Thus, if person A in a directly accessible thread makes a defamatory remark about person B in a media outlet covered by the Guiding Rules, person B cannot make a complaint directly to the Press Council – contrary to the situation where the remark appeared in an edited part of the media. However, if the media outlet either does not have any clear and published information as to how it is dealing with online comments or it does not act accordingly, person B may make a complaint to the Press Council. As for the latter situation, the Council has so far received no complaints, whereas it has rejected many complaints relating to unedited content.

Second, a new rule, B.8, states that:

> Statements published in digital media will often be available long after their publication. Upon request to the medium, the availability of such previously published sensitive or private information may be hampered if possible and deemed reasonable.[43]

The preparatory works[44] state that hindering the availability of statements may be done either by de-indexing, by anonymisation or by deletion. Technically, the Press Council now has the authority to criticise a media outlet for not de-indexing, not anonymising or not deleting media content after some time. The Council has declared that it will carefully weigh the interests and that criticism of non-deletion will be rare.[45] So far, the Council has only criticised the media

---

42 From the English version of the Press Council's website www.pressenaevnet.dk/press-ethical-rules/.s

43 From the English version of the Press Council's website www.pressenaevnet.dk/press-ethical-rules/.

44 Notat om justering af de vejledende regler for god presseskik 8. marts 2013 [Brief on the adjustment of the Guiding Rules for the Ethics of Journalism, 8 March 2013].

45 *Pressenævnets Årsberetning* [Annual Report of the Press Council], 2015, p. 20.

for not de-indexing or anonymising content that was already violating the Guiding Rules at the time of publishing. In other words, content that is against the Guiding Rules, such as unfounded allegations, may also be required to be de-indexed or made anonymous, whereas content that does not violate the Guiding Rules at the time of publishing will normally be acceptable even following the passing of time.

Final remarks

As indicated above, Danish media law can be quite complicated. The complicated state of affairs does not further the free flow of information while protecting relevant contradicting interests such as private life. The problem seems to be intensified for online media. It is difficult enough even for professional journalists to act according to the law, and for non-professional online actors it may be downright impossible, even if they wish to. A private person wanting to upload some pictures and comments must, in principle, check the 80-page EU General Data Protection Act, the Danish Supplement Act (presently in preparation) and a few provisions in the Criminal Code, only the last of which may be manageable. In addition, many online activists appear to have no intention of following the law, and implementation is difficult especially for private parties and even for the police. Also, the many institutions involved such as Danish and European courts, the Press Council, the Data Protection Agency and others, which deal with partly overlapping areas and cases, while not always applying similar standards to similar situations, may add to the confusion.

4 Estonia – raising high the roof beams of freedom of expression

New media environment in Estonia

Rain Veetõusme, Tiina Pajuste, and Mart Susi

Some introductory notes

Our goal is to map the Estonian human rights landscape from the perspective of safeguarding freedom of expression in new media. The answer to the question of whether a small country (in terms of population and territory) that is in a "complicated" location geopolitically[1] and has recently gone through a transition into a democratic society can do more than simply mirror the European and global developments, is not obvious. As a principle, neither a country's size nor its history is in direct correlation with its ability to influence global human rights law and policies.[2] In the context of freedom of expression and new media, Estonia, like any other country, can be viewed from the perspective of positive law, court practice and the practices of the new media stakeholders. In all these spheres, we can study whether the country is simply following in the footsteps of the European and global human rights communities – e.g. whether the country accepts international human rights law policies and norms without hesitation, whether national courts and stakeholders follow the practices of regional and international counterparts, or whether the country is a forerunner or engaging participant in some relevant human rights communities. Being a forerunner does not necessarily mean European or global outreach, since "progressive" national legal norms or best practice may simply not be visible from the outside.

Background

Estonia is a country of 1.3 million, which has earned a high international reputation both for its internet and press freedom. The Freedom on the Net 2016

---

1 Estonia's neighbour is Russia, and at the same time it is on the Eastern border of the EU and NATO.
2 Jensen demonstrates how in the 1960s Jamaica was instrumental in achieving a global breakthrough from simple human rights rhetoric towards the practical dimension of human rights – see Steven L.B. Jensen. *The Making of International Human Rights: The 1960s, Decolonization, and the Reconstruction of Global Values*, Cambridge: Cambridge University Press, 2016; or see the role of the South African Constitutional Court as one of the most advanced national human rights courts in the world despite it running opposite to the political winds. We refer to the landmark cases available through the website of the South African Constitutional Court.

Index, published by Freedom House, ranks Estonia first together with Iceland in the global context.[3] The Press Freedom Index ranked Estonia in 12th place in 2017.[4] Internet penetration in 2017 was about 91.6%.[5] Online media is growing in importance, demonstrated by the steady increase in the share of advertising.[6] Estonians have access to a wide array of online content, and there are few economic or political barriers to posting diverse types of content, including different types of news and opinions.[7] The majority of radio programmes can be listened to online. Some radio stations and television channels make their programmes available as on-demand archives.[8]

Most newspapers in Estonia have online versions, which limit the availability of stories from the print version that can be accessed free of charge online. Users have to pay to access the archive and the full version of all articles. One of the biggest and most influential news portals is *Delfi.ee*, operated by the Express Group. This portal produces some original content (including video and podcast) with the emphasis on headlines and the opportunity to comment on the news.[9] All other online versions of newspapers have the option to add comments, whereas some allow only comments by registered users and others allow comments both by registered and anonymous users.

Social media usage in Estonia is fairly widespread, and Estonians often make use of such sites to share news and information and to generate public discussion about current political debates.[10] Sixty five per cent of Estonians and 60 per cent of Russian speakers have at least one social media account.[11] The leading social network is Facebook. Russian speakers favour Russian social media, especially *Odnoklassniki* and *VKontakte*.[12]

We will not enter into a discussion in this article on whether the internet is a human right *per se*, or whether the right to internet access is a specific aspect of the right of access to and spreading of information and views. Despite the

---

3 Freedom on the Net Index, available online at https://freedomhouse.org/report/freedom-net/ freedom-net-2016 (accessed 1 February 2018).
4 Freedom of the Press Index, available online at https://rsf.org/en/ranking (last accessed 1 February 2018).
5 Internet World Stats Usage and Population Statistics, www.internetworldstats.com (last accessed 1 February 2018).
6 Currently, the market shares of different media forms in advertising are as follows: television 26%, newspapers 20%, internet 19%, radio 10%, outside advertising 10%, direct mailing 9% and magazines 6%. Statistics are available online at www.emor.ee (last accessed 1 February 2018).
7 Estonia Country Report, available online at https://freedomhouse.org/report/freedom-net/2015/ estonia (last accessed 1 February 2018).
8 Urmas Loit, Media Landscapes: Estonia, available online at http://ejc.net/media_landscapes/ estonia (last accessed 1 February 2018).
9 Delfi Website, www.delfi.ee (last accessed 1 February 2018).
10 Supra note 8.
11 Külliki Seppel, Meedia ja Infoväli, in *Eesti lõimumismonitooring 2015* (commissioned by the Estonian Ministry of Culture), available online at www.kul.ee/sites/kulminn/files/7peatykk. pdf (last accessed 1 February 2018), pp 88–89.
12 Supra note 8.

sometimes populist[13] rhetoric by some journalists and politicians[14] that the internet is a human right, such right has been recognised neither in positive law nor in national court practice. However, there was already a governmental policy in place in 2000 to secure the possibility of internet access in the countryside.[15] Partly due to a combination of various geopolitical factors, Estonia stands at the forefront of internet-related global challenges and initiatives. This is illustrated by the fact that the first cyberattacks in history occurred against Estonia in 2007,[16] and that the Tallinn Agenda for Freedom Online, which calls for governments to protect human rights online,[17] was adopted in Tallinn on 28 April 2014.[18]

The combination of these facts is sufficient to ascertain that new media communication is an integral part of everyday Estonian social reality. The enthusiasm related to the unprecedented communication possibilities of the internet has led, in our view, to a socially accepted preponderance of freedom of expression over the right to privacy in the digital reality. We will show below that academic writings addressing the relationship between the right to privacy and the freedom of expression give leave to the latter. There are no sociological studies into the social attitudes of Estonians regarding the importance of freedom of expression on the internet. Therefore, when Estonian academics in their writings emphasise that freedom of expression on the internet calls for a higher degree of protection, they speak on their own behalf or echo international views. It would be speculative to state that judicial "glorification" of the freedom of expression is a reaction to the high degree of governmental control over expression which existed during the socialist era.

National regulation on freedom of expression

General principles

Freedom of speech is laid down in paragraph 45 of the Constitution of Estonia.[19] This provision states that "[e]veryone has the right to freely disseminate

---

13 Read: academically not substantiated.
14 Referrals to these statements would take up too much room, so we rely here on our common observations of living together in Estonian society.
15 Eesti infopoliitika põhialused, adopted 13 May 1998, published in RT I 1998, 47, 700, paras 5–6, 11, 19.2.1. These Foundational Principles of the Estonian Information Policy include the aim to guarantee "equal reasonably priced access for all, irrespective of the geographical location, to means of communication" to avoid the creation of "information rich" and "information poor" regions or communities in Estonia.
16 For a detailed consideration of the 2007 cyberattacks, see Rain Ottis. Analysis of the 2007 Cyber Attacks against Estonia from the Information Warfare Perspective in Dan Remenyi (ed.), *Proceedings of the 7th European Conference on Information Warfare*, Reading, UK: Academic Conferences Limited, 2008.
17 Twenty three countries have joined the initiative.
18 Tallinn Agenda for Freedom Online Recommendations, available online at www.freedomonline. ee/foc-recommendations (last accessed 1 February 2018).
19 Constitution of the Republic of Estonia, entry into force 3 July 1992, RT 1992, 26, 349.

ideas, opinions, beliefs and other information by word, print, picture or other means". Estonian legal scholarship does not specifically address the question of whether the right to digital expression is protected under Article 45, limiting itself with the explanation that all forms of expression are protected.[20] Twenty years ago, the Estonian Supreme Court had already confirmed the fundamental importance of freedom of expression by declaring that this principle, which includes journalistic freedom of expression, is an indispensable guarantee of a democratic social order and thereby one of the most important social values.[21]

Like international human rights law, the Estonian Constitution also differentiates between "information" and "ideas", whereas both are afforded equal protection.[22] When interpreting the scope of protection inherent in the constitutional provision of freedom of expression, the Estonian commentators rely almost exclusively on the jurisprudence of the European Court of Human Rights (hereinafter "ECtHR"). For example, in the 2017 commentary to Article 45 of the Estonian Constitution,[23] the current Estonian Ombudsman, Ülle Madise, relied on dozens of judgments of the ECtHR, plus a handful of other sources. Rait Maruste, former judge at the ECtHR, points to the ECtHR standard that opinions cannot be vulgar or consciously insulting, or defaming of someone's honour or good name.[24] Elle Liiv explains, again with reference to the ECtHR jurisprudence, that not all shocking or insulting value judgments are unlawful.[25] The scholarly writings about the (offline) right to freedom of expression are not engaged in critical analysis of the international and European standards, nor are the Estonian courts engaged in "international dialogue" with the ECtHR.[26] For example, the Supreme Court has held that one specific expression can be both a factual statement and a value judgment, depending on the context of expressing

---

20 Ülle Madise et al. (eds.), *Eesti Vabariigi Põhiseadus: Kommenteeritud väljaanne*, Tallinn: Juura, 2017, Commentary to the Constitution of the Republic of Estonia, commentary to para 45.

21 Criminal Chamber of the Supreme Court, 26 August 1997, 3-1-1-80-97, section I.

22 The differentiation between "ideas" and "information" is in all major international human rights norms: European Human Rights Convention Article 10(1); International Covenant on Civil and Political Rights Article 19(2); EU Charter of Fundamental Rights Article 11(1); UN Universal Declaration of Human Rights Article 19.

23 Supra note 20, pp 456–467.

24 Rait Maruste, *Konstitutsionalism ning põhiõiguste ja −vabaduste kaitse*, Tallinn: Juura, 2004, p 547.

25 This is highlighted in Ele Liiv, *Väljendusvabaduse ja üldiste isikuõiguste konflikt veebipäevikute ja -foorumite näitel*, Tartu: Juridica, 2008/07, p 478.

26 One of the authors of this article has previously noted, writing about the role of the jurisprudence of the ECtHR in the case law of the Estonian Supreme Court

> The Estonian Supreme Court is not in a dialogue with the European courts. It sometimes credits the ECtHR with positions it does not have and has found in the jurisprudence of the European courts an instrument which can be used quite flexibly to substantiate its conclusions with a referral to an 'outside higher authority.
>
> see Mart Susi, Constitutional 'Trinity' for an EU Member State Stops at the Gates of National Sovereignty, *Journal of Comparative Politics*, 2013, Vol 6, No 2

it and on the audience towards which it is directed.[27] Neither Estonian scholarship nor court practice have produced novel interpretations of the right to freedom of expression, perhaps with the exception that Madis Ernits has expressed the view that intellectual freedom is also under constitutional protection.[28]

Limitations

The second part of paragraph 45 of the Constitution of Estonia lists the reasons for possible limitations:

> This right may be restricted by law to protect public order, morals, and the rights and freedoms, health, honour and good name of others. This right may also be restricted by law for state and local government public servants, to protect a state or business secret or information received in confidence, which has become known to them by reason of their office, and the family and private life of others, as well as in the interests of justice.

The reasons for limitations of the freedom of expression are narrower in the Estonian Constitution in comparison with the European Convention on Human Rights (hereinafter "ECHR"), which means that it provides wider protection than the ECHR. The Estonian Constitution does not include national security and territorial integrity in the list of potential reasons for limitations. The provisions also vary in relation to confidential information.[29] The ECHR states that freedom of expression can be restricted "for preventing the disclosure of information received in confidence",[30] whereas the Estonian Constitution proclaims that freedom of expression can be restricted "for state and local government public servants, to protect a state or business secret or information received in confidence, which has become known to them by reason of their office".[31]

Positive law and self-regulation

The Estonian media market is lightly regulated. No "media law" exists and issues regarding print media are covered by general laws, which sometimes results in gaps in regulation. Setting up a newspaper requires no license, permit or registration.[32] The written press relies mostly on self-regulation. In December 1997, the Estonian Newspaper Association passed a Code of Press Ethics. Two

---

27　Civil Chamber of the Supreme Court, 13 April 2007, 3-2-1-5-07, section 27.
28　This is highlighted in Madis Ernits, *Avalik väljendusvabadus ja demokraatia*, Tartu: Juridica 2007/1, p. 17.
29　Supra note 20.
30　Council of Europe, European Convention for the Protection of Human Rights and Fundamental Freedoms, as amended by Protocols Nos. 11 and 14, 4 November 1950, ETS 5, Article 10.
31　Supra note 19 §45.
32　Supra note 8.

self-regulation bodies enforce this Code – the Council of Public Word (Avaliku Sõna Nõukogu) and the Press Council (Pressinõukogu). The Supreme Court of Estonia has mentioned the Code of Press Ethics on three occasions in its jurisprudence, but as an additional source in interpreting the scope of the right to privacy *vis-à-vis* the interest of the public to know. One can conclude that the Supreme Court does not consider it a legally binding instrument.[33] As additional regulation, the Code of Press Ethics is supplemented by the agreements of good practice (Correction of errors online, Distinction of advertising and editorial content, Articles abstracting, Copyrights, Best practice agreement of phone sales, Best practice agreement of online comments, the main features of the newspapers), which regulate the correction of errors in web publications, commenting on online articles, the differentiation of advertisements and journalistic content, referring of articles, copyrights, the main attributes of newspapers and the criteria for membership in the Association. The existence of self-regulatory documents does not necessarily mean that these are up-to-date and are put into practice in reality. For example, the best practice agreement regarding online comments[34] stipulates that if a comment is not in accordance with good practices and is not deleted within a reasonable time, the online portal becomes liable in connection with the continuous publication of this comment. This document had already been adopted in 2008, which can lead us to conclude that the Estonian media community has not found it necessary to react to the *Delfi* judgment[35] and subsequent developments in Europe regarding online media responsibilities, at least formally. A statement establishing liability can be nothing more than a declaration, since it lacks an enforceability mechanism.

These two above-mentioned self-regulation bodies provide the public with the possibility of finding solutions to disagreements with the media without the need to go to court. The first body, the Council of Public Word, includes members from the printed media, some broadcasting channels and internet media. It aims to protect press freedom, examine complaints about mass media regarding good conduct and adherence to the good practices of journalism.[36] The Council both initiates examinations on its own and receives individual complaints. The second self-regulation body is the Press Council. It has ten members, including six from the media sector and four lay members from the non-media sectors. It is a voluntary body of media self-regulation that handles complaints from the public about material in the media. The Press Council discusses complaints about material that has appeared in the press, in online portals with journalistic content, and

---

33 Madis Ernits, *Põhiõigused, demokraatia, õigusriik*, Tartu: Tartu Ülikooli Kirjastus, 2011, p. 238.
34 Estonian Newspaper Association. The Agreements on Good Practices – Hea Tava Lepped: Best practice agreement of online comments, 2008, available online at http://eall.ee/lepped/online. html (last accessed 1 February 2018).
35 *Delfi vs Estonia*, ECtHR judgment of 16 June 2015 (Grand Chamber), no 64569/09.
36 More information about this entity is available on its website at www.asn.ee/english/in_ general.html (last accessed 1 February 2018).

on public service broadcasting stations.[37] The number of complaints sent to the Press Council has increased in recent years. In 2014, 51 complaints were filed, in 2015 – 75, and in 2016 – 84. In the first half of 2017, 37 complaints were filed.[38]

There are, however, statutory rules that regulate broadcasting and advertising. The Constitution lacks a clear norm regarding the right of the state to demand licensing of radio, television and film companies. But this can be deducted from §11 of the Constitution, which is the general provision regarding restrictions to the rights and freedoms laid down in the Constitution.[39] The Estonian broadcasting sector is governed directly by the Media Services Act and the Estonian Public Broadcasting Act and indirectly by the Copyright Act, the State Secrets Act, the Public Information Act and the Advertising Act. Following amendments made in 2001, there is no advertising in public service broadcasting; as of July 2002, it was excluded from public television. In 2005, ads were also removed from public radio.[40]

The Ministry of Culture is responsible for media and broadcasting policy. It also handles copyright issues and supervises compliance with the Act to Regulate Dissemination of Works which Contain Pornography or Promote Violence or Cruelty. The role of an independent media services controller is fulfilled by the Estonian Technical Surveillance Authority under the administration of the Ministry of Economic Affairs and Communications. Advertising issues are under the scrutiny of the Consumer Protection Board. And the Public Broadcasting Council, a body appointed by the Parliament, supervises public service broadcasting.[41]

Liability

Exercising the freedom of expression can also lead to abuse of that right. The Estonian Constitution, § 17 states that "[n]o one's honour or good name shall be defamed". The protection of a person's honour and good name is done through civil means laid down in the Law of Obligations Act. The Law of Obligations Act, § 1046(1) states that:

> The defamation of a person, inter alia by passing undue value judgement, by the unjustified use of the name or image of the person, or by breaching the inviolability of the private life or another personality right of the person is unlawful unless otherwise provided by law.

---

37 More information about the Press Council is available on its website at www.eall.ee/pressinoukogu/index-eng.html (last accessed 1 February 2018).
38 Press Council complaint statistic is available on its website at www.eall.ee/pressinoukogu/statistika.html
39 The wording of §11 is as follows, "Rights and freedoms may be restricted only in accordance with the Constitution. Such restrictions must be necessary in a democratic society and shall not distort the nature of the rights and freedoms restricted".
40 Supra note 8.
41 Ibid.

In case of defamation, the injured person has the option of filing a claim for the compensation of unlawfully caused damage (§ 1043), demanding that the person who disclosed such information refute the information or publish a correction at the person's expense (§ 1047(4)), demanding that damaging behaviour be terminated (§ 1055(1)), or filing a claim to ensure that damaging behaviour will be refrained from in the future (§ 1055(1)). A person can also file a claim to compensate non-pecuniary damage according to § 134(2) of the Law of Obligations Act. These options are not mutually exclusive and several of them can be used at the same time.

Compensation for an act of freedom of expression that infringes on someone else's rights can take place in two main ways: monetary compensation or an action, e.g. a public apology or refuting the information that damaged the honour or good name of a person. Monetary compensation can take place on the basis of mutual agreement or if the parties cannot agree, in which case it is assigned by a court.[42]

Although a person's honour and good name are no longer directly protected through the Penal Code (two relevant criminal acts were laid down in the old Criminal Code that was in force until 2002 – defamation and insulting the honour and dignity of another person), in certain cases defamation can amount to "incitement of hatred". This crime is defined in § 151(1) of the Penal Code:

> Activities which publicly incite to hatred, violence or discrimination on the basis of nationality, race, colour, sex, language, origin, religion, sexual orientation, political opinion, or financial or social status if this results in danger to the life, health or property of a person is punishable by a fine of up to three hundred fine units or by detention.[43]

The Criminal Chamber of the Supreme Court has given directions to interpret this provision. It held that the published message has to be such that it does not merely express the hostile attitude against some group mentioned in the provision, but it is also of a nature that could provoke hatred or violence in other people and bring about the spread of hatred or violence towards some social group. In addition, the published message needs to have the potential to find resonance in society. This means that the group with which the message might resonate should be of a certain size and have certain characteristics.[44]

In addition to incitement of hatred, freedom of expression can also have a connection with an aggravated breach of public order (§ 263 of the Penal Code), as this can include threats. Accordingly, someone was punished for promising on several occasions in the media to blow up the Bronze Soldier (a controversial Soviet World War II war memorial in Tallinn, Estonia).[45]

---

42 Supra note 24, p 333.
43 This implements § 12(2) of the Constitution which lays down that "[t]he incitement of national, racial, religious or political hatred, violence or discrimination shall, by law, be prohibited and punishable. The incitement of hatred, violence or discrimination between social strata shall, by law, also be prohibited and punishable."
44 Criminal Chamber of the Supreme Court, 10 April 2006, 3-1-1-117-05, section 20.
45 Supra note 33, p 22.

The Penal Code still includes the crimes of "defamation and insulting of persons enjoying international immunity" (§ 247), insulting representatives of state authority (§ 275), and insulting and defamation of court (§ 305, 305). However, despite these exceptions and the provisions mentioned above, public enforcement options remain very limited in the area of defamation.

Estonia in the European human rights landscape

Paragraph 3 of the Constitution of Estonia states that "[g]enerally recognized principles and rules of international law are an inseparable part of the Estonian legal system". In addition, § 123 states that "[i]f laws or other legislation of Estonia are in conflict with international treaties ratified by the Riigikogu /the Parliament/, the provisions of the international treaty shall apply". Therefore, international human rights instruments, such as the ECHR, the International Covenant on Civil and Political Rights, the International Covenant on Economic, Social and Cultural Rights and the EU Charter of Fundamental Rights are all applicable and part of the legal system of Estonia.

The first time the Supreme Court of Estonia referred to an ECtHR case was in December 1996, when the Constitutional Review Chamber referred to the 1984 decision in *Malone vs UK* in interpreting the principle of legality.[46] The first references to the ECHR and the jurisprudence of the Court included no introductions or explanations. The Supreme Court later confirmed that, on the basis of § 3(2) and § 123(2) of the Estonian Constitution, the ECHR and the positions of the ECtHR in interpreting the Convention are indivisible parts of the Estonian legal system, which take priority over Estonian laws and can also provide guidance in interpreting the Constitution itself.[47]

The ECHR was to a large extent the example for creating the catalogue of fundamental rights contained in the Estonian Constitution. Also, in interpreting the Constitution the Estonian legal scholarship has relied extensively on the ECHR and the jurisprudence of the ECtHR. This is also true of Article 10 regarding freedom of expression. However, Ernits has pointed out that there are no obstacles for Estonian courts to grant more freedom of expression in the Estonian legal order than that mandated by the European minimum.[48]

Emerging from its membership of the Council of Europe, Estonia has listed the following national priorities, amongst others:[49]

i securing the authority of the EHRC and the judgments of the ECtHR;
ii developing international law norms by focusing on media freedom and freedom of expression, including on the internet.

---

46 Constitutional Review Chamber of the Supreme Court, 10 December 1996, 3-4-1-3-96, section I.
47 Criminal Chamber of the Supreme Court, 20 September 2002, 3-1-1-88-02, section 7.1.
48 Supra note 33, pp. 16–17.
49 These priorities do not significantly differ from the priorities of other countries.

When holding the chairmanship of the Council, Estonia was prioritising the need for developing policies and standards governing the internet.[50] The measures included supporting the EuroDIG 2016 Conference in Brussels with the view of bringing to the attention of EuroDIG the most recent standard-setting work of the Council of Europe and its relevance for European citizens, as well as hosting a conference in 2016 on internet freedom.

The Tallinn Agenda for Freedom Online, adopted in Tallinn on 28 April 2014,[51] has the following introductory statement: "... the same rights that people have offline must also be protected online ..."[52] This agenda has remained largely unnoticed in the international arena – we have not noticed any referrals to this agenda in literature or in other policy documents. It reflects a growing global trend to address the internet-related policies via forums involving stakeholders, public and international organs and scholars.[53] The question of whether the concept of sameness between human rights online and offline is justified remains outside the scope of this article. For the purposes of this article, we can conclude that access to the internet and protecting freedom of expression on the internet is of high priority in the Estonian governmental level. This is exemplified by the Digital Agenda 2020 for Estonia, which the Estonian Government approved in November 2013 and which aims at establishing a well-working state information and communication technology environment and supporting the development of the Estonian information society.[54]

The European Commission against Racism and Intolerance criticised Estonia in 2015 for a provision in the Penal Code, which makes it impossible to prosecute incitement of hatred when it has no serious consequences – for example, via online media. The Commission recommended

> that the Estonian authorities introduce without delay in parliamentary proceedings a draft amendment to Article 151 of the Criminal Code, removing the restriction whereby an offence cannot be deemed to have taken place unless it is proven that it entails a risk to the health, life or property of the victim.[55]

---

50 Priorities of the Estonian Chairmanship, available online at www.vm.ee/en/priorities-estonian-chairmanship (last accessed 1 February 2018).
51 Supra note 18.
52 Ibid.
53 See, for example, the UN Internet Governance Forum, which is a multi-stakeholder platform to facilitate discussion of public policy issues pertaining to the internet, existing under the authority of the UN, of the Global Network Initiative, which is a civil forum involving companies, investors, civil society organisations and academics.
54 The aim is supported by four goals: (a) ICT infrastructure that supports economic growth, the development of the state and welfare of the population; (b) larger number of jobs with higher added value, improved international competitiveness and higher quality of life; (c) smarter governance; and (d) enhanced awareness of Estonia as an e-state all over the world. For more information, see the Ministry of Economic Affairs and Communications website at www.mkm.ee/en/objectives-activities/information-society (last accessed 1 February 2018) and the Digital Agenda 2020 for Estonia, available online at www.mkm.ee/sites/default/files/digital_agenda_2020_estonia_engf.pdf (last accessed 1 February 2018).
55 European Commission against Racism and Intolerance, Report on Estonia (fifth monitoring cycle), 16 June 2015, Doc no CRI(2015)36, recommendation 39.

At the time of completing this article in February 2018, there are no initiatives to follow the Commission's recommendation. Recent amendments to the Penal Code were adopted by the Parliament in 2017, but these recommendations were not part of the package.

We conclude that there is some degree of polarisation in Estonia's position in the European human rights landscape regarding freedom of expression. Estonia can be labelled an activist country in advancing freedom of expression for everyone and everywhere on the internet. This entails removing obstacles for internet access and setting standards for regulation of human rights protection online. On the other hand, when it comes to limiting freedom of expression via criminal law, Estonia does not comply with its apparent international obligations.

Court cases

Practice of the Estonian Supreme Court on (new) media issues

The Estonian Supreme Court has limited jurisprudence on freedom of expression matters. According to the index of the Supreme Court, since 2013 there have been no judgments of the Constitutional Review Chamber where Article 45 issues of the Constitution have emerged.[56] Prior to 2013 – when the Supreme Court was using a previous indexing system, there were also no entries concerning freedom of expression for Constitutional Review Chamber cases. According to the index, the Administrative Chamber has made no judgments regarding freedom of expression since 2013 and the Civil Chamber has made only two. These do not concern new media.

In an analysis of the jurisprudence of the Estonian Supreme Court, in 2012 Eve Rohtmets analysed the areas where the Supreme Court has relied upon the jurisprudence of the ECtHR.[57] There is not a single Supreme Court case in which it has relied on Strasbourg standards regarding freedom of expression. In an analysis reflecting the practice of the ECtHR, Rohtmets referred to the view that the internet environment cannot be subject to similar regulation with printed media.[58] This analysis does not indicate that Strasbourg standards have any role in the Estonian Supreme Court's jurisprudence on freedom of expression matters.

---

56 Accessible via Supreme Court website: www.riigikohus.ee/en/judgements/constitutional-judgments (last accessed 1 February 2018).

57 Eve Rohtmets, *Euroopa Inimõiguste Kohtu praktika Riigikohtu lahendites*, Tartu: Riigikohus, 2012, available via the website of the Supreme Court.

58 Eve Rohtmets, *Ajakirjandusvabaduse ja eraelu puutumatuse tasakaal Euroopa Inimõiguste Kohtu praktikas*, Tartu: Riigikohus, 2014, pp. 14–15, referring to *Węgrzynowski and Smolczewski vs Poland*, ECtHR judgment of 16 July 2013, no 33846/07, para 58. It may be noted here that the referral to this judgment is not correct. The ECtHR does not write in para 58 that there cannot be similar regulation of online and offline media regarding freedom of expression. It instead expresses hesitation on this matter: "Therefore, the policies governing reproduction of material from the printed media and the Internet may differ".

The previous data leads only to one main observation – the right to freedom of expression in Estonia has largely not been subject to judicial supervision. We have no data to address the reasons for this phenomenon. It is not possible to assess the impact of Strasbourg jurisprudence on the Estonian judicial system in the sphere of freedom of expression due to the absence of respective domestic case law. It is noteworthy that in the *Delfi* case the Supreme Court in its judgment from 10 June 2009 did not refer to any ECtHR judgments.

Estonian freedom of expression cases at the European Court of Human Rights

There are only two cases from Estonia regarding freedom of expression that have reached the ECtHR.[59] Both are highly significant in the Strasbourg jurisprudence, having become part of the Court's doctrinal arsenal in developing the scope and meaning of freedom of expression. These are the *Tammer vs Estonia*[60] and *Delfi vs Estonia*[61] cases. Overall, at the time of writing this article, there were 50 judgments on the merits by the Strasbourg Court against Estonia, so these cases represent about 4 per cent of the overall judgments.[62]

Tammer vs Estonia

This case concerned proceedings brought by a well-known journalist after being convicted for insulting the wife of a well-known Estonian politician as being an unfit and absent mother. The applicant was criminally convicted, although at the time of domestic proceedings the offence of insult was in the process of becoming decriminalised in the Estonian judicial system. The applicant argued that Ms. Laanaru, the wife of the well-known politician Mr. Savisaar, was a public figure and, therefore, the scope of her privacy was lessened.[63] The interference into the applicant's expression amounted to censorship, discouraging journalists in the future from writing critically about politicians.[64]

The ECtHR unanimously decided that there was no violation of ECHR Article 10. The Court presented the opinion that the applicant "could have formulated

---

59 There is also a third case dealing with an Article 10 violation – *Kalda vs Estonia*, ECtHR judgment of 19 January 2016, no 17429/10 – but this focused on the right of access to information, and accordingly is not directly relevant to our article. In that case, the Court concluded that prisoners should have access to some internet sites, even if the information contained there could be acquired by alternative means of communication, if it was difficult to get the information by alternative means.

60 *Tammer vs Estonia*, ECtHR judgment of 06 February 2001, no 41205/98.

61 Supra note 35.

62 In comparison, at the time of writing this article, the ECtHR had made 148 judgments against Lithuania, of which 8 concerned Article 10 (5.5%), the respective figures for Finland are 185 and 28 (15%), for Latvia 125 and 7 (5.5%) and for Hungary 315 and 24 (7.5%).

63 Supra note 60, para 46.

64 Ibid, para 48.

his criticism of Ms. Laanaru's actions without resorting to such insulting expressions,"[65] and that a public figure has the option of expressing views about one's private life in a private capacity, which then results in a different threshold of acceptable public scrutiny. This judgment has become a standard reference in the Strasbourg Court's subsequent jurisprudence and academic literature[66] by establishing the standard of "at least some private sphere" for a public figure.

The problematic aspect of this judgment lies in the acceptance by the ECtHR of the criminal sanction against the applicant as remaining within the margin of appreciation afforded to the Contracting States.[67] The Court did not address the question about the appropriateness of the criminal sanction at all. We can contrast this silence against the understanding reached by the Strasbourg Court about 10 years later, where a criminal sanction (imprisonment[68]) was considered compatible with the requirements of ECHR Article 10 only in exceptional circumstances, such as in the case of hate speech or incitement to violence.[69] The representative of the applicant may have overlooked the matter of the compatibility of a criminal sanction with the requirements of ECHR Article 10. Tammer may have been the last person in Estonia convicted for insult.

Delfi vs Estonia

This case is widely known in judicial and professional circles around the globe. It concerned the liability of an online news portal for anonymous insulting comments posted on its website, being the first case ever where the Strasbourg Court had to consider this issue. The Court established the obligation of a news portal, which has an economic interest in the online traffic, to act diligently and remove comments amounting to hate speech on its own initiative. The number of analyses of the impact of this case both for the internet service providers (hereinafter "ISPs") and more generally for human rights law is unprecedented – strictly academic analyses can be measured in tens, but if blogs and other new media formats are included, then definitely in hundreds. We will not engage in a discussion of whether the Court's judgment sufficiently took into account the constitutional aspects of the internet and human rights law and/or offered

---

65 Ibid, para 67.
66 Ronald J. Krotoszynski Jr., *Privacy Revisited: A Global Perspective on the Right to Be Left Alone*, New York: Oxford University Press, 2016, pp. 158–159; Dirk Voorhoof, The European Convention of Human Rights: The Right to Freedom of Expression and Information restricted by Duties and Responsibilities in a Democratic Society, EUI Working Paper, Florence, EUI RSCAS 2014/12, p. 19.
67 The Court uses expressly the "margin of appreciation" language in para 69 and in the subsequent paragraph expresses the view that the sanction was not disproportionate and pursued a legitimate aim.
68 In the *Tammer* case, the journalist was convicted under Criminal Code Article 130, which did foresee the possibility of detention in the form or arrest.
69 See *Amorim Giestas and Jesus Costa Bordalo vs Portugal*, ECtHR judgment of 03 April 2014, no 37840/10, para 36.

sufficient practical guidelines, since this is not the goal of the present article. We will briefly address three aspects, which have so far escaped scholarly attention when the *Delfi* case is scrutinised: was something "lost in translation", did the judgment change any practices of online portals in Estonia, and did *Delfi* miss a potentially decisive argument in front of the Strasbourg Court?

The position of the Estonian Supreme Court regarding the characterisation of the content of the debatable comments was "lost in translation". The ECtHR writes that the Estonian Supreme Court assessed the impugned comments as mainly constituting hate speech.[70] This is the imagination of the ECtHR at work, as the Estonian Supreme Court did nothing of the kind. The highest court in Estonia stated that the comments were inappropriate value judgments, meaning that they were vulgar, humiliating and taunting.[71] This is different from hate speech. However, the characterisation of some comments as hate speech was decisive enough for the Grand Chamber to reach the conclusion that these comments did not enjoy the protection of ECHR Article 10.[72] Therefore, the Grand Chamber interfered in the domestic assessment of the facts, deviating from the principle that domestic courts are more closely located and, therefore, better positioned to take a stand on relevant factual circumstances.

Second, what has been the impact of the *Delfi* judgment on the Estonian media environment? Our subsequent views stem from living in Estonia and using the media environment on almost a daily basis. Since there are no specific studies made on this subject, we cannot refer to any data and the reader has to rely on our collective understanding. Some online portals have ceased to offer the possibility of anonymous comments. Soon after the *Delfi* judgment, there was a "campaign" by one of the major daily newspapers *Postimees* with an apparent goal to influence the public opinion against anonymous comments. This campaign lasted for a few weeks and ended silently with neither a reaction from the legislature nor a visible reaction in the behaviour of the civil society. Some portals open articles for comments selectively. Delfi itself has not changed its policies – anonymous commenting is still possible. Delfi must operate automatic filtering or person-led monitoring or both, since once in a while a statement regarding the removal of a comment can be seen in the comments section. We have no reason to state that the *Delfi vs Estonia* case has led to a significant or perhaps even noticeable change in the practices of Estonian news portals regarding the issue of comments. It is our impression that the volume of anonymous comments has decreased, but we are unable to establish a causal link to the *Delfi* judgment.

Third, there was one fundamental question which was not raised by the *Delfi* team or at the initiative of domestic or international courts. This is the issue of the constitutionality of censorship. Censorship is prohibited by Article 45(2) of the Estonian Constitution by a simple sentence, "There is no censorship". Our

---

70 Supra note 35, para 117.
71 Estonian Supreme Court judgment (the *Delfi* judgment), no 3-2-1-43-09, para 16, 1st paragraph.
72 Supra note 35, para 140.

comparative study shows that with the exception of Finland, there is a constitutional level prohibition of censorship in all Baltic and Scandinavian countries.[73] In some countries (at least in the Baltics), this prohibition may originate from the constitutional benchmarking with Germany,[74] as the German Grundgesetz prohibits censorship in Article 5. The unraised question in the *Delfi* proceedings was not whether monitoring anonymous comments and deleting these after the assessment by an online news portal is censorship, but whether the constitutional prohibition of censorship by itself excludes the option of shifting the responsibility to monitor and take action to online portals? The argument of censorship was raised by *Delfi* during the Strasbourg proceedings,[75] but not in reference to the constitutional prohibition. The Grand Chamber adopted the position that the requirement to take measures for limiting expressions on the internet portal "… can by no means be equated to 'private censorship'",[76] but left the reasoning behind it unexplained. Judges Sajó and Tsotsoria were critical of this lack of explanation and expressed the view that the Grand Chamber's judgment was "an invitation to self-censorship at its worst",[77] elegantly drawing a comparison between internet censorship and censorial regulation during the English Reformation, where licensing provided a tool to easily convict offenders.[78] In the discussion section of this article, we will raise the question of whether the uneven constitutional prohibition of censorship may lead to the uneven protection of freedom of expression among the Council of Europe's Member States.

Discussion of the lessons emerging from the Estonian new media environment

The matter of censorship

The *Delfi* case raises a dilemma. On the one hand, if internet censorship is expressly not prohibited by European human rights principles and EU law, then it cannot be excluded that under certain conditions private ISPs can have constitutional legitimacy to exercise such censorship. On the other hand, if censorship

---

73 For the purposes of this article, it is sufficient to note the constitutional character of the prohibition of censorship. The actual wording and scope may vary in different countries – for example, in Sweden this prohibition is given in Chapter 1, Article 2 of the Freedom of the Press Act, which has the status of fundamental law. In Denmark the prohibition refers to some historical reasons stating that this shall never be introduced again (section 77 of the Danish Constitution) and Lithuania's Constitution Article 44 censorship is prohibited regarding mass information.

74 There are several constitutional norms in the Baltic constitutions which copy German wording – take, for example, the protection of marriage. The German Constitution was used as one of the main references when the Baltic constitutions were written or revised after the collapse of the socialist system.

75 Supra note 35, paras 73 and 78.

76 Ibid, para 157.

77 Ibid, joint dissenting opinion para 1.

78 Ibid, joint dissenting opinion's appendix.

is expressly prohibited in a particular national constitution, then within this particular country's jurisdiction censorship cannot be undertaken in whatever format. A conflict between supranational law and national constitutional law inevitably emerges. The dilemma is the following: in order to secure the principle of equal protection of human rights in Europe, either the European human rights regime may have to return to the safe harbour principle, which excludes the option of private online censorship ("anything goes" principle in our view), or there may be an unbearable and unrealistic goal to eliminate the prohibition of censorship from national constitutions.

The matter of delegating censorship of internet traffic to private ISPs is one of the principal areas of disagreement within the debate concerning the role of ISPs in the horizontal protection of fundamental rights on the internet. Some argue that the obligation to censor has to remain in the hands of the state only. La Rue has categorically objected to using or forcing internet intermediaries to exercise censorship on behalf of the public authority.[79] Academics seem to object to the delegation as well. Coudert and Werkers are critical of the ability of ISPs to protect fundamental rights, since these are not binding for private entities, and of the legitimacy of any balancing conducted by private entities.[80] Angepoulus has analysed the efficiency of the notice-and-action systems in the context of the practice of European regional courts – which in his view support the doctrine of balancing – and concluded that the proper answer to the intermediary liability question must be in the vertical approach, where the states carry the burden of implementing fundamental rights protection formulas and not the private intermediaries.[81] European policy-making bodies, the EU and the Council of Europe, as well as the global internet stakeholders, may be viewed as legal realists when advancing the understanding that the role of the public institutions should be handing down the criteria to the ISPs to properly balance conflicting rights. The Council of Europe explicitly asserts that balancing is the appropriate method to be applied on the internet, as it uses the "balancing" language when recommending compliance methods with the freedom of expression on the internet.[82] The *Google* judgment of the Court of Justice of the European Union expressly establishes the obligation of the data controller (the online internet

---

79 UN Human Rights Council's Special Rapporteur Frank La Rue's report of 16 May 2011, where in para 43 he writes that censorship measures should never be delegated to a private entity.

80 Fanny Coudert and Evi Werkers, In the Aftermath of the Promusicae Case: How to Strike the Balance? *International Journal of Law and Information Technology*, 2010, Vol 18, No 1, 50–71 – the authors prudently point out that restricting a fundamental right online is a sanction, but in order to have the sanction averted, should internet subscribers be required to prove innocence in front of a private entity?

81 Christina Angelopoulos and Stijn Smet, Notice-and-fair-balance: How to Reach a Aompromise between Fundamental Rights in European Intermediary Liability, *Journal of Media Law*, 2016, Vol 8, No 2, 266–301, at 300–301

82 Appendix to Recommendation CM/Rec(2016)5 of the Committee of Ministers to Member States on Internet Freedom, adopted by the Committee of Ministers on 13 April 2016 at the 1253rd meeting of the Ministers' Deputies), para 2.4.1.

company) to duly examine the merits of requests for ending the online intrusion into privacy by displaying personal data.[83] At the time of writing this article, the European Council's Committee of Ministers has not yet approved the Recommendation on Internet Intermediaries. In paragraph 1.3.5. of this Recommendation, the Committee of Ministers is expected to express the opinion that "State authorities should not directly or indirectly impose a general obligation on intermediaries to monitor content which they merely give access to, or which they transmit or store, be it by automated means or not. " This means a change in the Council's position – back to the vertical approach regarding the protection of fundamental rights on the internet. As soon as the Committee of Ministers adopts this Recommendation, it will signify European level acceptance of the fact that private censorship is a practice which occurs on the internet in reality in some Contracting Countries. Whether or not it is compelled by state authority or law is not decisive in this context. If it was different – not a practice occurring within some countries – there would be no reason to write about its unsuitability from the perspective of human rights law.

The argument that can be immediately raised against this background, which might also be the opportunity that *Delfi* missed, is to state that any requirement to assess the legality of comments and subsequently delete comments, if conducted by a non-judicial entity, is censorship and, as such, against any constitution which has a provision prohibiting censorship. It is our prediction that sooner or later the European and perhaps global community will accept the understanding that ISPs are practicing censorship of digital content. This will lead to the constitutional objection from the ISPs operating in countries where censorship is prohibited by constitutional norms. They will simply argue that the obligation to monitor user-generated content is unconstitutional. It may also mean geographically uneven protection of fundamental rights, where the watershed is whether censorship in a particular country is constitutionally prohibited or not. Ironically, the protection of fundamental rights will be higher in the countries where censorship is not prohibited in the national constitutions, since this situation will allow private ISPs to implement the obligation of protecting fundamental rights online.

Does a lack of strict regulation mean higher protection of freedom of expression?

The information presented above shows that freedom of expression in new media has not been the subject of sizeable court practice in Estonia – to say the least. In fact, there are few court cases regarding this. Positive law has few specific norms to regulate new media from the perspective of freedom of expression protection. Yet, international observers praise Estonia as a country where the roof beams of

---

83 Google Spain SL, *Google Inc. vs. Agencia Española de Protección de Datos* (AEPD), Mario Costeja Gonzáles (Grand Chamber), C-131/12, judgment of 13 May 2014, para 77.

freedom of expression protection are raised high. Is there a correlation, does less formal regulation and jurisprudence mean a higher degree of protection? The Estonian new media landscape brings us to a somewhat surprising conclusion that this appears to be the case.

Our explanation is that since human rights law is not limited to concrete legal norms, but is also comprised of policies which emerge and develop through discursive practice, the key to understanding the Estonian situation is hidden in the proportionately high emphasis in public policy on supporting the idea of freedom of expression as opposed to formal regulation. More formal regulation and courts' jurisprudence may lead, in contrast, to the principle of freedom of expression being lost in definitive commands, which lack the ability to adapt to a rapidly changing new media environment.

5 Finland

*Riku Neuvonen, Jukka Viljanen,
and Mikko Hoikka*

Media environment in Finland

The Finnish media environment is generally considered free and pluralistic. Finland was ranked number one for six consecutive years in the World Press Freedom Index (2011–2016), compiled by Reporters Without Borders. In the latest index (2017), Finland dropped to third place behind Norway and Sweden. With more than 4000 print publication titles, Finland also holds first place in the global comparison of press titles per capita.[1] The media landscape consists of a great diversity of politically, culturally, ethically and regionally divergent media.

When measuring media pluralism by concentration of media ownership, as done recently in the EU Media Pluralism Monitor, however, Finland tends to get a relatively high risk assessment. The concentration of ownership is partly due to the small language and market area, with an audience of 5.3 million, and to the relatively broad part of market coverage by public service media. Thus, reaching a profitable market size and ability to invest in service development may require a company size that counts for a strikingly large market share in a European comparison. Finland is also a bilingual culture, with a Swedish-speaking minority and also the language rights of the Sami people guaranteed in the Constitution. Twelve newspapers are published in Swedish, eight of which are dailies. Sami media, especially the news programme Oddasat, is mainly published in cooperation with Swedish and Norwegian partners in Northern Finland.[2]

The variety of Finnish media is traditionally based on a very high penetration of press subscriptions. In a country with a low population density, this is due to the combination of a relatively efficient postal system, a low VAT rate for press subscriptions, permissive telemarketing regulation and most prominently, a vivid culture of reading. This combination has, however, already started to erode, not only due to being substituted by mostly free internet content, but also through

---

1 Reporters Without Borders, Country Profile of Finland 2017, https://rsf.org/en/finland (last accessed 5 February 2018).
2 EU Media Pluralism Monitor, Country Profile of Finland 2015, http://monitor.cmpf.eui.eu/mpm2015/results/finland/ (last accessed 5 February 2018).

the rapid price increases in postal services and an increase of the press VAT rate in 2012. Nonetheless, the figures for newspaper subscriptions are still quite high.

The size of the Finnish media market is around 4 billion euros. In media types, the biggest shares belong to television (27%), newspapers (25%), magazines (14%) and books (14%).[3] Internet advertising covers around 8% of the media market value. In corporate turnovers, the biggest media players are Sanoma (1717 million euros), the public broadcasting service Yleisradio (468 million), Otava (293 million), Alma Media (292 million) and MTV (230 million). Around 50 different media companies reach a turnover of over 10 million euros.

The main challenge of the media landscape is the digital revolution, which is slowly changing the way media content is consumed, but more crucially and certainly more rapidly, it is moving advertising investment to digital channels other than mass media. Most of these digital platforms are owned by multinational companies. One strategy of media companies in adapting to the situation is stronger involvement in the content marketing business. This trend helps publishing houses to create new revenues and keep investing in creative skills that have evident synergy with journalism, but it does not solve the problem of profitable digital journalism itself.

Finland is traditionally considered one of the top countries in the digital environment. The number of internet connections per capita is relatively high in Finland. In 2015, 90% of households had a broadband connection, whereas the average in the EU is 80%, with only the Netherlands, Luxembourg, Norway and the United Kingdom ahead of Finland. Another important factor is the number of fast mobile networks that supplement fixed broadband networks. In 2014, there were 138 mobile broadband subscriptions per 100 inhabitants (Sweden had 113, Estonia 114 and the EU average was 72). One of the key findings in the European Commission study on the prices of broadband subscriptions was that prices in Finland in that area are relatively low.[4]

Freedom of speech doctrine in Finland

Section 12.1 of the Finnish Constitution guarantees the freedom of expression as the fundamental right of sananvapaus, literally translating to freedom of the word. The definition dates back to the comprehensive fundamental rights reform in 1995, following the Finnish ratification of the European Convention on Human Rights (ECHR) in 1989. Section 12.1 defines freedom of expression as follows:

> Everyone has the freedom of expression. Freedom of expression entails the right to express, disseminate and receive information, opinions and other

---

3 NORDICOM (Nordic Information Centre for Media and Communications Research) 2016 statistics, www.nordicom.gu.se.
4 Finland Media Landscape, European Journalism Centre, ecj.net/media_landscapes/finland

communications without prior prevention by anyone. More detailed provisions on the exercise of the freedom of expression are laid down by an Act. Provisions on restrictions relating to pictorial programmes that are necessary for the protection of children may be laid down by an Act.

The Finnish term being nearer to the common law term freedom of speech, the definition is more closely linked to the ECHR Article 10 definition of freedom of expression and, further in the continental constitutional tradition, to Article 11 of the French Declaration of the Rights of Man and Citizen of 1793. The fundamental rights protection covers the communication chain from expressing and disseminating to receiving, as well as all content in the form of any information, opinion or communication. Prior prevention of using the freedom is prohibited. Since the scope a priori covers all types and forms of communication, all limitations have to be legitimated through the general limitation requirements of fundamental rights. Section 12.1 also provides for specification of the freedom in legislation, as well as a special mandate for audiovisual content restrictions necessary for the protection of children.[5]

The concept of freedom of the press goes back to the Swedish (Finland was part of Sweden until 1809) law of 1766, inaugurating freedom of the writing and of the press (skriff- och tryckfrihet), with the emphasis being predominantly on the authorisation of text media as a form of free communication. Two scholars originating from the Finnish part of the kingdom, Peter Forsskål and Anders Chydenius, are considered to have had an important role in defining and promoting the concept in the politics of the time. The statute of 1766 was repealed in 1772 by the new Constitution of Gustav III. Censorship was restored in 1774. From 1809 to 1917, Finland was an autonomous entity in the Russian Empire, however, during the first decades of Russian rule censorship from the Swedish period remained. The complete preventive censorship system was enacted in 1829 and lasted until the end of the Russian period. The only exceptions were the short periods of freedom in 1865 and 1905.

Before the fundamental rights reform in 1995, the Finnish constitutional statutes included an act on the freedom of the press from 1919, which was actually written during the Russian regime in 1906 and modified after the Civil War. Originally linked to printing as a technical form of expression and disseminating information, it had de facto already developed into a guarantee of the free press in the form of publishing houses and professional journalism. The evolution of the former rules of freedom of the press into the fundamental right of freedom of expression was, however, a considerable leap in the Finnish freedom of speech concept. It opened the doors to a new, technology neutral way of seeing free communication through different media, covering printed publications,

---

5 Analysis of freedom of speech in the Finnish context: R. Neuvonen: Sananvapauden sääntely Suomessa. Lakimiesliiton kustannus, Helsinki 2012 (only in Finnish but includes a brief summary in English).

commercial and public broadcasting services, as well as the internet. A lot of the constitutional tradition of free printing was intellectually expanded to cover all known forms of communication. At the same time, some of the questions that were more or less solved in the old context were left more open in the new one, notably, the relevance of amateurs versus professional journalists when it comes to their level of protection.

Besides freedom of expression, the Finnish Constitution guarantees the fundamental rights of access to information and the freedom of science, the arts and higher education:

> Documents and recordings in the possession of the authorities are public, unless their publication has for compelling reasons been specifically restricted by an Act. Everyone has the right of access to public documents and recordings.
>
> (Section 12.2)

> The freedom of science, the arts and higher education is guaranteed.
>
> (Section 16.3)[6]

On access to information, the Finnish Constitution includes a fundamental right of julkisuus (public nature of documents), closely linked to the freedom of expression in the same Section 12, and the right of access as one of its components. Access to public documents has a strong tradition in Finnish democracy and in Nordic countries, but it guarantees access more in the sense of transparency of the state, rather than as a subjective right of being informed. As for the right to information in a broader sense, there is no explicit constitutional guarantee.[7]

The scope of the freedom of science, the arts and education has mostly been left for courts to define. In addition to presenting a further constitutional argument in weighing freedom of expression in fields of artistic, scientific and educational expression, Section 16.3 has normally been considered as guaranteeing at least some degree of institutional independence for art institutions and universities. Due to the lack of an applicable norm in the ECHR, the cases in freedom of arts and sciences are often seen in light of Article 10 of the Convention and, thereby, in light of Section 12 rather than Section 16.3 of the Finnish Constitution.

The relationship between the Strasbourg Court and the Finnish courts and the Finnish legislator has been complicated. Over the years, the tendency in the relationship between Finnish and European human rights law has promoted greater freedom of expression and, due to cuts to the former, a relatively broad

---

6 Unofficial translation by the Finnish Ministry of Justice for Finlex, the public information service for legislation.

7 For more on the public nature of documents, see O. Mäenpää: Julkisuusperiaate. WSOY, Helsinki 2016.

scope of privacy. The legislative reaction to several cases confirming breaches of Article 10 of the ECHR can be called a conformist one. In 2013, the Penal Code definitions of defamation and dissemination of information offending private life were amended with sentences allowing a more general balancing of interests than before. The amendments made it easier to interpret the national code in harmony with the case law of the European Court of Human Rights (ECtHR), but also diminished the legal certainty connected to the previous definitions and the already existing case law.[8]

There is an interesting contradiction between the breaches of Article 10 of the ECHR by Finland and the long-lasting number one ranking position of Finland in the Press Freedom Index, compiled by Reporters Without Borders. The two phenomena clearly measure different aspects of freedom of expression. The level of privacy protection is not key when measuring the actual freedom of journalistic work in the sense of the Index.

There have been several Finnish cases related to Article 10 of the Convention. The statistics show that freedom of expression forms a significant number of Finnish cases before the ECtHR. There have been 28 judgments in the field of freedom of expression between 1990 and 2017, 20 of which the Court found a violation against Finland.[9] Eight freedom of expression cases have resulted in a finding of non-violation of Article 10.[10] Two of the judgments were referred to the Grand Chamber, Pentikäinen and Satakunnan Markkinapörssi Oy and Satamedia Oy, whereas the latter was decided on 27 June 2017. In both of these Grand Chamber judgments, the Court found no violation of Article 10 of the Convention. However, in the Satakunnan Markkinapörssi case there was a breach of Article 6 § 1 of the Convention on account of the length of the proceedings.

The cases are mostly about the rights of journalists to report on public figures, defamation and right to privacy. Some of the cases are related to political leaders or other public figures and their right to private life. The principal problem that

---

8 Government proposal HE 19/2013. This government proposal contains an extensive part dealing with comparative criminal law, which is exceptional for a proposal by the Finnish Government, and also a good analysis of ECtHR case law.

9 See from oldest to newest case: Nikula v. Finland, 21.3.2002; Karhuvaara and Iltalehti v. Finland, 16.11.2004; Selistö v. Finland, 16.11.2004; Soini and others v. Finland, 17.1.2006; Goussev and Marenk v. Finland, 17.1.2006; Juppala v. Finland, 2.12.2008; Eerikäinen and Others v. Finland, 10.2.2009; Tuomela and Others v. Finland, 6.4.2010; Soila v. Finland, 6.4.2010; Iltalehti and Karhuvaara v. Finland, 6.4.2010; Jokitaipale and Others v. Finland, 6.4.2010; Flinkkilä and Others v. Finland, 6.4.2010; Mariapori v. Finland, 6.7.2010; Niskasaari and Others v. Finland, 6.7.2010; Saaristo and Others v. Finland, 12.10.2010; Reinboth and Others v. Finland, 25.1.2011; Lahtonen v. Finland, 17.1.2012; Ristamäki and Korvola v. Finland, 29.10.2013; Niskasaari and Otavamedia Oy v. Finland, 23.6.2015; M.P. v. Finland, 15.12.2016.

10 The judgments in the cases of Ruokanen and Others v. Finland, 6.4.2010; Ruusunen v. Finland, 14.1.2014; Ojala and Etukeno Oy v. Finland, 14.1.2014; Pentikäinen v. Finland, 4.2.2014 (referred to Grand Chamber (GC)); Salumäki v. Finland, 29.4.2014; Satakunnan Markkinapörssi Oy and Satamedia Oy v. Finland, 21.7.2015 (referred to GC); Pentikäinen v. Finland 20.10.2015 (GC); Satakunnan Markkinapörssi Oy and Satamedia Oy v. Finland, 27.6.2017 (GC).

can first be identified in the case law is that the Finnish Courts have not applied the ECtHR case law and failed in the balancing process between the rights of others and the freedom of expression. Second, there has been a clear systemic problem with criminal sanctions against journalists. While the Strasbourg Court has reserved certain criminal sanctions (especially imprisonment) for incitement to hatred and violence, Finnish legislation has allowed it in other circumstances, such as defamation procedures. The legislative amendments have resolved part of this problem.

Most recent cases, like those of Ruusunen and Ojala and Etukeno, have also indicated that the problem with balancing and relying on the established case law has also been resolved to some extent. In these cases, the applicants were convicted of revealing information on the private life of the Finnish Prime Minister in a book. The applicants had received criminal convictions for writing and publishing an autobiographical work, which contained details of the relationship between the former Prime Minister of Finland and his former girlfriend Ms Ruusunen. The Court considered that the Finnish courts had fairly balanced freedom of expression and the Prime Minister's right to private life. The Court referred to the doctrine stating that it needed strong reasons to substitute its view for that of the domestic courts in circumstances where domestic courts had established restrictions on the exercise of freedom of expression convincingly and the Court also took into account existing Strasbourg case law.

In the case of Ristamäki and Korvola v. Finland (29.10.2013), related to YLE (Finnish Broadcasting Company), the two journalists had been convicted of defamation in the case of a well-known Finnish businessman, standing trial for economic offences at the time. In a programme broadcasted on national television, the businessman was made an example in a story that focused on the lack of cooperation between different authorities investigating economic crimes. According to the Court, the domestic courts failed to strike a fair balance between the applicants' rights and the right to reputation. The Court criticised the reasoning for the fact that it did not reveal the pressing social need and did not address whether the interference was proportionate.

Several other cases relate to reporting on the private lives of politicians or high profile civil servants. The case of Saaristo and others (12.10.2010) revealed an affair of a presidential campaign advisor. Taking into account that the article had been published during the presidential election campaign and, therefore, had been closely linked to it at the time, the Court considered that the article did not only satisfy the curiosity of certain readers but it also contributed to an important matter of public interest in the form of political background information. The Court thus found a violation of Article 10 of the Convention. Stories published two years later about the same incident were considered in the case of Reinboth and others (25.1.2011), and the Court found a violation of Article 10 in this case as well.

The events relating to the private life of the former National Conciliator and his female friend were revealed in several newspapers and magazines, which led to various cases. In the cases of Flinkkilä and Others v. Finland, Tuomela and

Others v. Finland, Jokitaipale and Others v. Finland, Iltalehti and Karhuvaara v. Finland and Soila v. Finland (all 06.04.2010), different forms of media received criminal sanctions for having disclosed the identity of a public figure's partner. Violations of Article 10 were found in all five cases. In the earlier case of Karhuvaara and Iltalehti (16.11.2004), the newspaper revealed information about the private life of a Member of Parliament's husband. The Finnish courts relied on the provision that focused on protecting the rights of members of the Parliament, which did not allow for any balancing between the freedom of expression and the right to private life. The Court considered that the severe penalties and a limited interference disclosed a striking disproportion between the competing interests of the right to private life and the right to freedom of expression.[11]

In the case of Eerikäinen and Others v. Finland (10.2.2009), a newspaper was ordered to pay damages for the publication of an article about ongoing criminal proceedings, disclosing the identity of the accused. The Court stated once again that the reasoning of the Finnish Supreme Court did not reveal what was relevant in the balancing process and how much weight was placed on the facts that the story was based on the prosecutor's statement and that pictures were taken with the consent of the applicant, although for a different story.

The Selistö v. Finland (16.11.2004) case related to the defamation proceedings in the case of a surgeon and a medical malpractice claim made by a journalist in successive articles on alcohol consumption in the workplace. The purpose of the applicant's articles was to discuss matters of patient safety. The case, relating to the surgeon and an operation that ended with the death of a patient, served to highlight a more general problem. The Court considered that it could not find the factual statements either excessive or misleading. Nor was there any indication that the applicant had acted mala fide. The interest of protecting the surgeon's professional reputation was not sufficient to outweigh matters of legitimate public concern.

In the case of Juppala v. Finland (02.12.2008), the applicant was convicted for defamation "without better knowledge" of her son-in-law, after she had taken her three-year-old grandson to a doctor and voiced a suspicion that he might have been hit by his father. The Court found a violation of Article 10 if the threat of conviction might prevent taking action against child abuse and a risk of exposure to claims by a distressed parent if the suspicion of abuse proves unfounded. The Court found that the threat of an ex post facto review in criminal proceedings for a statement that had been given in good faith was alarming. The Court considered that this kind of mechanism should be available to individuals without the potentially chilling effect of a criminal conviction or compensation for harms suffered or costs incurred. In a more recent case of M.P. v. Finland (15.12.2016), the Court also found a violation in a case where the applicant had been convicted for defamation based on a confidential telephone conversation

11 J. Viljanen: Karhuvaara ja Iltalehti vs. Suomi; Selistö vs. Suomi – Suomalaiset sananvapausrajoitukset Euroopan ihmisoikeustuomioistuimen testissä. Lakimies 4/2005, pp. 636–650, Lakimies, Helsinki 2005.

with a public official, where she voiced her concerns about a child and her suspicions of sexual abuse. According to the Court, bringing criminal charges against the applicant and convicting her for defamation was a course of action that cannot be considered proportionate with a view to the requirements of Article 10 of the Convention. The Court noted that it was relevant to the proportionality assessment that the insinuation was made to a public official who was bound by confidentiality.

The non-violation findings have related to the most recent cases and a few earlier decisions. In the case of Ruokanen and others (6.4.2010), there was an article in a weekly magazine, where an alleged rape was presented as a fact, although the criminal investigation only started after the publication of the article. Article 6 §2 requires that everyone charged with a criminal offence shall be presumed innocent until proven guilty according to law. The Court, therefore, decided that the article violated the presumption of innocence of the parties and defamed them by stating something that had not yet been established as a fact.

In a case of reporting on criminal proceedings, Salumäki v. Finland[12], the ECtHR also found no violation of Article 10. In a story by the applicant, who was a journalist with the nation wide evening newspaper, about the murder of a businessman (P.O.), two unrelated criminal investigations were juxtaposed, with headlines clearly suggesting to the ordinary reader that there was more to P.O.'s murder than what was actually being stated in the text of the articles. The story was found to be defamatory, since it implied that the businessman K.U. was somehow responsible for P.O.'s murder. It amounted to stating, by innuendo, a fact which was highly damaging to the reputation of K.U. At no time did the applicant attempt to prove the truth of the insinuated fact, nor did she plead that the insinuation was a fair comment based on relevant facts.

The Pentikäinen case was the first Grand Chamber judgment relating to Finnish freedom of expression case law and, therefore, a very interesting precedent. The Court considered for the first time a photojournalist's rights in demonstrations. The applicant was detained during a demonstration and kept in detention for 17.5 hours. The basic argument behind the non-violation finding was that the authorities had not prevented the media from covering the demonstration. In the case of the applicant, he was not prevented from carrying out his work as a journalist during or after the demonstration. The Court tried to avoid any more general interpretations of the photographer's rights within a demonstration and remarked that the conclusion must be seen in light of the particular circumstances, where there were due regards to avoid any impairment of the media's role as a public watchdog.

The second Finnish case reviewed by the Grand Chamber is the case of Satakunnan Markkinapörssi Oy and Satamedia Oy (27.6.2017). The applicant company was the publisher of the newspaper Veropörssi (Tax Stock Exchange), which published the tax data of over 1.2 million people and their earned and

12 Salumäki v. Finland, 29.4.2014.

unearned income, as well as their taxable net assets. In addition to the paper version, the data was available on CD-ROMs and via an SMS service. Satakunnan Markkinapörssi was prohibited from processing taxation data in the manner and to the extent that had been the case in 2002 and from forwarding that information to an SMS service. Satamedia Oy was prohibited from collecting, storing or forwarding to an SMS service any data received from Satakunnan Markkinapörssi's database and published in Veropörssi.

The core issue of the case is how much margin of appreciation is left to the courts in order to assess what counts as "journalistic activity" under data protection legislation. The Personal Data Act allowed derogation under Section 2(5) for "purposes of journalism or artistic or literary expression". As Finland is a member of the European Union, the Finnish data protection legislation was based on the EU Data Protection Directive (95/46/EC).[13] During the domestic proceedings, the case was also referred to the Court of Justice of the European Union (CJEU). The Grand Chamber of the CJEU[14] gave a preliminary ruling on issues like the journalistic activities and journalistic purposes of derogation under the EU's Data Protection Directive. It left it for the national court to decide whether or not activities could be classified as "journalistic activities" in this case.

In the context of publishing tax information, national courts considered that the applicant companies publishing the Veropörssi newspaper did not have solely journalistic purposes. The Strasbourg Court agreed with the Finnish Administrative Court that the impugned publication could not be regarded as contributing to a debate of public interest or similar kind of speech. One of the criticised points mentioned in the judgment is the reference to the publication of information on people's economic status as a form of sensationalism, even voyeurism.[15] The Court also specifically refers to very detailed issues related to circumstances of the case, such as the layout of the publication, its form, content and extent of data enclosed as factors that lead to the conclusion that the sole object of the publication was not the disclosure of information, opinions and ideas to the public.[16] The Court also considered that the SMS service rendered data accessible in a manner and to an extent not intended by the legislator.[17]

---

13 Directive 95/46/EC of the European Parliament and of the Council on the protection of individuals with regard to the processing of personal data and on the free movement of such data was adopted (OJ 1995 L 281, p. 31, hereafter "the Data Protection Directive"
14 Case C-73-07 Tietosuojavaltuutettu v. Satakunnan Markkinapörssi Oy and Satamedia Oy, 16 December 2008.
15 The Grand Chamber referred to the case of *Couderc and Hachette Filipacchi Associés v. France* [GC] 10.11.2015, § 101. However, as in Satakunnan Markkinapörssi Oy and Satamedia Oy v. Finland, [GC] supra note 10, the dissenting opinions of Judges Sajó and Karakas rightly point out, the case is different because the Court relates voyeurism generally to sexual curiosity.
16 See Satakunnan Markkinapörssi Oy and Satamedia Oy v. Finland, [GC] 27.6.2017 supra note 10, § 178.
17 See ibid § 190.

One of the most relevant aspects highlighted in the Satakunnan Mark-kinapörssi judgment is related to the legislative choices and, in that context, the quality of parliamentary and judicial review of the necessity of the legislation and the measures adopted.[18] The Grand Chamber observed that balancing the private and public interests involved in the Parliament does not mean that data protection considerations should become irrelevant. The Court founded its interpretation on the approach taken in the case of Animal Defenders International,[19] which provides a wide margin of appreciation, and external supervision has to take into account the constitutional choice and the interest of transparency to make taxation data accessible. In addition, the analysis and careful application of Strasbourg and Luxembourg case law by the Supreme Administrative Court was particularly noted.[20] Thus, there were no strong reasons which would require the Court to substitute its view for that of the domestic courts and set aside the balancing done by the Finnish judiciary.[21]

One of the inadmissibility decisions has been widely referred to in the commentaries. The decision was made in the case of Karttunen v. Finland (10.5.2011), where the applicant was convicted for displaying child pornography. In her artistic work "The Virgin-Whore-Church", she tried to criticise easy access to child pornography on the internet. However, this was only taken into account as a mitigating factor and led to no sanctions being imposed.

The European Court found in the Karttunen case that the domestic courts had adequately balanced the artist's freedom of expression with the countervailing interests. The Court referred to the finding by the Finnish courts that the possession and public display of child pornography was still subject to criminal liability, the criminalisation of child pornography and the artist's conviction being mainly based on the need to protect children against sexual abuse, as well as the violation of their privacy and on moral considerations.

Media regulation in Finland

The general statute concerning media law is the 2003 Act on the Exercise of Freedom of Expression in Mass Media, often referred to as the Freedom of Expression Act (sananvapauslaki), due to its historical background as the replacement for the 1919 Press Freedom Act (painovapauslaki). The 2003 Act consists of a horizontal regulation of mass media responsibilities a priori in all printed

---

18 See ibid § 192.
19 Legislative choices are mentioned in § 192 of *Satakunnan Markkinapörssi* case (GC). In the case of Animal Defenders International v. the United Kingdom, [GC] 22.4.2013, the Court similarly refers to "legislative choices" in paragraphs 108, "It emerges from that case law that, in order to determine the proportionality of a general measure, the Court must primarily assess the legislative choices underlying it", and 111, "Country-specific and complex assessment, which is of central relevance to the legislative choices at issue in the present case".
20 See ibid § 195–196.
21 See ibid § 198.

and digital media as well as in all broadcasting media. In digital publishing, the scope is, however, defined by a concept of internet publication (verkkojulkaisu), which is already out of date in some aspects, e.g. concerning professional journalistic use of social media channels.[22]

The 2003 Act, as well as the Finnish media law in general, applies equally to professional journalism and to all kinds of publishing. The status of a media outlet and being or not being a journalist has no direct legal consequences. Anyone can appoint himself or herself a journalist and the responsible editor of his or her own publication, regardless of its volume or financing. However, to benefit from the protection of journalistic sources, one must at least be able to show the journalistic purpose of collecting information. For example, the protection of sources was also applied to a book in court practice. A credible publishing purpose is relevant in some aspects of copyright law as well.

Factually, the most important limitations of freedom of expression are based on the Penal Code, mostly breaches of privacy and hate crimes but also defamation and blasphemy are part of the Penal Code. Civil liability of publications is rarely tried in courts, but there are some cases of abuse of personality rights and of damages to brand goodwill by critical media content.

While the regulation of journalistic content is horizontal, the regulation of advertising is very sectoral, lacking a general view of communications policy. Strict rules on alcohol advertising are seen as a part of alcohol policy, rules on gambling advertising as a part of gambling policy, etc. With the exception of product placement, the restrictions are generally broader for television and narrower for print media.

The classification of audiovisual programmes (movies, television programmes, games, DVDs/Blu-rays or other content intended for viewing as moving images by technical means) for protecting minors is organised as co-regulation. The Act on Audiovisual Programmes (kuvaohjelmalaki) (710/2011) applies to other audiovisual programme provision and its supervision in Finland if the programmes are provided by Finnish legal or natural persons or if the decision on the provision of programmes has been made in Finland. Audiovisual programmes may only be provided if they have been classified in accordance with the Act. The classification is executed by approved and trained audiovisual programme classifiers. The National Audiovisual Institute (Kansallinen audiovisuaalinen instituutti; KAVI) is responsible for the supervision and classification duties pursuant to the Act and it trains and maintains a register of classifiers. The Act on Audiovisual Programmes was drafted in accordance with the Audiovisual Media Services Directive (2007/65/EC).[23]

---

22 General view of Finnish media law: R. Neuvonen: Viestintä- ja informaatio-oikeuden perusteet. Lakimiesliiton kustannus, Helsinki 2013.

23 Directive 2007/65/EC of the European Parliament and of the Council of 11 December 2007 amending Council Directive 89/552/EEC on the coordination of certain provisions laid down by law, regulation or administrative action in Member States concerning the pursuit of television broadcasting activities(Text with EEA relevance) OJ 18.12.2007, L 332/27.

The Finnish Mass Media Council JSN (julkisen sanan neuvosto) is a media self-regulation body that interprets the rules of ethics in journalism and covers all major publishers and broadcasters, including the public broadcasting service. The system is governed by both journalist and publisher organisations and it receives a part of its financing through state aid. The rulings of the Council are implemented broadly and efficiently, which is a predictor of the continuity of the self-regulation system.

The Act on Yleisradio Oy (Finnish Broadcasting Company) (1380/1993) de-fines the nature of public service programming and regulates the YLE. Commer-cial television, radio and telecommunication are regulated by the Information Society Code (tietoyhteiskuntakaari, 917/2014). This Code implements the EU's Audiovisual Media Services Directive (AVMSD) (2010/13/EU).[24] The law gathers six laws relating to electronic media, privacy in telecommunications and e-commerce regulation under one umbrella.[25] The Code also renews the jurisdiction of the Finnish Communications Regulatory Authority (FICORA, Viestintävirasto). The Code is relatively new and there is not much case law or decisions yet. Following the division of duties between FICORA, consumer protection authorities and KAVI, FICORA is responsible for technical regula-tions, KAVI is responsible for content, and commercial issues are part of general commercial law and consumer protection.

In the Finnish media environment and particularly in online media, there has been heated discussion about propaganda media and hate speech. This phenom-enon has related to stories that have not been written in the mainstream media. The fact that stories from this propaganda media have a sizeable number of fol-lowers is a cause for concern.

The most famous of these media publications are MV-lehti and Magneettime-dia. In addition, there are magazines that concentrate on alternative medicine stories questioning the mainstream medical science, especially vaccination. The content of these outlets is a mix of antisemitism, islamophobia, racist hate speech and it also includes more general conspiracy theories and movements such as the anti-vaccination movement and other forms of "unconventional" medicine.

Mainstream media has been concerned about these media outlets and a group of editors-in-chief published a common statement (1 March 2016).[26] In their statement supporting responsible media, they pointed out that the way top-ics are debated has been rapidly changing. They used the word "fake media" (valemedia) and committed to taking action against media that is trying to fal-sify and obscure information. They also intend to protect individual journalists

24 Directive 2010/13/EU of the European Parliament and of the Council of 10 March 2010 on the coordination of certain provisions laid down by law, regulation or administrative action in Member States concerning the provision of audiovisual media services (Audiovisual Media Ser-vices Directive) (codified version) (Text with EEA relevance) OJ 15.4.2010, L 95/1.
25 Analysis of Information Society Code and regulation of Finnish media market legislation: M. Hoikka, R. Neuvonen, P. Rautiainen: Viestintämarkkinaoikeus. Kauppakamari, Helsinkii 2016.
26 Only in Finnish, www.paatoimittajat.fi/luotettavan-median-puolesta/

who are pressured by these fake media outlets as that kind of pressure leads to chilling effects.

The Finnish national prosecutor's office is currently leading criminal investigations in relation to stories distributed via these media outlets. MV-lehti is commonly considered to be racist, and it is being investigated for incitement to hatred under the provision of the Criminal Code. Magneettimedia has been convicted for publishing anti-Semitic articles in Fall 2013. There are also problems relating to the alleged copyright violations, because most of the stories are taken from other websites or social media. The veracity of these stories has not been checked in the same way as is happening in other media outlets, according to the ethical codes of journalists. One of the issues that complicates the matter in these criminal proceedings is that the owner of MV-lehti is operating outside of Finland, which means that it is not easy to prosecute him under the Finnish Criminal Code. The case is essentially a test case, to gauge how the new legislation on freedom of expression works. Case law concerning issues specific to online publishing or online communication is scarce.

In the Finnish legal debate, it has been considered whether we should apply a provision that prohibits the abuse of rights in these kinds of cases, as is included in the ECHR (Art. 17). In such case, fake media would not be considered within the scope of freedom of expression. The argument derives from the premise that fake media is using the freedom of expression to deflect Article 10 of the Convention from its real purpose by using the right to freedom of expression for ends that are contrary to the text and spirit of the Convention. Such ends, if admitted, would contribute to the destruction of the rights and freedoms guaranteed by the Convention.[27] At the moment, there is no concept of abuse of rights or the fundamental right of human dignity (like, for example, in the German Constitution) in the Finnish Constitution.

The Strasbourg influence on the Finnish freedom of expression

Introduction

The Finnish legal history on freedom of expression dates back 250 years, but the application of constitutional rights by the Finnish judiciary was uncommon, and it was not until after the ratification of the ECHR in 1990 that the application of international human rights provisions or constitutional rights developed to become a regular element in reasoning.

The Finnish freedom of expression discussion included a special element related to foreign policy considerations and prohibition of publication that would in some way harm friendly relations between Finland and other countries, especially the Soviet Union. In the aftermath of the fundamental rights reform

---

27 See Garaudy v. France (dec.), no. 65831/01, 24.6.2003, ECHR 2003-IX.

in 1995, first freedom of expression cases did not include argumentation that would take into account human rights or constitutional rights; instead, argumentation still heavily relied on criminal law provisions (Criminal Code Chapter 27:3 a §, KKO1997:80 and KKO1997:81). The argumentation changed only after the first judgments were decided by the Strasbourg Court in 2004. In the subsequent case law by the Supreme Court (KKO:2005:82, KKO:2005:136), there are frequent references to particular judgments in the field of freedom of expression.

The main lessons from the Finland – Strasbourg dialogue

The first basic lesson was that Finnish courts failed to strike a fair balance between the freedom of expression and the right to respect for private life.[28] It was closely related to the general approach to human rights and constitutional rights and recognising what balancing requires. This finding of a systemic failure in balancing can be identified in the early freedom of expression judgments of Karhuvaara and Iltalehti (16.11.2004) and Selistö v. Finland (16.11.2004). In the Karhuvaara case, the interference was justified before the national courts by relying on the clear formulation of the parliamentary immunity clause. As a consequence of this clear formulation, interpretation was also rigid and lacked normal balancing. The courts abstained from giving any guidance as to how the provision was to be applied when it conflicted with other important competing interests and went on to state that "The automatic and unqualified application of section 15 by the domestic courts effectively nullified the competing interests guaranteed by Article 10 of the Convention".[29] The national courts failed to strike a fair balance because they also did not consider the severity of the sanction in light of a proportionality test.[30] In the subsequent case law, the Court has recurrently referred to the problems in balancing the two rights before Finnish courts. This balancing failure is often due to not taking all relevant factors, such as public interest, into account or imposing excessive consequences, such as severe sanctions, on the applicants.[31]

The second recurring lesson has been the lack of transparent reasoning on the analysis made by the domestic courts. Therefore, it is difficult to follow the reasoning of the decision because Finnish courts are not providing a detailed basis for their balancing process. These failures to provide sufficient reasons for the interference have been found both in the context of the existence of a pressing

---

28 In Finland, respect for private life is part of the protection of privacy, as in Article 8 of the ECHR. Other parts of privacy are domestic privacy, privacy in public premises, data protection and the right to confidential correspondence. See R. Neuvonen: Yksityisyyden suoja Suomessa. Lakimiesliiton kustannus, Helsinki 2014.

29 See Karhuvaara and Iltalehti v. Finland, supra note 7, § 52.

30 Ibid § 53.

31 See e.g. Iltalehti and Karhuvaara, supra note 7, § 68.

social need and in how different relevant factors[32] mentioned in the criteria laid down by the Strasbourg Court have been applied in the particular circumstances of a case. The Von Hannover II/Axel Springer (introduced in 2012) criteria introduce six factors to be taken into account while balancing competing interests and rights under Articles 8 and 10, and they are as follows: (i) contribution to a debate of general interest; (ii) how well-known is the person concerned and what is the subject of the report; (iii) prior conduct of the person concerned; (iv) method of obtaining the information and its veracity; (v) content, form and consequences of the publication; and (vi) severity of the sanction imposed.[33]

The third recurring fault has been that Finnish courts did not sufficiently refer to the relevant Strasbourg case law.[34] They presumed that even general references, like "according to the established case law of the ECtHR", were sufficiently precise without making a detailed reference to individual judgments and explaining how these cases have influenced the national Court in its reasoning. This more transparent approach was openly recognised by the Court in more recent judgments, in which the Finnish courts were also allowed to have a "strong reasons" presumption as in the Axel Springer/MGN Limited cases.[35] However, even among the latest cases, there is a different message that questions how Finnish courts applied criteria in case law.[36] In the Niskasaari and Otavamedia (23.6.2015) case, the problem is that there are limited references to case law, but there is no evaluation made according to the criteria set out in the Strasbourg case law.[37] Similarly, in the case of Ristamäki and Korvola (29.10.2013), the

---

32 See e.g. Eerikäinen v. Finland, supra note 7, § 69.

> [I]t is not evident that the Supreme Court in its analysis as to whether the applicant's privacy had been invaded attached any importance to the fact that the information given was based on a bill of indictment prepared by the public prosecutor and that the article clearly stated that the applicant had merely been charged.

33 The Court has mentioned several times Von Hannover II/Axel Springer criteria, which are relevant to balancing competing interests. See e.g. in Ristamäki and Korvola, supra note 7, § 48; Salumäki, supra note 8, § 50; Niskasaari and Otavamedia, supra note 7, § 49.

34 See e.g. formulation "limited reference … to case law" in Niskasaari and Otavamedia Oy, supra note 7, § 58.

35 See e.g. Ruusunen v. Finland, supra note 8, § 52. The restrictions of the exercise of the applicant's freedom of expression were convincingly established by the Supreme Court, taking into account the Court's case law. The Court recalls its recent case law, according to which the Court would require, in such circumstances, strong reasons to substitute its view for that of the domestic courts. A similar reference can be found in the case of Ojala and Etukeno Oy, supra note 8, § 57; Satakunnan Markkinapörssi Oy and Satamedia Oy v. Finland (GC), 27.6.2017, supra note 8, § 164 and 198. See also Von Hannover v. Germany (no. 2) [GC], § 107; and Axel Springer AG v. Germany [GC], § 88.

36 However, in the case of Niskasaari and Otavamedia oy, supra note 7, the Court mentions the doctrine (§ 49), but finds that criteria were not applied in order to balance the applicant's rights.

37 See ibid § 58:

> While the Appeal Court made some limited reference to Article 10 of the Convention and to case law and legal literature on Article 10 in its judgment (see paragraph 18 above), thereby recognising as a matter of principle the relevance of Article 10 for the domestic

74   *Riku Neuvonen et al.*

Court did find a violation despite the strong reasons that the doctrine mentioned. The basic problem also in this judgment was related to the inadequate importance placed on the applicants' freedom of expression and also other parts of reasoning that did not reveal what the pressing need was and whether the interference was proportionate.[38]

The fourth major systemic freedom of expression theme indicated in the Finnish cases has been criminal sanctions related to defamation and their "chilling effect".[39] This has been clearly mentioned in a number of cases before the Court. In the case of Mariapori v. Finland (6.7.2010), the Court mentioned that the classic case of defamation presented

> no justification whatsoever for the imposition of a prison sentence. Such a sanction, by its very nature, will inevitably have a chilling effect on public debate. The fact that the applicant's prison sentence was conditional and that she did not in fact serve it does not alter that conclusion.[40]

Similar findings were brought up, e.g. in the case of Saaristo and others (12.10.2010)[41] and Reinboth and others (25.1.2011).[42] In several Finnish cases, it has not been indicated that "exceptional circumstances" required for criminal sanctions to be justified were present.[43] In these judgments, references have also been made to the Parliamentary Assembly of the Council of Europe Resolution 1577 (2007). This Resolution urged those Member States that still give prison sentences for defamation, even if they are not actually imposed, to abolish them

---

decision whether to convict the first applicant of defamation, it did not, as required by Article 10, proceed to a sufficient evaluation of the actual impact of the first applicant's right to freedom of expression on the outcome of the case.

38 Ristamäki and Korvola v. Finland, supra note 7, § 56. The Court observes that the domestic courts did not, in their analysis, attach any importance to the applicants' right to freedom of expression, nor did they balance it in any considered way against K.U.'s right to reputation. It is not clear in the reasoning of the domestic courts what pressing social need in the present case justified protecting K.U.'s rights over the rights of the applicants. Nor is it clear whether, according to the domestic courts, the interference in issue was proportionate to the legitimate aim pursued. (K.U. was a well-known businessman who, at the time, was standing for a trial for economic offences).

39 R. Ollila: Vankeutta kunnianloukkauksista. Lakimies 2/2011 pp. 365–386, Lakimies, Helsinki 2011.

40 See Mariapori v. Finland, supra note 7, § 68. According to the Court, the criminal sanction and the accompanying obligation to pay compensation "were manifestly disproportionate in their nature and severity".

41 Saaristo and others, supra note 7, § 69.

42 Reinboth, supra note 7, § 90:

the Court points out that the imposition of a prison sentence for a press offence will be compatible with journalists' freedom of expression as guaranteed by Article 10 only in exceptional circumstances, notably where other fundamental rights have been impaired as, for example, in the case of hate speech or incitement to violence.

43 See e.g. Lahtonen v. Finland, supra note 7, § 79 ... "No such exceptional circumstances exist in the present case".

without delay (Resolution Towards decriminalisation of defamation adopted on 4 October 2007). These findings were in the background of the legislative reform.

In the previous provisions of the Criminal Code (Chapter 24, section 8), it was mentioned that

A person who unlawfully
(1) through the use of the mass media, or
(2) otherwise by making available to many persons
disseminates information, an insinuation or an image of the private life of another person, so that the act is conducive to causing that person damage or suffering, or subjecting that person to contempt, shall be sentenced for dissemination of information violating personal privacy to a fine or to imprisonment for at most two years.

The spreading of information, an insinuation or an image of the private life of a person in politics, business, public office or public position, or in a comparable position, does not constitute dissemination of information violating personal privacy, if it may affect the evaluation of that person's activities in the position in question and if it is necessary for purposes of dealing with a matter with importance to society.

The Ruusunen case (Ruusunen v. Finland and Ojala and Etukeno Oy v. Finland (14.1.2014)), involving a book that disclosed information on the private life of Prime Minister Matti Vanhanen, is the leading case to show a turning point in the Strasbourg freedom of expression case law concerning Finland. It confirmed a message of acknowledging the lessons learned by the domestic courts, especially in the reasoning taken by the Finnish Supreme Court. According to the Ruusunen judgment, the domestic courts had finally achieved an adequate standard in their balancing exercise. The Strasbourg Court considered that the restrictions of the exercise of the applicant's freedom of expression were convincingly established by the Supreme Court, taking into account the Court's case law.[44]

In the original judgment (KKO:2010:39), the lessons learned from the Strasbourg case law are easily displayed. The Supreme Court carefully analyses several relevant arguments, e.g. the alleged consent, the relevance of the nature of the publication and information and the relevance of the Prime Minister's social status. The Supreme Court recognised information that had relevance to general public discussion, when arising issues pointed at the question of whether Prime Minister Vanhanen had been dishonest and lacked judgment. The Strasbourg Court also recapped and agreed with the Supreme Court's finding that the information concerning the great differences in the standard of living between the applicant and the former Prime Minister, his lifestyle, the data protection

---

44 Conversation and analysis of Finnish penal code reform: R. Neuvonen: Uudistettu yksityiselämän ja kunniansuoja Suomessa. Defensor Legis 5/2015 pp. 864–882, Defensor Legis, Helsinki 2015.

concerns and the protection of the highest political authorities in general had relevance to a general public discussion.[45]

The Strasbourg Court goes into detail in its analysis of the domestic courts' decisions and, in particular, whether the balancing process follows the established principles mentioned in the Axel Springer/Von Hannover II cases. The Strasbourg Court points out that in their analysis the domestic courts attached importance both to the applicant's right to freedom of expression as well as to the former Prime Minister's right to respect for his private life. On the one hand, the Court acknowledged that there were elements that have to be taken into account, such as whether certain private family information had been disclosed earlier by the Prime Minister himself, when he had published his autobiography in 2005. On the other hand, certain information about the former Prime Minister's sex life, intimate events and his children's feelings and behaviour had not been disclosed to the public before. However, the Supreme Court found that only the references to the sex life and intimate events between the applicant and the former Prime Minister were illegal.

An important aspect of the analysis is that the Supreme Court narrowed down the scope of the problematic passages in the book. It clearly departed from the broader approach to restrictions of freedom of expression taken by the Court of Appeals. According to the Supreme Court, the issues relating to the Prime Minister's children did not deal with the children's feelings or privacy in a manner that would cause suffering and contempt. Thus, the Supreme Court enumerated only certain parts of the book which it considered to contain information falling within the core area of the private life of the former Prime Minister. The Supreme Court found that such information and hints and their unauthorised publication was conducive of causing the former Prime Minister suffering and contempt.

The legislative reforms have also been reflecting the established case law of the Strasbourg Court. This is especially evident in government proposal 19/2013. The reformed provisions entered into force on 1 January 2014 (Act 879/2013).

One of the major differences, pointed out in the legislative proposal, was the understanding of what constitutes a "matter with importance to society". In Finnish law, this does not normally include information relating to a politician's intimate relationships. However, the Strasbourg Court is more flexible on these issues and has a wider understanding of what political activity is.

The second interesting argument is related to the decriminalisation of defamation, especially the requirement of abandoning imprisonment in defamation cases. The Finnish system has been pressured by the Court (Niskasaari and others v. Finland (6.7.2010) §§ 76–77), and the Council of Europe Resolution 1577 (2007) has echoed a similar message. This Resolution was also mentioned in the Supreme Court decision 2011:100, which was related to Mariapori v. Finland (6.7.2010) and the annulment procedure of a legally final judgment after the Strasbourg judgment. The Government referred to the case law and found that

---

45 See Ruusunen v. Finland, supra note 8, § 49.

the use of imprisonment would not be restricted, that in normal forms the punishment would be a fine and that only in the aggravated forms of these crimes would imprisonment be possible.

Concluding remarks

The deepest transformation in the Finnish freedom of expression doctrine has been in understanding the essential role of balancing different competing rights in freedom of expression cases. This has been the result of an open and on-going dialogue with the ECtHR. The public debate on freedom of expression has received a much-needed outside catalyst with a relatively high number of Article 10 cases brought before the Strasbourg Court. In a per capita comparison, Austria and Finland have been over-represented in freedom of expression case law. After the critique, the domestic courts chose to cooperate with the Strasbourg criteria rather than openly disagree with the ECtHR.

The scope of freedom of expression cases has broadened during the more than 25-year period in which the Convention has been an incremental part of Finnish law. While the first textbook from 1991 (Pellonpää: Euroopan ihmisoikeussopimus) concentrated on whether Finnish law was in compliance with the requirements, the most recent editions of textbooks have very extensive descriptions of the different aspects of case law and, especially, of the balancing process. Domestic courts have taken a stronger role in developing national doctrine, while in the past the freedom of expression law was mostly left to the national legislator's discretion.

The domestic case law in the field of freedom of expression has set a standard for other fields of human rights law, demonstrating how to refer convincingly to the European case law. Although some high Finnish judges have also criticised the Strasbourg Court, there seems to be a great deal of respect between the national courts and the Court in Strasbourg. This was presented in the lessons learned part.

There are still many open questions in the Finnish freedom of expression law. One of the issues relates to online media and whether there should be a source neutral approach or whether there should be certain specific rules in order to cope with the challenges of the new media environment. From the European Union perspective, the Single European Digital Market is one of the EU's priorities. Under this strategy, Finland has a proactive stance towards broadband development.

Even after the recent Satakunnan Markkinapörssi judgment by the Grand Chamber, there are still many unanswered questions. However, the prevailing doctrine seems to be that there must be strong reasons for the Strasbourg Court to substitute its views for that of Finnish courts. It is interesting that the Grand Chamber seems to acknowledge not just the domestic courts, but also the careful assessment made by the Finnish legislator, sending a message of trust in the Finnish system. However, complacency over the quality of freedom of expression can be detrimental to the enhancement of improved standards. Past practices show that the Finnish legal system clearly needs an outside catalyst in order to develop and reform established structures.

6 Icelandic online media law and the ECHR

Eiríkur Jónsson

Main features of the legal environment

The media environment

The media environment in Iceland is rather diverse and multiform. There are several national newspapers, of which the biggest is *Fréttabladid*, delivered free in the capital area six days a week. According to the website Gallup in June 2017, 44.6% of the Icelandic population reads the paper. The second largest newspaper is *Morgunbladid*, which is available by subscription. It is published daily and read by 25.7% of the population.[1]

The state-owned Icelandic National Broadcasting Service runs the most watched television station.[2] It also runs three radio stations and the news website ruv.is. There are several private television stations and radio stations; the biggest one is the media corporation 365, which also runs the above-mentioned newspaper *Fréttabladid*.

There are several Icelandic news websites. The newspapers mentioned above run some of them. The biggest in terms of hits are mbl.is and visir.is.[3] Most of the websites allow readers to comment on the news posted, generally through the readers' Facebook accounts. Such comments are not monitored before they appear online, but the websites generally reserve their right to remove defamatory and improper comments and seem to close certain types of news for comments. It is safe to say that the online media play a significant role in the Icelandic media landscape and are commonly used. A recent survey also shows that out of all Europeans, Icelanders use the internet the most.[4] Interestingly, however, advertising has not moved as quickly to the internet as in neighbouring countries. In 2014, online media only received 14.9% of the advertising fees spent, whereas the printed media received 37.4% and television stations 29.7%. Most of

---

1 See www.gallup.is/nidurstodur/prentmidlar/ (last accessed 6 February 2018).
2 See www.gallup.is/nidurstodur/utvarp/ (last accessed 6 February 2018).
3 See http://topplistar.gallup.is/ (last accessed 6 February 2018).
4 See the website of Statistics Iceland, https://hagstofa.is/utgafur/frettasafn/visindi-og-taekni/ tolvu-og-netnotkun-mest-a-islandi-af-ollum-evropulondum/ (last accessed 6 February 2018).

the online advertising fees went to Icelandic media (82.4%), whereas 17.6% went to companies abroad like Google and Facebook.[5]

In recent years, the increased concentration of amalgamated media and tele-communication services is worth mentioning. For example, the corporation 365 that runs the above-mentioned media also provides telecommunications services. However, different authorities regulate these services. The Media Commission sees to the media, and the Post and Telecom Administration sees to telecommunication services.

The freedom of speech doctrine

Article 73 of the Icelandic Constitution ensures freedom of expression but also allows for exceptions to this freedom under certain conditions. The roots of the article date back to 1874, when the king of Denmark enacted the first Constitution of Iceland. It included an article on freedom of expression in print and a ban against censorship. The article was, in fact, based on a similar article in the Danish Constitution of 1849.[6] The article remained in later constitutions, including the one enacted in 1944 when Iceland became an independent republic. This Constitution, as amended, is still in place. The article was as follows, translated by the European Court of Human Rights (ECtHR):[7]

> Every person has the right to express his thoughts in print. However, he may be held responsible for them in court. Censorship or other limitations on the freedom of the press may never be imposed.

In 1995, the human rights chapter of the Icelandic Constitution was revised, including a new Article 73 on freedom of expression. The article is as follows, translated by the government offices of Iceland:[8]

> Everyone has the right to freedom of opinion and belief.
> Everyone shall be free to express his thoughts, but shall also be liable to answer for them in court. The law may never provide for censorship or other similar limitations to freedom of expression.
> Freedom of expression may only be restricted by law in the interests of public order or the security of the State, for the protection of health or morals, or for the protection of the rights or reputation of others, if such restrictions are deemed necessary and in agreement with democratic traditions.

---

5 "Skipting birtingarfjár milli miðla 2014", published on the website of the Icelandic Media Commission, see http://fjolmidlanefnd.is/2015/09/23/skipting-birtingafjar-milli-midla-2014/ (last accessed 6 February 2018).

6 Thorarensen, Björg: *Stjórnskipunarréttur – Mannréttindi*, Reykjavík: Bókaútgáfan Codex, 2008, p. 348.

7 See *Thorgeirson v. Iceland*, Application No. 13778/88, 25 June 1992.

8 See www.government.is/constitution/ (last accessed 6 February 2018).

Unlike the older provision, the article is not limited to freedom of expression in print. Rather, paragraph 2 ensures freedom of expression generally. Paragraph 1 also prescribes that everyone has the right to freedom of opinion and belief. This freedom is closely connected to freedom of religion, which Articles 63 and 64 ensure. Paragraph 1 is of limited practical importance, since it is difficult to limit freedom of opinion and belief until opinions and beliefs are expressed — and then paragraph 2 applies.[9] The second sentence of paragraph 2 proscribes censorship and other similar limitations, just like the older article did. This proscription can also be said to have little practical importance in everyday legal application, since the concept of "censorship and other similar limitations" has been quite narrowly construed.[10]

Therefore, the former sentence in paragraph 2 is of greater importance. It ensures freedom of expression in general, and it is clear that it covers expression on the internet, just as expression elsewhere.[11] Although narrowly worded ("shall be free to express his thoughts"), the scope of the article is considered to be very broad. It covers all kinds of expression and includes freedom to receive and impart information. It is even deemed to guarantee a certain right of the general public to access information from the authorities.[12] This freedom is not unlimited, since paragraph 3 allows restrictions if the criteria set out there are met. As can be seen from the foregoing direct quote, paragraph 3 is quite similar to Article 10, paragraph 2, of the European Convention on Human Rights (ECHR) and demands law, legitimate aim and necessity. In fact, one of the principal aims of the revision of the human rights chapter in 1995 was to increase its coherence with international conventions on human rights to which Iceland is a member.[13] The ECHR had already been given the status of general law, under Act No. 62/1994, and it is clear that, after the revision in 1995, Icelandic courts tend to take notice of the Convention's articles when interpreting similar articles in the Icelandic Constitution.[14] This is clearly the case when it comes to Article 73, where the Supreme Court often refers to Article 10 of the ECHR and sometimes to the interpretation of the ECtHR when resolving issues involving the limits of the freedom of expression.[15]

---

9 Thorarensen, supra note 6, pp. 352–353.
10 Jónsson, Eiríkur: *Mannréttindi lögaðila. Vernd lögaðila samkvæmt mannréttindaákvæðum stjórnarskrárinnar, einkum 71. og 73. gr.*, Reykjavík: Bókaútgáfan Codex, 2011, pp. 152–153.
11 Many defamation cases from the Icelandic courts could be mentioned, where people have successfully defended their online expression on the grounds of Article 73. As a recent example, see *SC (Supreme Court of Iceland) 17 March 2016 (Case No. 610/2015)*.
12 See Thorarensen, supra note 6, p. 358 and 362. See also on the right to information from authorities Jónsson, supra note 10, pp. 271–276.
13 See, for example, Parliamentary Record (*Alþingistíðindi*), 1993–1994, A-section, p. 5222.
14 Some have even said that the Convention can be seen as a "constitutional equivalence". See Sigurður, Líndal: *Um lög og lögfræði. Grundvöllur laga – Réttarheimildir I*, Reykjavík: Hið íslenzka bókmenntafélag, 2007, p. 85. This can, however, hardly be said to be the view of the courts, see for example *SC 14 November 2002 (Case No. 167/2002)*, although the Convention and the case law of the ECtHR clearly seem to influence constitutional interpretation.
15 See as recent examples *SC 18 December 2014 (Case No. 215/2014)* and *SC 20 November2014 (Case No. 214/2014)*, where the Supreme Court referred to both Article 73 of the Constitution and

Influence of international human rights instruments

As already explained, the ECHR has an influence on cases concerning freedom of expression in Iceland. Judgments from the ECtHR have also influenced changes to legislation. Thus, the judgment in *Thorgeirson v. Iceland*,[16] where Iceland was found to have violated Article 10 by convicting Thorgeirson for two newspaper articles on police brutality, seems to have had quite an influence. First, changes were made to the General Penal Code (Act No. 19/1940), by Act No. 71/1995, which repealed Article 108 of the Penal Code. That article dealt specifically with the defamation of civil servants. Second, the judgment influenced the enactment of the aforementioned Act No. 62/1994, where the ECHRwas given the status of general law.[17]

Since 2012, the ECtHR has handed down six judgments where Iceland has been found to have violated Article 10: *Björk Eidsdóttir v. Iceland*[18]; *Erla Hlynsdóttir v. Iceland*[19]; *Erla Hlynsdóttir v. Iceland (No. 2)*[20]; *Erla Hlynsdóttir v. Iceland (No. 3)*[21]; *Steingrímur Sævarr Ólafsson v. Iceland*[22]; and *Reynir Traustason and others v. Iceland*.[23] All these cases concerned Icelandic judgments in defamation cases, ordering journalists to pay non-pecuniary damages for media coverage. In addition, certain statements were declared null and void. The situation in the first case had already led to certain changes of liability rules with Media Act No. 38/2011, and it can be strongly argued that these changes would have led to the Icelandic Courts' acquittal of the journalists in three of the six cases, if the new rules had been in force.[24] Otherwise, no changes have been made to domestic legislation due to these cases. However, according to what has already been described, it has to be assumed that the Icelandic Supreme Court will take notice of these judgments in future defamation cases. In fact, in summer of 2017 the ECtHR handed down two judgments where it denied that Iceland had violated Article 10 by judgments in defamation cases: *Ólafur Arnarson v. Iceland*[25] and *Svavar Halldórsson v. Iceland*.[26]

Iceland is also bound by other international conventions on human rights, for example, the UN International Covenant on Civil and Political Rights. The Icelandic legal system is based on the theory of dualism. Therefore, such conventions do not become binding in national law unless the legislature enacts them.

Article 10 of the ECHR and took among other things into account "how article 10 has been interpreted by the European Court of Human Rights" (author´s translation).

16 See *Thorgeirson*, supra note 7.
17 See for example Parliamentary Record (*Alþingistíðindi*), 1993–1994, A-section, p. 779.
18 *Björk Eidsdóttir v. Iceland*, Application No. 46443/09, 10 July 2012.
19 *Erla Hlynsdóttir v. Iceland*, Application No. 43380/10, 10 July 2012.
20 *Erla Hlynsdóttir v. Iceland (No. 2)*, Application No. 54125/10, 21 October 2014.
21 *Erla Hlynsdóttir v. Iceland (No. 3)*, Application No. 54145/10, 2 June 2015.
22 *Steingrímur Sævarr Ólafsson v. Iceland*, Application No. 58493/13, 16 March 2017.
23 *Reynir Traustason and others v. Iceland*, Application No. 44081/13, 4 May 2017.
24 See Jónsson, Eiríkur: "Ábyrgðarreglur fjölmiðlalaga", *Afmælisrit Páll Sigurðsson sjötugur 16. ágúst 2014*, Reykjavík: Bókaútgáfan Codex, 2014, p. 198.
25 *Ólafur Arnarson v. Iceland*, Application No. 58781/13, 13 June 2017.
26 *Svavar Halldórsson v. Iceland*, Application No. 44322/13, 4 July 2017.

The ECHR and the UN Convention on the Rights of the Child are the only human rights conventions having such status. Therefore, other conventions are not in force as general law in Icelandic national law. It is, however, a recognised principle of interpretation that national law shall be interpreted in accordance with Iceland's obligation under public international law,[27] and the Supreme Court has cited Article 19 of the International Covenant on Civil and Political Rights in connection with Article 73 of the Constitution and Article 10 of the ECHR.[28] Iceland is a member of the Agreement on the European Economic Area but not a member of the European Union. Therefore, the EU Charter of Fundamental Rights is of limited relevance in Icelandic law.

Media law

In 2011, the Icelandic Parliament enacted Media Act No. 38/2011. According to Article 1, the objective of the Act is to promote freedom of expression, freedom of information, media literacy, diversity and pluralism in media and enhance consumer protection in this area. A further objective of the Act is to establish a coordinated regulatory framework for media services, irrespective of the type of media employed. Before the enactment of the Media Act, different acts covered audiovisual media and print media. Print media came under the Right of Publication Act No. 57/1956, and audiovisual media was covered in the Act on Broadcasting No. 53/2000. The Media Act incorporated the provisions of Directive 2010/13/EU (the Audiovisual Media Services Directive).[29] However, it does more since it also regulates print media and, to some extent online media, which were not previously regulated. Determining to what extent the Act covers online media is somewhat complicated. This question will be further discussed later in this chapter. However, the short answer is that the Act applies to the most traditional online media, but does not apply to personal communication on social media, and the same is often true with regards to personal blogs.

The Media Act requires that audiovisual media service providers have a licence from the Media Commission, whereas other media service providers do not require a licence, although they do have to be registered with the Media Commission (see Articles 14 and 16). The Media Commission is an independent administrative committee. It consists of five persons appointed by the Minister of Education, Science and Culture. The Supreme Court of Iceland nominates two members, the Standing Committee of the Rectors of Icelandic Higher

---

27 See for example Thorarensen, supra note 6, p. 85, and Spanó, Róbert: *Túlkun lagaákvæða*, Reykjavík: Bókaútgáfan Codex, 2007, pp. 248–251.
28 See *SC 25 February 1999 (Case No. 415/1998)*.
29 Directive 2010/13/EU of the European Parliament and of the Council of 10 March 2010 on the coordination of certain provisions laid down by law, regulation or administrative action in Member States concerning the provision of audiovisual media services (Audiovisual Media Services Directive) (OJ L 95, 15.4.2010, pp. 1–24).

Education Institutions one member and the National Union of Icelandic Journalists one member (Articles 7 and 8).

Section V of the Act includes many rules on the rights and obligations of media service providers. For example, under Article 24, media service providers shall lay down their own rules on the editorial independence of those on their staff involved in news and current affairs programming, and these rules shall be submitted to the Media Commission for confirmation. Article 25 concerns the protection of sources. Article 26 prescribes that media service providers shall uphold democratic principles and ensure freedom of expression, and Article 27 includes prohibition of hate speech and incitement to criminal activity. Section V also includes rules on the protection of minors against harmful content (Article 28), duties to promote the Icelandic language (Article 29), obligations to preserve media content (Article 35) and rules on the right to reply (Article 36). Section VI of the Act includes detailed rules on commercial communications and teleshopping.

As the regulatory authority, the Media Commission can take action if media service providers do not obey the aforementioned rules. It has certain special investigative powers under Article 12 and can impose administrative fines under Article 54 and *per diem* fines under Article 53. It can also lodge a complaint with the police, potentially leading to criminal prosecution. Due to principles of *ne bis in idem*, however, the Media Commission shall either impose administrative sanctions or lodge a complaint with the police, but not both. Section Xa of the Media Act includes rules on media ownership, with the Competition Authority as the main regulatory authority, although the Media Commission also plays a certain role. The Media Commission also has a role under Act No. 62/2006 on the Supervision of Children's Access to Movies and Video Games, but the Act in principle establishes a self-regulatory system, with the Media Commission playing a certain supervisory role.

Articles 50 and 51 of the Media Act include rules on liability. The scope of these articles extends beyond the scope of the aforementioned articles, since Articles 50 and 51 generally prescribe who bears the liability if content "contravenes the law" (not only the Media Act). For example, if an expression violates an article in the General Penal Code (Act No. 19/1940), Articles 50 and 51 of the Media Act answer who shall bear the criminal responsibility for the violation. Article 51 concerns liability for text content. It is as follows:[30]

> Where text content contravenes the law, criminal and compensatory liability shall apply as follows:
> a. Individuals shall be liable for content which they write in their own name or with which they clearly identify themselves if they are domiciled in

---

30 The English translation of the Media Act, which is used here, can be found at the website of the Media Commission, see http://fjolmidlanefnd.is/wp-content/uploads/2011/12/Log-um-fjolmidla_ensk-thyding_mai2015.pdf (last accessed 6 February 2018).

Iceland or subject to Icelandic jurisdiction on other grounds. If text content is correctly quoted as being that of named individuals, the persons quoted shall be liable for their own expressions if they have given consent for the communication thereof and are either domiciled in Iceland or subject to Icelandic jurisdiction on other grounds;

b. The purchaser of a commercial communication, whether an individual or a legal person, shall be liable for its content if domiciled in Iceland or subject to Icelandic jurisdiction on other grounds;

c. In other cases the responsibility for distributed content lies with the responsible editor of the media outlet in question.

Media service providers shall be liable for the payment of fines and compensation payments that their employees may be ordered to pay under this Article.

Media service providers shall be obliged to provide all persons who consider that their rights have been prejudiced by the publication of text content with information indicating who is liable for the content.

Article 50 concerns liability for audiovisual content and has a similar structure. According to paragraph 1a, individuals making a statement in their own name, or presenting or conveying content of their own composition and/or presenting content by another party by their own decision, shall be liable for it if they are domiciled in Iceland or subject to Icelandic jurisdiction on other grounds. The purchaser of an audio or audiovisual commercial communication is liable for its content. Otherwise, the responsibility lies with the responsible editor. See paragraphs 1a and 1b, which are similar to the same paragraphs of Article 51. Article 50 then includes the same paragraphs 2 and 3 as cited from Article 51 above. These rules will be further discussed later in this chapter.

There are many articles in Icelandic legislation, outside the Media Act, that set boundaries to expression in the media. The General Penal Code includes a special chapter on defamation and violation of personal privacy, i.e. chapter XXV. To mention some examples from the chapter, Article 229 prescribes that any person publicly disclosing the private affairs of another person, in the absence of sufficient justification, the action shall be subject to a fine or imprisonment for up to one year. Article 234 prescribes the same punishment for defaming another person by insults in word or deed, and Article 235 for making insinuations about another person of a nature that would damage his or her reputation. According to Article 241, in action for libel, offensive remarks may be judged null and void if the injured party so requests. It should also be mentioned that according to Article 233a, hate speech can lead to fines or imprisonment, and the same is true with regards to the distribution of pornography according to Article 210. Until recently, Article 125 also criminalised blasphemy, but this Article was repealed in 2015 by Act No. 43/2015.[31]

---

31 In this regard, it should also be mentioned that Article 136 prescribes that a civil servant revealing anything which is to be treated as secret that he/she learned of in the course of his/her work, or that pertains to his/her office or function, shall be subject to imprisonment for up to one year.

Legal proceedings for most of the offences in chapter XXV of the Penal Code may only be instituted by the injured party. However, violations of Article 233a (hate speech) shall be prosecuted by indictments, and if a defamatory insult or insinuation has been directed at a civil servant and has some bearing on his or her work, such an offence shall be subject to indictment at his/her request. Finally, there is an exception in Article 242 stating that if a defamatory insinuation has been made in writing, but either anonymously or with an incorrect or fabricated signature, the offence shall be made the subject of an indictment if the injured party so requests. This exception could, of course, have a bearing on the online environment, where anonymous comments are quite common, but it does not seem to have been used in that context so far. Questions on liability for such comments will be discussed below.

Although imprisonment is a possible punishment under the aforementioned articles of the Penal Code, such a sentence has not been handed down for decades. In fact, in recent years the Icelandic courts have even showed a certain tendency to refrain from imposing fines under the Penal Code, and defamation cases have been moving more towards non-pecuniary damages.[32] There has also been ongoing discussion on whether the legislature should decriminalise defamation.[33] Under Article 26 of the Tort Damages Act No. 50/1993, courts can order the one responsible for defamation (or other intrusion of privacy) to pay non-pecuniary damages to the defamed person. This is the article most used in defamation cases, along with the allowance in Article 241 of the Penal Code, to declare remarks null and void.

There are also several provisions outside the Media Act setting boundaries to commercial advertising, like Article 20 of the Alcohol Act No. 75/1998. This article prohibits alcohol advertisements, and Article 7 of the Act on Tobacco Prevention No. 6/2002, prohibiting tobacco advertisements. Several rules on advertisement are also found in Act No. 57/2005 on Supervision of Unfair Commercial Practices and Transparency of the Market, which is to a great extent based on Directive 2005/29/EC (the Unfair Commercial Practices Directive),[34] with the Consumer Agency as the regulatory authority.

---

32 The following are recent examples of judgments not imposing fines even though the expression involved was deemed to have gone too far, *SC 18 December 2014 (Case No. 215/2014)* and *SC 7 November 2013 (Case No. 200/2013)*. See also on the development towards tort law, Jónsson, Eiríkur: "Ábyrgð á birtu efni á Internetinu", *Afmælisrit Björn Þ. Guðmundsson sjötugur 13. júlí 2009*, Reykjavík: Bókaútgáfan Codex, 2009. p. 121.

33 See, for example, a letter from the Criminal Law Commission to the Ministry of Justice 12 November 2012, available at www.menntamalaraduneyti.is/media/MRN-pdf/Alit-refsirettarnefndar-IRR.pdf (last accessed 6 February 2018).

34 Directive 2005/29/EC of the European Parliament and of the Council of 11 May 2005 concerning unfair business-to-consumer commercial practices in the internal market and amending Council Directive 84/450/EEC, Directives 97/7/EC, 98/27/EC and 2002/65/EC of the European Parliament and of the Council and Regulation (EC) No 2006/2004 of the European Parliament and of the Council ('Unfair Commercial Practices Directive') (OJ L 149, 11.6.2005, pp. 22–39).

All the aforementioned articles apply to online media, just like other media. To illustrate this, some recent judgments can be mentioned:

> *SC 2 June 2016 (Case No. 705/2015)*. An individual was fined (ISK 100,000) for violating Article 235 of the Penal Code (insinuation) by having employed and published certain comments on his Facebook wall about a civil servant.
>
> *SC 17 December 2015 (Case No. 239/2015)*. The case concerned statements that an individual made in a blog area he had on the website of an online medium. The Supreme Court declared two statements null and void under Article 241 of the Penal Code and ordered the individual to pay non-pecuniary damages under Article 26 of the Tort Damages Act.
>
> *SC 18 December 2014 (Case No. 215/2014)*. A statement that an individual made on Facebook was declared null and void under Article 241 of the Penal Code.

In all these cases, the defendants referred to their rights under Article 73 of the Constitution. Some recent judgments can also be mentioned, where defendants have successfully claimed that their online expression did not exceed the rights they enjoyed under Article 73, see for example *SC 22 October 2015 (Case No. 101/2015)*, *SC 31 March 2015 (Case No. 421/2014)* and *SC 20 November 2014 (Case No. 214/2014)*. In fact, the courts do not seem to make any distinction between online expression and other kinds of expression in this regard. The courts apply the aforementioned articles, in both general law and the Constitution, in the same manner.

Until now there do not seem to have been any court cases concerning online hate speech. In fact, to date there appears to be only one conviction under Article 233a of the Penal Code, i.e. *SC 24 April 2002 (Case No. 461/2001)*. This case concerned statements in a newspaper interview. However, a great deal of discussion on the subject has been held lately, and a special section dealing with hate crimes has recently been established by the police in the capital area. Forum shopping does not seem to have been a problem. About a decade ago, there was a rather high-profile lawsuit that an Icelandic business man pursued in the United Kingdom against an Icelandic professor for statements in English that he published on his website (see *SC 1 March 2006 (80/2006)*, concerning his attempts to enforce the UK libel judgment in Iceland.) However, this seems to have been an isolated instance, since no similar cases have arisen since then.

In addition to legal rules, the National Union of Icelandic Journalists adapted ethical rules long ago. The Union runs an ethics committee that issues opinions on whether these rules have been broken.[35]

Finally, it is worth pointing out that the parliamentary bill for the Media Act garnered quite a lot of criticism in 2010–2011. It was somewhat revised before

---

35 See the website of the National Union of Icelandic Journalists, http://press.is/index.php/sidhavefur (last accessed 6 February 2018).

being enacted into law. A temporary provision was added to the Act, stating that the Act should be reviewed within three years of its enactment. Although a couple of changes have been made to the Act since its enactment, the aforementioned review has not yet taken place. It seems that the criticism of the Act has subsided and that no major changes are likely in the near future.

Specific questions on liability for online media

Introduction

Some of the most relevant questions regarding the legal environment of online media in Iceland relate to the scope of the Media Act. To the extent that the Act covers online media, the media service providers are obliged to register with the Media Commission and adhere to the many duties prescribed in the Act. Some of these duties have been described above. Furthermore, although the liability rules in Articles 50 and 51 generally prescribe who is liable if content contravenes the law (whether it contravenes the Media Act or other legislation), the rules pertain solely to content that is provided by a *media outlet* within the meaning of the Act (this follows from Articles 2 and 3).[36] The foregoing makes it important to try to answer to what extent online media fall under the Act. It also raises the question of what rules apply to online media not falling under the Act.

This section will discuss these questions. First, it will look at the question of the Act's scope with regards to online media. Second, there will be a brief description of the liability rules applying to online media covered by the Act. Third, this section will discuss what rules apply to online media not falling under the Act. Finally, this section will present some thoughts on how recent judgments from the ECtHR will affect domestic liability rules in Iceland.

To what extent do online media fall under the Media Act?

Article 2 of the Media Act includes the following definition of *media outlet* (2–13):

> [A]ny media outlet which regularly provides the public with content which is subject to editorial control. Media outlets include, among other things, newspapers and periodicals, together with their supplements, internet media, audiovisual media and other comparable media.

Although the examples of internet media in the latter sentence might at first be understood as including internet media in general, the definition includes a requirement of "editorial control", which Article 2 (2–35) defines as "control over the selection and organisation of the content made available". This requirement,

---

36 See Jónsson, supra note 24, p. 188.

in fact, excludes a lot of internet communication. The Media Commission's working rules set forth certain criteria for evaluating whether distribution of content falls under the concept of "media outlet". Paragraphs 4 and 5 of Article 2 are as follows (author's translation):

> The fact that a media service provider's profession is to distribute media content and is in that way responsible for the editorial structure and the final composition of the media outlet is a clear indication that its distribution of content falls under the concept of media outlet. On the other hand, service not having this primary purpose rarely falls under the concept of media outlet within the meaning of the Act.
>
> Personal blogs generally fall outside the concept of media outlet within the meaning of the Act. Individual and personal communications on the internet, for example, on Facebook, also fall outside the concept.

These criteria are in many ways helpful and some judgments have viewed comments on Facebook as falling outside the concept of media outlet within the meaning of the Act (for example, see *SC 18 December 2014 (Case No. 215/2014)*). However, uncertainties remain. In addition, due to technical changes and the evolvement of online media, uncertainties keep arising. For example, in recent years quite big groups have formed on Facebook. Some have more than 50,000 members (Iceland's population is just over 330,000). These groups have certain administrators, who write and distribute material, which is then available to all the group members. It can be argued that this content is "subject to editorial control" within the meaning of the Act, and the groups should therefore be considered as media outlets under the aforementioned definition. It should also be pointed out that the Media Commission's working rules do not wholly preclude communication on Facebook, only "[i]ndividual and personal communication". Similar questions could also be raised about distribution through accounts on sites other than Facebook, for example, through YouTube and Snapchat accounts. It is, however, clear from the list of media registered on the Media Commission's website that the Commission has taken a rather restrictive approach, and the registered online media seem to be limited to rather traditional websites distributing news and articles.[37] This is no surprise since it is clear that if the Media Commission started including registrations of certain aspects of social media, it would be rather difficult to draw the line and it could also raise some jurisdictional issues.[38]

---

37 See http://fjolmidlanefnd.is/leyfi-og-skraning/listi-yfir-skrada-fjolmidla/ (last accessed 6 February 2018).

38 According to Article 3, the Act applies to "all media outlets and media service providers established in Iceland which make content available to the Icelandic public, subject to the provisions of Article 4". Article 4 then states, "Iceland shall have jurisdiction over audiovisual media service providers established in Iceland", and includes further clarifications on when such entities should be regarded as being established in Iceland.

As described above, the Media Commission's working rules also exclude personal blogs for the most part, i.e. they state that such blogs generally fall outside the concept of media outlet. However, some blogs are connected to registered media outlets. In *SC 17 December 2015 (Case No. 239/2015)*, the Supreme Court concluded that since the website www.dv.is was a media outlet under the Media Act, an article, written by an individual in an area on the website that he had the right to use, had been published in a media outlet, therefore, Article 51 of the Act applied. This brings some personal blogs under the scope of the Act, i.e. those that are directly connected to media outlets. However, most personal blogs are still not covered by the Act.

It should be stressed that this rather narrow scope regarding online media not only affects the application of liability rules, which will be discussed below, but it also means that the Media Act's articles on the duties of media service providers only apply to the most traditional online media. As an important example, the prohibition of surreptitious commercial communications in Article 37 does not apply to online media not covered by the Act. Therefore, the Media Commission does not seem to be able to take direct action against such advertisements, which seem to be increasing in the online media environment. In fact, the Media Act can be criticised for having a kind of on-off structure. Either you are operating a media outlet and have to be registered and have all the rights and duties prescribed in the Act, or you are not operating a media outlet within the meaning of the Act and then none of its articles apply. It might be preferable to moderate the scope somewhat, for example, by keeping a narrow definition of the media service providers required to register, but broadening the scope of some general principles in the Act so they apply to more actors than the registered media service providers.

What are the liability rules for online media falling under the Media Act?

To the extent that online media fall under the scope of the Media Act, Article 51 on liability for text content most often answers the question of who is liable for content that contravenes law.[39] However, Article 50 on liability for audiovisual content might also apply in some instances.

Descriptions of these articles appear in the section entitled *Media law* on p. 82. Both primarily assume the author's liability, i.e. it is the author of a statement or content that is generally responsible for it, if the author is known. However, the purchaser of a commercial communication is liable for its content. In other cases, the "responsible editor" bears the responsibility. This is a chain of responsibility, i.e. the liability of one of the persons in the chain exhausts other liability. So, if there is an author falling under paragraph 1a of Article 50 or 51,

---

39 See, as an example of Article 51's application to online media, *SC 21 February 2013 (Case No. 525/2012)* and *SC 7 November 2013 (Case No. 200/2013)*.

a claimant cannot go further down the chain. The author simply bears the responsibility. This arrangement deviates from general rules — for example, the principle of undivided responsibility in tort law and the principle in criminal law that everyone fulfilling the criteria for criminal liability shall be held criminally liable.[40]

Through the years it was somewhat unclear what requirements applied to the first person in the chain, i.e. the author.[41] However, the general practice was that the full name of an author of printed content (in newspapers and magazines) was a requirement for his liability. The Media Act was supposed to change this strict requirement, and paragraph 1a of Article 51 now prescribes that individuals shall be liable for content which they write in their own name or one "with which they clearly identify themselves",[42] if they are domiciled in Iceland or subject to Icelandic jurisdiction on other grounds.[43] This means that the authors of statements will be liable more often than before. However, it should be pointed out that many of the registered online media outlets in Iceland use Facebook accounts for comments, i.e. allow readers to comment through their Facebook accounts. It is well and generally recognised that many comments are made through fake Facebook accounts and, therefore, it is unclear who the author really is, although a full name appears with the comment. In such cases, the responsible editor would likely bear liability, under paragraph 1c of Article 51. However, according to paragraph 2 of the same article, the media service provider would be liable for payment of the fine or compensation payment that the responsible editor would be ordered to pay under the article.

Article 2 (2–3) defines the concept of "responsible editor" as "a medium employee having editorial responsibility for content and the choice thereof and who decides on its organisation, such as an editor-in-chief, a programme director or a director of a radio or television station". According to Article 14 of the

---

40 See Jónsson, supra note 32, p. 107, Matthíasson, Viðar Már: *Skaðabótaréttur*, Reykjavík: Bókaútgáfan Codex, 2005, p. 425, and Þórmundsson, Jónatan: *Afbrot og refsiábyrgð I*, Reykjavík: Háskólaútgáfan, 1999, pp. 138–139.

41 See, for example, Jónsson, Eiríkur: "Miskabætur vegna ólögmætrar meingerðar gegn æru samkvæmt b-lið 1. mgr. 26. gr. Skaðabótalaga", *Úlfljótur*, Reykjavík: Úlfljótur, tímarit laganema, 2007, pp. 70–71.

42 A similar provision on an author's liability in paragraph 1a of Article 50 prescribes that individuals "making a statement in their own name, or presenting or conveying content of their own composition and/or presenting content by another party by their own decision" shall be liable for it.

43 Paragraph 1a then continues as follows:

> If text content is correctly quoted as being that of named individuals, the persons quoted shall be liable for their own expressions if they have consented to the communication thereof and are either domiciled in Iceland or subject to Icelandic jurisdiction on other grounds. This was supposed to change the practice of often holding journalists liable for quotes they distributed. This was, for example, the situation in *Björk Eidsdóttir v. Iceland*, supra note 18. If the aforementioned provision had been in force at that time, the Supreme Court would probably have ruled in favour of the applicant and no case would, therefore, have arisen in Strasbourg.

Media Act, a media service provider shall provide information on the media outlet's responsible editor upon registration, and the Media Commission shall then publish this information on its website. This means that it is generally easy for an individual who thinks he has been defamed by anonymous comments on a registered online media outlet to find out who the responsible editor is and, therefore, who is liable. He simply goes to the Media Commission's website and sees who is listed there as the responsible editor.

What are the rules on online media falling outside the Media Act?

The legal situation described above makes it important to answer what rules apply to online media that are not within the scope of the Media Act. This question is not new since the Media Act's predecessors did not address online media at all. Of course, that did not hinder people from carrying out lawsuits because of expression on the internet. Courts then faced questions on the application of existing legal provisions to the internet, which, in many instances, did not even exist when the provisions were enacted. As explained in the section entitled *Media law* on p. 82, the courts have had no problems with applying the legal provisions mentioned there to the internet, for example, the provisions on defamation, as well as Article 73 of the Constitution on freedom of expression (the same is true with regards to Article 71, which ensures the right to privacy). In fact, it seems that the courts have for the most part taken it as self-evident that these articles apply to expression on the internet as elsewhere and there does not seem to be any similar discussion yet in the case law on the particularities of the internet with regards to freedom of expression, as in the *Delfi* case at the ECtHR.[44]

As explained above, it is, however, clear that the liability rules of the Media Act only apply to some parts of the online environment. Of course, this does not mean that no liability rules apply in other instances. It simply means that the special rules on liability in the Media Act do not apply, but instead the general rules apply, which derive from general principles in tort and penal law as well as the wording of the legislation that is allegedly violated.[45]

It is clear that the main principle of these general rules is that the author of an unlawful expression bears legal responsibility for it. This can be seen in many judgments. For example, in *SC 24 November 2011 (100/2011)*, the Supreme Court stated in general (author's translation):

> The principle that an author is liable for his comments on the grounds of general rules, particularly the culpa rule, has been deemed to apply to content that is published on the internet...[46]

---

44 *Delfi AS v. Estonia*, Application No. 64569/09, 16 June 2015 (Grand Chamber).
45 See Jónsson, supra note 32, p. 120.
46 The Court referred in this context to *SC 30 March 2006 (490/2005)* and *SC 29 January 2009 (321/2008)* as examples.

According to this and the description in the previous section, it is clear that the same principle applies whether or not online media falls under the scope of the Media Act. In both instances, the author, if known, bears liability for unlawful content. Some differences are still apparent. First, an author's liability under the Media Act exhausts other liability, whereas other people could also be liable under general rules. Second, the situation is different if the author is unknown. In that situation, the Media Act clearly and simply makes the responsible editor liable, whereas the general rules raise more complicated questions.

It is safe to say that it can often be difficult to find out who wrote what on the internet. It may be difficult, but technically possible, for example, when comments are anonymous or stem from fake social media accounts as there are ways to track down the device used for making the comment. It can, however, for many reasons, be difficult for a defamed individual to obtain such information. This has raised questions with regard to the general rules — more precisely, to what extent persons other than the author can be held liable. Can a blogger, for example, be held liable for anonymous comments made on his blog which he does not remove, or an internet discussion board operator who does not remove comments? What about a Facebook user who does not remove comments made by others on his wall through a fake Facebook account? Can he be held liable? So far, there are no direct judgments on this kind of situation. However, the author thinks that such liability is by no means impossible. It is more unlikely that such liability would be recognised under the Penal Code, but tort liability under such circumstances does not seem a distant possibility. The main condition for an award of non-pecuniary damages for defamation under Article 26 of the Tort Damages Act seems to be the tortfeasor's culpable conduct, involving a certain roughness that is defamatory to the tort claimant.[47] It seems that this could apply, for example, to a website operator who does not remove clearly defamatory statements that others have written on the website — if he is aware of the statements and is able to remove them. In certain instances, such conduct could clearly be considered culpable and rough enough to establish tort liability. Of course, the situation's facts would determine the result in each and every case, but at least nothing in the article precludes such liability. However, the application of such liability would, of course, always have to fulfil the requirements of Article 73 of the Constitution and Article 10 of the ECHR. Although there are still no direct judgments on the above-mentioned situation, there are examples of the liability of individuals other than the author for an online expression, supporting the foregoing conclusions, like the following judgment:

> *SC 24 November 2011 (100/2011).* The case, among other things, concerned content published at the news website www.dv.is. It is clear that the website now falls under the Media Act, but at that time it did not fall under the

---

47 See Jónsson, supra note 41, p. 32.

relevant legislation, i.e., the Right of Publication Act No. 57/1956. The Supreme Court rejected that the rule on editor's liability in Article 15, paragraph 3, of the Act could be applied by analogy. The Court nevertheless concluded that the editors of the website would be liable if the content violated law, on the grounds of general rules. Thus, the Court continued after rejecting argument by analogy (author's translation): "However, it has to be taken into account that the [editors] of the website had a duty to supervise. They were obliged to handle the editorial so as to avoid its content causing others pain or distorting privacy. Their culpable neglect in fulfilling this duty of supervision could therefore make them liable, and the case is therefore not wrongly directed against them." However, the result was that the content was within the limits of Article 73 of the Constitution, so there was no liability for it.

This judgment clearly shows that others besides the author of an online expression can be held liable, on the grounds of general rules.[48]

Notwithstanding the foregoing conclusions, a person who is simply providing technical services, for example, hosting and communicating, without knowledge of the relevant defamatory material or the possibility of influencing it, will not be held liable. This is, in fact, due to several reasons. First, Directive 2000/31/EC (the Electronic Commerce Directive),[49] which was legalised in Iceland with Act No. 30/2002, excludes such liability to a certain extent. Second, such liability can be seen as violating the aforementioned articles on freedom of expression, both in the Constitution and the ECHR, as they have been construed. Third, such liability can be seen as contravening basic principles in tort and penal law, where some kind of culpable behaviour is generally required before liability is established. This all boils down to the same thing: an individual's conduct must be in some way culpable before he can be held liable for it. As previously stated, this requirement can clearly be met for a website operator who does not remove clear defamation that he knows about. On the other hand, this requirement will never be met for a person simply providing technical assistance who has no knowledge of the content of the material.

---

48 See also *SC 21 February 2013 (525/2012)*. Jónsson, supra note 24, pp. 205–206. See also further discussion in Jónsson, supra note 32, pp. 121–124, where *SC 29 January 2009 (321/12008)* and several other judgments are also discussed in this context. See also pp. 124–128 in the same article on criminal liability. It should also be mentioned that a case that ended with the judgment from the *District Court of Reykjanes 8 February 2008 (Case No. E-1257/2007)* was almost directly on point here, where a claim was made against a website operator (Internet discussion board) that was not the author of the defamatory statements. The case was, however, dismissed on procedural grounds, so there was no result on the substance.

49 Directive 2000/31/EC of the European Parliament and of the Council of 8 June 2000 on certain legal aspects of information society services, in particular electronic commerce, in the Internal Market ('Directive on electronic commerce') (OJ L 178, 17.7.2000, pp. 1–16).

What is the effect of recent Strasbourg judgments on liability rules in Iceland?

After this brief description of the liability rules in Icelandic national law, some words are in order on the recent judgments from the ECtHR concerning online media. The *Delfi* case has raised many questions with regard to the liability of online media providers for comments made by others on their websites.[50] The ECtHR concluded that holding *Delfi AS* liable for third-party comments posted on its internet news portal did not violate Article 10. In fact, it is pretty hard to derive from the judgment, as tailored as it is to the particular facts of the case, general rules on the liability of online media for third-party comments. It can also be argued that subsequent case law further complicates the picture, particularly *Magyar Tartalomszolgáltatók Egyesülete and Index.hu Zrt v. Hungary*.[51] There the Court found that holding the applicants liable for third-party comments on their portals violated Article 10. The judgment can hardly be described as anything other than a small step back from *Delfi*, although the result, just as in *Delfi*, was highly tailored to the particular facts of the case, and the Court stressed that the cases were different. Among other things, the Court found that the nature of the comments in the *Magyar* case was not as serious as in the *Delfi* case. For example, it stated that although offensive and vulgar, the comments at issue did not constitute clearly unlawful speech and certainly did not amount to hate speech or incitement to violence.

If we consider how these cases would have turned out in Iceland, it seems rather clear that the portals of *Delfi AS* and Index.hu Zrt would have fallen under the scope of the Media Act and been registered by the Media Commission. This would have meant that the authors of the comments would have been liable and exhausted other liability, if they wrote the comments in their own name or if the authors clearly identified themselves with the comments in another way. In other instances, liability would have rested with the responsible editor, but the media service provider would have been liable for the compensation payments that the responsible editor would have been ordered to pay. The situation of the first applicant in the *Magyar* case is more complicated but would probably have been governed by general rules rather than the Media Act. That would have meant that the principal liability would have rested with the authors of the comments. However, liability of the website operator would not have been impossible, but would have required establishing culpable behaviour on its behalf.

Although the recent judgments from the ECtHR can be seen as unclear, they do not seem to create many problems for the application of the domestic liability rules described here. The requirement of culpable behaviour under the general rules should, for the most part, prevent establishing liability for

---

50 *Delfi AS v. Estonia*, supra note 44.
51 *Magyar Tartalomszolgáltatók Egyesülete and Index.hu Zrt v. Hungary*, Application No. 22947/13, 2 February 2016. See also the decision in *Rolf Anders Daniel Pihl v. Sweden*, Application No. 74742/14, 7 February 2017.

third-party comments in contravention of Article 10 of the ECHR. To the extent that online media falls under the scope of the Media Act, the responsible editor surely becomes liable for anonymous third-party comments contravening law, and the media service provider is then liable for the payment of fines and compensation payments that the responsible editor may be ordered to pay. However, *Delfi* makes it clear that liability for third-party comments can be fully in accordance with Article 10. The principal concern might be cases where the comments in question are not of a very serious nature, since the latter of the aforementioned judgments indicates that the direct application of the Media Act's rule in these cases might be problematic. Problems might also arise in cases of small, non-commercial websites. It remains to be seen how the case law of the ECtHR will evolve and clarify itself, but it at least seems that the Icelandic liability rules described in this article do not create any serious problems with regards to Article 10 of the ECHR.

Conclusions and remarks

As has been explained, the current legislation on the media in force in Iceland is relatively new. The Constitution includes a rather recent provision on freedom of expression, i.e. Article 73, and a new Media Act was enacted only five years ago.

Article 10 of the ECHR heavily influenced the constitutional article, and this also tends to have an effect on constitutional interpretation. The same is true with regard to the right to privacy, which Article 71 of the Constitution guarantees, along similar lines as Article 8 of the ECHR. Articles 71 and 73 apply to the internet, i.e. they guarantee freedom of expression and the right to privacy on the internet, just as elsewhere. Until now, the Supreme Court's judgments do not include any discussion on the particularities of the internet similar to the ECtHR's discussion in the *Delfi* case.

The Media Act covers some online media but not all. Broadly put, the Act covers the most traditional online media, whereas personal online communication falls outside the Act. To the extent that online media falls under the Act, it prescribes its duties and rights. Many provisions in other acts limit expression and extend to online media, whether or not it falls under the Media Act, for example, articles on defamation in the General Penal Code and the Tort Damages Act.

If online content contravenes law, for example, the aforementioned articles, it raises the question of who is liable for this. It then matters whether or not the Media Act applies to the relevant online media since the Act includes rules on liability, with a chain of responsibility. Outside the scope of the Media Act, questions on liability must be resolved on the grounds of general rules. In both instances, the principal rule is that it is the author of a statement or comment who is liable for it. However, there are differences between these two sets of rules. For example, the liability of one person under the rules of the Media Act exhausts others' liability, whereas more than one person can be held liable under the general rules. The rules in the Media Act also mean that if the author is unknown, it is generally the responsible editor who becomes liable (and the media service provider is liable for the compensation payments that the responsible editor is ordered to pay), whereas the general rules here are more complicated.

It has to be said that the ECtHR's recent judgments on liability for online third-party comments are somewhat unclear, and it is difficult to derive general rules from them. However, it seems that the rules on liability for online expression in Iceland will generally not create many problems with regard to Article 10 of the ECHR.

7 Regulation of online media in Latvia

Lolita Bērziņa, Linda Bīriņa, Laura Jambuševa, and Artūrs Kučs

Media environment in Latvia

Media environment in general

The field of media has been divided into Russian speaking or writing and Latvian speaking or writing media mainly because of historical events in Latvia in the last millennium, including the russification and migration policy implemented during the Soviet occupation. As a result, Latvians comprise a little more than 60% of the population. The gap between the media targeting the Latvian-speaking audience and the Russian-speaking audience is wide. This split makes the available market for media even smaller, because these two groups demand different products.[1] Several media formats, especially online media, have made use of this situation offering their outlets in both Russian and Latvian languages.[2] Additionally, the television and radio stations from Russia are competing with the local media.[3] Compared to Latvian media companies, these channels have more financial resources, allowing them to provide more diverse content.

The most popular types of media in Latvia are television and internet. Within different age groups, one prevails over the other.[4] Time spent watching television, in general, has a tendency to decrease, while the usage of internet is growing annually.[5] The number of daily internet users in Latvia is above average

---

1 Ilze Šulmane, "The Russian language media in Latvia", In: *Latvian-Russian Relations: Domestic and International Dimensions*, Nils Muižnieks (ed.), Riga, LU Akadēmiskais apgāds, 2006.

2 All the biggest online media platforms, such as Delfi and TVNET are available in both languages.

3 Media itself has described the issue quite broadly, for example: "Krievijas TV kanāli pārņem Latvijas auditoriju" (Latvijas Avīze, 5 August 2016) www.la.lv/krievijas-tv-kanali-parnem-latvijas-auditoriju/ (last accessed 6 February 2018).

4 "TNS Latvijas mediju petijumu gadagramata 2013/2014" (TNS, 2014) www.tns.lv/wwwtnslv_resources/images/Mediju_petijumu_gadagramata/TNS_Latvia_mediju_petijumu_gadagramata_2013-2014.pdf (last accessed 6 February 2018); A.Rožukalne, Medial pluralism monitor 2016: Latvia http://cmpf.eui.eu/media-pluralism-monitor/mpm-2016-results/latvia/ (accessed 14 February 2018).

5 "TNS Latvijas mediju petijumu gadagramata 2013/2014", supra note 4; "Media Use in the European Union" (Standard Eurobarometer 82 Autumn 2014, European Commission, November

among Eastern and Central European countries.[6] Almost 75% of the population use the internet regularly.[7] TV channels are trying to catch up with this phenomenon, and now almost all TV channels offer at least some part of their content online. Among the 20 most visited online sites, four are news platforms and one platform which offers to watch the content of some of the TV channels.[8]

Although the radio has lost its significance, it is still a very popular medium, and the average listener spends more than four hours daily listening to the radio.[9] As almost everywhere in Europe, the number of people reading newspapers and magazines is decreasing. However, it must be emphasised that the readership of weekly magazines is decreasing much slower than that of daily newspapers.[10]

Key players in the media market

There are three big audiovisual media groups in Latvia. The biggest one, owning more than half of the TV market, is *Modern Times Group* or *MTG*,[11] an international entertainment group, which provides several TV channels in Latvia, such as *TV3*, *LNT* and *TV6*, a radio station *Star FM*, as well as the online video platform *TvPlay* and *Skaties.lv*. The second biggest is *Baltijas Mediju Alianse*, which provides several TV channels mainly in the Russian language and the newspaper *MK Latvija*. Additionally, it provides content for the TV sets installed in Riga's public transportation system.[12] The third one is the public broadcaster *Latvijas Televīzija*, which has two TV channels – one broadcasting mainly news, documentaries and educational programmes in Latvian, and the other offering content in both Russian and Latvian.

The share of the media market offering radio is more diverse. The biggest market share belongs to the public broadcaster *Latvijas Radio*. It has several radio stations, the most popular of which is a radio station broadcasting mostly music in the Latvian language, *Latvijas Radio 2*.[13] Additionally, there are several other bigger private radio stations, such as *Radio SWH*, *Radio Skonto*, *European Hit Radio*, *Hiti Rossii/Russkoje radio*, also mainly concentrating on music, and

---

2014) http://ec.europa.eu/public_opinion/archives/eb/eb82/eb82_media_en.pdf (last accessed 7 February 2018).

6 Ianis Bucholtz, "Media Use Among Social Networking Site Users in Latvia" (2015) 9 *International Journal of Communication* 2653.

7 "Information Technologies – Key Indicators" (Central Statistical Bureau, 13 November 2015) www.csb.gov.lv/en/statistikas-temas/information-technologies-key-indicators-30744.html (last accessed 7 February 2018).

8 "Regulāri internetu lieto jau 68% Latvijas iedzīvotāju" (TNS, 29 May 2015) www.tns.lv/?lang=lv&fullarticle=true&category=showuid&id=4797 (last accessed 7 February 2018).

9 "TNS Latvijas mediju petijumu gadagramata 2013/2014" supra note 4.

10 Ibid.

11 "Latvijas 2015. gada II ceturkšņa TV tirgus apskats" (Baltijas Mediju Alianse, 2015) http://1bma.lv/files/2015/07/Latvija_Q2_2015_LV.pdf (last accessed 7 February 2018).

12 More information about Baltijas Mediju Alianse is available at the webpage: "Par BMA" http://1bma.lv/lv/par-holdingu/par-mums/ (last accessed 7 February 2018).

13 "TNS Latvijas mediju petijumu gadagramata 2013/2014" supra note 4.

quite a few smaller radio stations and regional radio stations, such as *Latvijas Kristīgais Radio*, *Kurzemes Radio* and others providing information and other material to more specific groups of society.

The most read printed media are weekly magazines. As with the TV stations, the most popular printed media differ between Latvian and Russian readers. Latvian speakers most often choose *Ieva*, a magazine generally targeting women, and *Privātā dzīve* and *Kas jauns* are magazines providing entertainment and ce-lebrity news. The most popular printed media read by Russian readers are *MK Latvija (rus)*, a newspaper discussing news, everyday issues and entertainment and *Televizor* and *Latvijskaja TV-programma*, a guide for TV shows, movies and entertainment.[14]

The biggest online news platforms – *Delfi*, *TVNET* and *Apollo* – are in fourth, seventh and tenth place, respectively, among the most visited websites. The field in which Latvia differs the most from other countries is social media. Up un-til 2014, *Draugiem.lv*, one of the few local social networking sites still operat-ing, was more popular than *Facebook* itself.[15] However, in the spring of 2015, *Facebook* received 2% more daily visitors than *Draugiem.lv*.[16] Among the Russian-speaking public, the Russian social network *odnoklassniki.ru* is also of-ten visited.

Television receives most of the funds spent on advertisement. In 2014, it re-ceived 44% of the market share[17] and in 2015 increased this share by 0.2%. However, the internet has received the biggest increase of the advertisements – in 2015, its market share had grown by 38.2% and it has become the second biggest advertising platform after television, pushing back the radio and magazines to third and fourth place respectively on this list.[18]

Brief introduction to freedom of speech doctrine

Historical background

The importance and roots of freedom of expression in the Latvian legal sys-tem date back to the very first documents establishing the Latvian state.[19] The Soviet occupation of Latvia in 1940 eliminated any possibility for freedom of

---

14 "Nacionālā preses auditorijas pētījuma rezultāti 2015. gada vasarā" (TNS, 17 August 2015) www. tns.lv/?lang=lv&fullarticle=true&category=showuid&id=4833 (last accessed 7 February 2018).
15 Bucholtz, supra note 6.
16 "Regulāri internetu lieto jau 68% Latvijas iedzīvotāju" supra note 8.
17 "Mediju reklāmas tirgus 2014.gadā ir audzis par 3% un sasniedzis 75,63 miljonus eiro" (TNS, 10 April 2015) www.tns.lv/?lang=lv&fullarticle=true&category=showuid&id=4774 (last accessed 7 February 2018).
18 "2015.gadā Baltijas mediju reklāmas tirgus pieauga par 3,1% un sasniedza 270,9 miljonus eiro" (TNS, 11 May 2016) www.tns.lv/?lang=lv&fullarticle=true&category=showuid&id=4974 (last accessed 7 February 2018).
19 Latvijas Tautas padomes politiskā platforma. Pagaidu Valdības Vēstnesis, 14 December 1918, Nr. 1.

expression, subjecting all press under the control and censorship of the communist party and persecuting anyone criticising the policies of the Soviet regime. However, freedom of expression, free press and freedom of assembly played a crucial role at the end of the 1980s during the transformation of the Soviet regime and coincided with the attempts to re-establish the independence of the Republic of Latvia and struggle against the regime, russification and suppression of the Latvian language. Even prior to the restoration of independence, the first democratically elected parliament adhered to core human rights documents guaranteeing the freedom of expression as a way to illustrate the democratic nature of the new political regime. This was evidenced by the fact that on 4 May 1990, when the Supreme Soviet of the Latvia SSR adopted a Declaration of the Renewal of the Independence of the Republic of Latvia, it also issued a Declaration on the Accession of the Republic of Latvia to International Instruments Relating to Human Rights.[20] According to this document, the Republic of Latvia joined the 51 human rights instruments adopted by the United Nations (UN) and the Organization for Security and Co-operation in Europe (OSCE).

Contrary to the neighbouring Baltic States, the Latvian Parliament did not adopt a new constitution, but restored the pre-war Constitution of the Republic of Latvia, which did not contain a fundamental rights chapter.[21] Therefore, initially the fundamental rights were granted in the constitutional law titled the Rights and Obligations of a Citizen and a Person, which was adopted on 10 December 1991. Article 30 of this law guaranteed the right to the freedom of expression.[22]

The Constitution was amended only in 1998, when Chapter 8 entitled "Fundamental Rights" was adopted and integrated within the pre-war Constitution of the Republic of Latvia.

Scope and limitations of the freedom of speech in national constitutional doctrine

Article 100 of the present Constitution reads as follows:

> Everyone has the right to freedom of expression, which includes the right to freely receive, keep and distribute information and to express their views. Censorship is prohibited.[23]

---

20 Declaration on the Accession of Latvia to International Instruments Relating to Human Rights. Adopted on 4 May 1990. Latvijas Republikas Augstākās Padomes un Valdības Ziņotājs, 17 May 1990, Nr. 20. The text of the Declaration is available in English at: www.humanrights.lv/doc/latlik/dokdekl.htm (last accessed 7 February 2018).

21 Artūrs Kučs and Jānis Pleps, "Latvia: Second Part of the Constitution as a Project for Next Generations", In: *First Fundamental Rights Documents in Europe*, Markku Suksi, Kalliope Agapiou-Josephides, Jean-Paul Lehners, Manfred Nowak (ed.), Intersentia, Cambridge-Antwerp-Portland, 2015, pp. 329–343.

22 Constitutional Law "The Rights and Obligations of a Citizen and a Person". Adopted on 10 December 1991. An English translation of the law is available at: www.uta.edu/cpsees/latconst.htm (accessed 20 February 2018).

23 The Constitution of the Republic of Latvia. www.saeima.lv/en/legislation/constitution (accessed 20 February 2018).

During the drafting of the text for Article 100, a number of proposals were made. For instance, the state's Human Rights Bureau advised to supplement the article with the prohibition to force a person to reveal his or her membership in a political party, to discover one's political, religious, ethical or other opinions.[24] Furthermore, the Latvian judge at the European Court of Human Rights (ECtHR) at the time, Egils Levits, proposed to insert within the text of the article guarantees for freedom of press and independence of public television and radio.[25] Due to time constraints, the parliamentary working group did not manage to consider the latter proposal. However, the interpretation of Article 100 in the practice of the Constitutional Court allows us to conclude that both the right to remain silent and freedom of press are protected within the scope of Article 100. The right to the freedom of expression is not absolute. At the same time, the Constitutional Court has emphasised that freedom of expression has a rather wide scope[26] and it can be limited only in cases provided for and in accordance with the procedure established by the Constitution, where the key principle is the proportionality of limitations.[27] The scope of freedom of expression in the Constitution is largely influenced by two factors.

First, it is influenced by the jurisprudence of the Latvian Constitutional Court, which interprets the fundamental rights guaranteed in the Constitution. The Constitutional Court has invoked Article 100 in four cases up until 2017. Contrary to the freedom of expression, it has found for the restriction of local private radio and television channels to broadcast in foreign languages no more than 25% of broadcasting time.[28] The law prescribing administrative liability for persons refusing to display the state flag next to their homes during the national holidays or days of commemoration has also been declared invalid.[29] Furthermore, the Court has found deficiencies in the provisions of the Criminal Law, which dealt specifically with the defamation of civil servants and public officials.[30]

The Court has also recognised that restrictions on political advertising one day prior to elections are in conformity with freedom of expression.[31] Furthermore,

---

24 Valsts Cilvēktiesību biroja atzinums Latvijas Republikas Satversmes otrās daļas projekta 'Par cilvēktiesībām' izstrādes komisijai. 1997. gada 25. jūlijs, Nr. 1-14Z/83.

25 Levits E. Piezīmes par Satversmes 8.nodaļu - Cilvēka pamattiesības. Satversme un cilvēktiesības: gadagrāmata 1999, Cilvēktiesību Žurnāls. Rīga: Juridiskās fakultātes Cilvēktiesību institūts, 1999, Nr. 9–12. 11.lpp.

26 Judgment of the Constitutional Court of the Republic of Latvia of 2 July 2015, No. 2015-01-01, para. 11.4.

27 Judgment of the Constitutional Court of the Republic of Latvia of 29 October 2003, No. 2003-05-01, para. 31.3.

28 Judgment of the Constitutional Court of the Republic of Latvia of 5 June 2003, No. 2003-02-0106.

29 Judgment of the Constitutional Court of the Republic of Latvia of 2 July 2015, No. 2015-01-01.

30 Judgment of the Constitutional Court of the Republic of Latvia of 29 October 2003, No. 2003-05-01.

31 Judgment of the Constitutional Court of the Republic of Latvia of 22 February 2010, No. 2009-45-01.

in 2003 the Constitutional Court has already concluded that "Article 100 of the Constitution envisages not only the right of freely expressing one's viewpoint and distributing information but also the right to freely receive it".[32] The Supreme Court of the Republic of Latvia has added that "Article 100 of the Latvian Constitution includes the scope of the human right to information in a broad sense – namely, not only to receive public information provided, but also to actively seek it".[33]

Second, international human rights bodies have played an enormous role in interpreting the Constitution, most notably the ECtHR, due to direct application of international human rights treaties at a national level. The Constitutional Court has declared that for a restriction of freedom of expression to be legitimate it must comply with the objectives mentioned in Article 10 of the Convention.[34] However, while the European Convention on Human Rights sets the boundaries for the limitation of the freedom of expression, the Constitution may contain wider guarantees for freedom of expression.

Regulation of media

Scope of media law

Latvian media law consists of two core legislative acts adopted by Parliament; namely, the Law on the Press and other Mass Media (adopted in 1991) and the Electronic Mass Media Law (adopted in 2010). While the Law on the Press and other Mass Media has a broader scope and its general principles are applicable to all media, including online media,[35] the Electronic Mass Media Law additionally contains specific legal provisions for electronic mass media (media providing audio and/or audiovisual programmes).[36]

Mass media are registered in the Mass Media Register; however, the registration is not mandatory for online media.[37] No such registration procedure has been introduced for journalists. In order to recognise a person as a journalist, it is sufficient to ascertain that this person prepares materials for a mass medium and has entered into an employment relationship or acts upon the instruction

---

32 Judgment of the Constitutional Court of the Republic of Latvia of 29 October 2003, No. 2003-05-01, para. 31.

33 2007.gada 8.jūnija SPRIEDUMS Lietā, Nr.SKA-194/2007.

34 Judgment of the Constitutional Court of the Republic of Latvia of 22 February 2010, No. 2009-45-01, para. 9.

35 Law on the Press and Other Mass Media, Article 2. In force from 1 January 1991 http://likumi. lv/doc.php?id=64879 (last accessed 7 February 2018); about online media as part of mass media in a broader sense, please see the Civil Department of the Supreme Court's judgment of 17 October 2012 No. SKC-637/2012 at: at.gov.lv/files/uploads/files/637-skc-2012.doc (last accessed 7 February 2018).

36 Electronic Mass Media Law, Articles 1-2.

37 Law on the Press and Other Mass Media, Articles 2 (1), 9.

of this mass medium.[38] Bloggers are not endowed with a specific status under Latvian media law, and in practice they are equated with private individuals exercising freedom of expression.

Regulatory and self-regulatory bodies

There are two self-regulatory authorities, which aim to protect journalists and their press freedom. Both the Latvian Association of Journalists[39] and the Latvian Union of Journalists[40] have developed their codes of ethics,[41] containing such sections as a journalist's main tasks and their relationship with information sources. The Latvian Association of Journalists may review complaints about journalists' activities and breaches of the Code of Ethics. Possible sanctions may include, for example, condemnation in a public announcement to mass media or expulsion of the journalist from the Latvian Association of Journalists.[42] However, a journalist is not obliged to become a member of these self-regulatory bodies.

In the area of television and radio, the Latvian Association of Broadcasting is a self-regulatory body promoting broadcasters' freedom and rights,[43] whereas the Latvian Association of Press Publishers unites publishers of printed media. The Latvian Association of Press Publishers promotes the development of printed media and the publishing industry and seeks to determine the policy and standards of the development of the industry.[44] Involvement in both these organisations is not mandatory.

The National Electronic Mass Media Council as a regulatory body is authorised to review complaints about and apply sanctions to electronic mass media. The Council has the right to suspend the operation of an electronic mass medium for a period of up to seven days if it has repeatedly violated the Electronic Mass Media Law (including breaches of obligations to provide only veritable information and to respect human rights and privacy). Furthermore, the National Electronic Mass Media Council has the right to annul a broadcasting permit or retransmission permit, if an electronic mass medium has severely and repeatedly

---

38 Ibid, Article 23.
39 For information about the aims and principles of the Latvian Journalists Association, please see: www.latvijaszurnalisti.lv/par-asociaciju/ (last accessed 7 February 2018).
40 For information about the aims and principles of the Latvian Journalists Union, please see: www.zurnalistusavieniba.lv/?p=3519&pp=3712&lang=923 (last accessed 7 February 2018).
41 Code of Ethics of the Latvian Journalists Union www.zurnalistusavieniba.lv/index.php?p=3519&lang=923&pp=3768 (accessed 20 February 2018); Code of Ethics of the Latvian Journalists Association www.latvijaszurnalisti.lv/etikas-kodekss/ (last accessed 7 February 2018).
42 Code of Ethics of the Latvian Journalists Association, ibid, Article 6.3.
43 For information about the aims and principles of the Latvian Broadcasters Association, please see: www.tvradio.lv/index.php (last accessed 7 February 2018).
44 For information about the aims and principles of the Latvian Press Publishers Association, please see: www.lpia.lv/eng/ (last accessed 7 February 2018).

breached the Law.[45] It is also authorised to apply penalty fees in accordance with the Latvian Code of Administrative Violations.[46] While the Council applies the penalty fees relatively often, there have been no suspensions or annulments of a broadcasting permit or retransmission permit so far.[47]

Media liability

Liability rules for breach of privacy and defamation in mass media are applicable not only to mass media and journalists, but also to unregistered online media platforms and private individuals, including bloggers, who have published their statements in mass media. Therefore, the Latvian legislator has not made registration a precondition for liability concerning violations of privacy and defamation.

Breach of privacy

According to the Law on the Press and Other Mass Media, "The use of the mass media to interfere in the private life of citizens is prohibited and shall be punished in accordance with the law."[48] There are no regulations specifically designed for wrongful acts committed by the media, which have resulted in violations of privacy. The applicable norm in the Latvian Civil Law regulates a person's responsibility for every wrongful act, as a result of which harm has been caused, including moral injury.[49] A claimant may sue the responsible medium in civil proceedings and ask for a civil remedy, which usually includes monetary compensation or an apology published in the medium.

According to the Law on the Press and Other Mass Media, the editor is responsible for the content published in the medium and represents the medium in relationship with other persons.[50] However, the claimant's choice against whom to submit a claim is not restricted. The claim may be submitted against the medium (as a legal entity), the editor, the author/journalist and the source of information/individual (if it can be identified) – against one of the aforementioned persons or against several of them in different combinations. In practice, the claim is usually submitted against the medium itself[51] or the individual who has directly expressed the information, which has breached the claimant's right

45 Electronic Mass Media Law, Articles 21 (2), 21 (3) and 60 (2), Nr. 1.
46 Latvian Code of Administrative Violations, Article 201.
47 For information about the decisions made by the National Electronic Mass Media Council, please see: http://neplpadome.lv/lv/sakums/normativie-akti/nozari-regulejosie-neplp-lemumi. html (last accessed 7 February 2018).
48 Law on the Press and Other Mass Media, Article 7 (4).
49 Civil Law, Article 1635. In force from 1 September 1992.
50 Law on the Press and Other Mass Media, Article 16. In force from 1 January 1991.
51 Judgment of the Civil Department of the Supreme Court of the Republic of Latvia of 5 October 2011, No. SKC-209/2011 [not published].

to privacy.[52] There have also been cases in which the claimant files a lawsuit against the media, editor and journalist simultaneously but, interestingly, not against the author of the statements,[53] as well as cases in which the claim is brought against the media outlet and the journalist simultaneously.[54] The internal relationship between the medium and journalist is usually regulated through a specific (labour/services) agreement.[55] Thus, parallel to the civil proceedings in the court initiated by the claimant, the internal liability between the medium and the journalist may be determined in accordance with the clauses of the agreement and other regulations stipulated in the Latvian Civil Law. Similarly, a regress claim can be later submitted by the medium against the author of the publication.

Defamation and libel

According to the Law on the Press and Other Mass Media, "It is prohibited to publish information that injures the honour and dignity of natural persons and legal persons or defames them."[56] A claimant has the right to ask the medium to retract the untrue statements of fact or publish an apology for the defamatory opinion. However, mass media are not liable for the dissemination of false information, if it is included in official documents and announcements of the state authorities, and political and public organisations.[57]

A claimant may also sue the responsible medium in civil proceedings and ask for a civil remedy, which usually includes a retraction of information and a monetary compensation/apology published in the medium.[58] Similarly, as in the case of a breach of privacy, the claimant's choice against whom to submit a claim is not restricted. In practice, the claim is usually submitted against the medium itself or the individual who has directly made the defamatory statements. According to the Latvian Criminal Law, criminal liability applies in case of an intentional dissemination of defamatory statements, which contain untrue allegations (libel), providing community service or a fine as a punishment. For defamation in mass media, the applicable punishment is the temporary deprivation of liberty, community service or a fine.[59]

---

52 Judgment of the Riga city Vidzeme district court of 6 April 2016, No. C30606413 [not published]; Judgment of the Riga city Centre district court of 8 November 2012, No. C27195012 [not published].
53 Judgment of the Division of Civil cases of the Riga Regional court of 9 November 2015, No. C27123413 [not published].
54 Judgment of the Division of Civil cases of the Riga Regional court of 20 June 2014, No. C27230712 [not published].
55 Law on the Press and Other Mass Media, Article 23. In force from January 1991.
56 Ibid, Article 7 (5).
57 Ibid, Article 29.
58 Civil Law, Article 2352. Civil Law, Article 1635. In force from 1 September 1992.
59 Criminal Law, Article 157. In force from 1 April 1999.

Influence of the case law of the ECtHR

As mentioned before, the case law of the ECtHR has had a great influence in Latvia. It has been established by national courts that cases relating to freedom of expression or right to privacy have to be considered taking into account the principles and interpretation established by the ECtHR.[60] Therefore, in almost any national cases that concern media or journalists' rights and obligations the case law of the ECtHR is cited and evaluated.

There are three judgments from the ECtHR against Latvia that directly relate to media law and journalists' rights issues. In all the cases, the ECtHR unanimously held that there had been a violation of Article 10 of the Convention.[61] Though the cases have not lead to any changes in law, they have definitely influenced the case law, the application of the law and the media environment in Latvia.

Defamation

In the case of *Vides Aizsardzības Klubs v Latvia*,[62] the applicant association for environmental protection adopted a resolution addressed to the relevant authorities, expressing its concerns about the conservation of an area of dunes along a stretch of coastline. The resolution was published in a regional newspaper and accused the chair of the district council of various illegal activities in this regard. The chair of the district council initiated civil litigation claiming compensation from the applicant association and requesting an official retraction. The national court found that although some illegalities had occurred, there was no proof that the chairman had contributed to them, *inter alia* taking into account that the respective documents were considered as a collective decision of the council. Consequently, the court ruled against the applicant association.

The ECtHR held that the judgment constituted interference with the exercise of the applicant's right to freedom of expression. The applicant association had fulfilled the role of "watchdog" by drawing attention to a sensitive matter of public interest. Like the role of the press, such participation by a voluntary association is essential in a democratic society. It was also stated that the fact of criticising the mayor for the policy of the local authority could not be described as abuse of freedom of expression. Moreover, the usage of word "illegal" when describing the mayor's behaviour was recognised as a value judgment, whose truthfulness could not be proven.

---

60 LR Augstākās tiesas Plēnuma un tiesu prakses vispārināšanas daļas Tiesu prakse lietās par personas goda un cieņas civiltiesisko aizsardzību 2003/2004.
61 *Vides Aizsardzības Klubs v Latvia* App no. 57829/00 (ECtHR, 27 May 2004); *a/s Diena and Ozoliņš v Latvia* App no. 16657/03 (ECtHR, 12 July 2007); *Nagla v Latvia* App no. 73469/10 (ECtHR, 16 July 2013).
62 *Vides Aizsardzības Klubs v Latvia*, ibid.

In the case of *a/s Diena and Ozoliņš v Latvia*,[63] the applicants included a daily newspaper and its journalist, a political commentator, who in 1998 published several articles criticising the Minister of Economic Affairs and accusing him of abuse of authority and bribery in connection with the privatisation of a state-owned company. The minister initiated civil litigation and the national court ordered the applicant company to pay compensation and to retract four of the seven articles in question.

The ECtHR held that the judgment constituted interference with the exercise of the applicants' right to freedom of expression. It noted that the offending articles had concerned a sensitive matter of public interest – the privatisation of a major state-owned commercial corporation and the conduct of the minister responsible for overseeing the process. In their capacities as publishing company of the leading Latvian newspaper and journalist, the applicants had exercised the role of "watchdog". Moreover, the ECtHR observed that the articles concerned the minister as a public figure and that the limits of acceptable criticism were, therefore, wider. It was also constituted that the statements were value judgments that had been based on information reported to the general public and, subsequently, discussed widely in the press and in Parliament. Whilst the language used by the applicant journalist had admittedly constituted a personal attack on the minister, it could not be regarded as completely excessive because the journalist had provided an objective explanation for his remarks.

As regards the defamation cases, Latvian courts have faced difficulties with interpreting and correctly applying criteria established by the ECtHR to balance rights provided by Article 8 and Article 10 of the Convention. In many cases, disputed statements were mainly evaluated based on the grammatical interpretation, not the context.[64] Though there are still cases when it is not easy for the national courts to make a distinction between value judgments and statements of fact, the above-mentioned cases have contributed towards greater compliance with the approach used by the ECtHR. Additionally, the respective judgments established a broader understanding of media and journalists' rights to alert the public about matters of public interest, even if it is done by criticising public figures.

Protection of information sources

The case of *Nagla v Latvia*[65] concerned an applicant journalist who was working for the national television broadcaster, producing and hosting a weekly investigative news programme. In February 2010, she publicly announced during this programme that she had been contacted by an anonymous source, who revealed that there were serious security flaws in a database maintained by the

---

63 *a/s Diena and Ozoliņš v Latvia* supra note 62.
64 LR Augstākās tiesas Plēnuma un tiesu prakses vispārināšanas daļas Tiesu prakse lietās par personas goda un cieņas civiltiesisko aizsardzību 2003/2004.
65 *Nagla v Latvia* supra note 62.

State Revenue Service and a subsequent data leak. Almost three months after the broadcast, the applicant's home was searched and her data storage devices were seized in connection with the criminal investigation of the data leak. The search warrant suggested that the applicant may have had information concerning the data leaks and such evidence could be at risk of destruction.

The ECtHR held that there had been an interference with the applicant's freedom to receive and impart information. It stated that the right of journalists not to disclose their sources of information could not be considered a privilege, depending on the lawfulness or unlawfulness of the sources. Moreover, any search involving the seizure of data storage devices belonging to a journalist raises the question of a journalist's freedom of expression, including source protection, and access to the information contained therein had to be protected by sufficient and adequate safeguards against abuse.

The case of *Nagla v Latvia* was the first case in Latvia regarding the search of a journalist's premises and seizure of their devices in a case relating to the performance of the journalist's professional duties. Following the judgment, the Government called for special educational courses to be held for the law enforcement bodies in order to raise awareness of the application of the ECtHR principles deriving from Article 10 of the Convention. Additionally, there was a debate relating to the need to introduce criminal procedural immunity for journalists, so that they could properly protect their information sources.[66]

Issues concerning the applicability of liability rules regarding online media

In the area of hate speech, defamation and privacy, Latvian courts follow the European approach in applying the same rules to offline and online cases. This is even more so in regards to hate speech – the Latvian Criminal Law provides stricter punishment for hate speech spread online.[67] The case law in this regard is quite consistent – in a majority of the cases, the courts at least formally analyse the same factors, including the intent of the person and the audience reached.[68]

However, the nature of the internet and the opportunities it gives to upload content and comment anonymously has made the applicability of these rules more complicated, especially as the status of the online media entities is not always clear.

---

66 See for example a letter of 2nd of March 2012 by the Ministry of Justice to the Ombudsman of the Republic of Latvia: http://titania.saeima.lv/LIVS11/saeimalivs11.nsf/0/741af4897197ab-d2c22579b800387382/$FILE/2_651.pdf/ (accessed 20 February 2018).
67 Criminal Law, Article 78 (2). In force from 1 April 1999.
68 See for example: Decision of the Supreme Court of the Republic of Latvia of 24 April 2014 in case SKK-0088-14 2016 and Judgment of Riga District Court of 6 June 2014 in case No. 11840001013.

Status of online media

It is only since 2011 that the Law on the Press and Other Mass Media provides that internet sites can be registered as mass media.[69] However, the Law does not state that the registration is mandatory, nor does it provide criteria that have to be met by the internet site so that it could or should register as mass media. Considering that being a media comes not only with rights, but also obligations, such as liability for the content including content created by third parties, this has led to a situation where even the biggest online news platforms have not registered their internet sites as mass media in Latvia.[70] However, the court practice has acknowledged such platforms as mass media and has applied the Law on the Press and Other Mass Media to the activities carried out by such news platforms.

In 2012, in probably the most important judgment regarding online media, the Supreme Court of the Republic of Latvia expressly explained the particular provision of the Law on the Press and Other Mass Media, which had raised questions regarding the status of online platforms.[71]

The judgment concerned a defamation case against an online news platform. The Supreme Court recognised that the rapid development of the internet must be taken into account and that the Law on the Press and Other Mass Media must be read in light of that development. More specifically, even though the Law does not expressly include online media in the list of press and other mass media, it should be considered as one. As an additional argument, the Court added that during the time of the proceedings before the Court the legislator had amended the Law providing that online platforms are also allowed to register as mass media. The Supreme Court also rejected the argument of the online news platform that it had not registered as mass media. The Court stated that the new amendments merely allowed registering the already existing situation, therefore, only declaring but not creating legal fact.

Therefore, the particular judgment stipulates that the online news platforms are also considered mass media even if they have not been registered as such. Though the Law and the court practice is in a way contradictory, currently the claims against online news platforms are brought and heard based on the Law on the Press and Other Mass Media, and the issue of formal registration as mass media is not being highly debated.

Hate speech

In recent years, the online environment has been a major source for hate speech. For instance, in 2015 all hate speech cases in courts were related to hate speech

---

69 See the amendments of the Law on the Press and Other Mass Media of 22 September 2011. In force from 20 October 2011.
70 According to information from the Lursoft database at www.lursoft.lv (last accessed 7 February 2018).
71 Judgment of the Civil Department of the Supreme Court of 17 October 2012 in case No. SKC-637/2012.

online.[72] This is explained by the fact that compared to traditional media, where there are editorial boards that edit the text prior to its publication, on the internet each individual can freely publish his/her opinion. Another explanation is related to the fact that people often feel anonymous on the internet. This is evidenced by the fact that the absolute majority of instances of incitement to hatred have been disseminated through anonymous comments in online news platforms, social media platforms or other websites.

In 2013, a monitoring session conducted by the Latvian Centre for Human Rights (a non-governmental organisation) showed that the main target groups of hate speech were persons with dark skin colour, ethnic Latvians, Russians, Jews and sexual minorities.[73] Upon contacting the site administrators, the majority of the sites were willing to comply with the requests to delete the hateful comments. However, more than 30% of the material was not removed. The second phase of the monitoring in 2014–2015 showed that only 41.4% of the hateful content reported was deleted by the content providers. At that time, the majority of the hateful content was aimed at asylum seekers and refugees.

There are no special rules in Latvia regarding prohibition of hate speech in online media, but traditional rules of criminal liability enshrined in Article 78 of the Latvian Criminal Law apply at least to the authors or disseminators of such expressions if there is intent to incite racial hatred. The fact that the crime has been committed online and the hate expressions are available to a sizeable audience is considered by the Law as an aggravating circumstance.[74]

While the online environment is a major source of expressions inciting hatred, all criminal proceedings so far were instituted against authors or disseminators of such expressions and not against online media hosting these expressions. This is explained by the fact that the Latvian Criminal Law requires proof of the intent to incite hatred in order to hold the person accountable. The question would arise if an online media platform is notified about the "hate expression" on its platform but refuses to delete such a comment. This might be a rare case because, according to the statements expressed by the editors of the largest online news platforms, they delete the hateful comments if they are informed about them. Yet, according to the Latvian Criminal Law legal persons can only be subject to such form of punishment as coercive measures[75] and, according to the case law, responsibility still lies with individual persons.[76]

---

72 "Pārskats par attīstību naida noziegumu un naida runas novēršanā". Latvijas Cilvēktiesību centrs, http://cilvektiesibas.org.lv/media/attachments/21/12/2015/Parskats_Naida_noziegumi. pdf (last accessed 7 February 2018).

73 Information about the results of the project is available from: "The LCHR concluded the first stage of online hate speech monitoring project" (Latvian Centre for Human Rights, 18 December 2014) at http://cilvektiesibas.org.lv/en/news/the-lchr-concluded-the-first-stage-of-online-hate--325/ (last accessed 7 February 2018).

74 Latvijas Republikas Augstākās tiesas Tiesu prakses apkopojums krimināllietās par nacionālā, etniskā un rasu naida izraisīšanu. Rīga, 2012.

75 Criminal Law, Article 70. In force from 1 April 1999.

76 Latvijas Republikas Augstākās, supra note 75.

The online media outlets themselves have started to monitor the comments sections more carefully. The previously mentioned research of the Latvian Centre for Human Rights allows us to compare the situation throughout a period of three years, and it has been recognised that the situation has improved with media policy towards hateful comments, for example, terms of use have been introduced or improved and the enforcement of these rules was carried out more comprehensively in 2015 than in 2013.[77] In the incidents involving severely hateful comments or repeated hate speech, the online news portals decide whether it is necessary to involve the Security Police of the State Police.

Another tendency visible in online media is limiting the possibility to comment on the content either for some specific articles, topics or on sensitive dates. Before the famous *Delfi* judgment of the ECtHR,[78] the issue of hateful and harmful comments online was already topical. Several ideas were proposed to fight the issue – from banning anonymous comments[79] to making the IP addresses of the users expressing hate publicly available.[80] None of these ideas were introduced as amendments of law, and none of the online news media showed an inclination towards closure of the comments section in general.

Privacy and defamation

While hate speech is relatively easy to spot and recognise for the online news platforms, defamatory comments and comments violating someone's honour and dignity might not be so obvious. Additionally, if a person wishes to pursue civil litigation against the author of a harmful comment, it might be difficult to identify the defendant. Although the legal framework provides the solution for the issue, the enforcement of the mechanism is often the weak spot for Latvian authorities.

The Electronic Communications Law provides that the internet provider must comply with a court's order to disclose any information it has about a particular user in order to ensure the protection of the rights and legal interests of the infringed individual.[81] Additionally, the Latvian Civil Procedure Law provides the right of a claimant to ask a court to ensure the evidence without summoning potential participants if it is impossible to determine the defendant.[82] Nonetheless, the courts are often reluctant to apply this mechanism. The

---

77 Outcomes of the research are available from: "Noslēdzies Latvijas Cilvēktiesību centra veiktā interneta portālos publicētā satura un komentāru monitoringa otrais posms" (Latvian Centre for Human Rights, 20 October 2015).
78 *Delfi AS v Estonia* App no. 64569/09 (ECtHR, 10 October 2013).
79 See, for example, the discussion in 2012: "Anonīmie komentētāji. Grib aizliegt" (TvNet, 25 May 2012).
80 "Rosina publiskot naidu kurinošu interneta komentētāju IP adreses" (TvNet, 25 March 2013).
81 Electronic Communications Law, Article 71. In force from 1 December 2014.
82 Civil Procedure Law, Article 100 (3). In force from 1 March 1999.

inquiries made by the Ombudsman's office of the Republic of Latvia show that until September 2014 at least no civil cases have been initiated regarding anonymous defamatory comments.[83] The reasoning of the courts regarding these statistics also includes the opinions that the claimant should find out himself/ herself who the defendant would be in the case and that the regulations of law are not clear enough.[84]

Another relevant issue is liability for the publication of an article by anonymous authors. One of the recent court cases relating to the publication of an anonymous author included an article published by one of the biggest online news platforms TVNET. The publication strongly criticised the private birthday party of a well-known Russian artist that took place in the Latvian National Opera house.

Representatives of the Opera filed a claim against TVNET for the retraction of defamatory statements and compensation of moral damage. The Court partly satisfied the claim against TVNET, arguing *inter alia* that TVNET is liable as a publisher and disseminator of the defamatory publication.[85] The judgment has been appealed by TVNET. It has to be taken into account that in case an online media platform does not reveal the identity of the author or does not know the identity, it has to take full liability if the published material is recognised as defamatory.

When talking about online privacy, one of the newest trends in data protection – the right to be forgotten – must be mentioned. There is no case law regarding this right from the Latvian courts, mainly because according to the Data State Inspectorate of the Republic of Latvia it has no jurisdiction to hear cases regarding the actions of *Google*, which is registered in the USA.[86] Namely, the Latvian Personal Data Protection Law, which implements the EU Data Protection Directive,[87] states that the administrator has to be registered in Latvia or has to use equipment situated in Latvia for the Latvian law to be applicable.[88] As the Data Protection Directive does not require the registration of the data administrator as a precondition of the applicability of national legislation,[89] one might only conclude that the previously described situation arises from the inappropriate implementation of EU Law.

---

83 Apart from one case where the claimant had learned the identity of the commentator with the help of the police, the full study is available from: Kristīne Pakārkle, "Kā noskaidrot anonīmā komentētāja identitāti, ja komentārs aizskāris personas godu un cieņu?" (Ombudsman's office of the Republic of Latvia, 14 January 2015).

84 Pakārkle, ibid.

85 Judgment of Riga city Vidzeme district court of 10 March 2016 in case No. C30292615 [not published].

86 Letter of Data State Inspectorate of the Republic of Latvia (19 March 2015).

87 Directive 95/46/EC of the European Parliament and of the Council of 24 October 1995 on the protection of individuals with regard to the processing of personal data and on the free movement of such data, Article 4 [1995] OJ L 281/0031.

88 Personal Data Protection Law of the Republic of Latvia, Article 3. In force of 20 April 2000.

89 Directive 95/46/EC, supra note 88.

Social networks

Although big international companies, such as *Facebook, Twitter, YouTube, Spotify* and quite recently also *Netflix*, are successfully operating in Latvia, there are no noteworthy cases in Latvia where these companies are directly involved as parties. Nonetheless, social networks, such as *Twitter* and *Facebook*, are quite often mentioned in the judgments of national courts. There have been instances where the applicant has appealed to *Twitter* posts of the State Police containing interpretation of law[90] or when information about a *Facebook* event has been used as evidence against organisers, who had not received permission for the event they organised.[91] Also, the privacy issue has been touched upon. For example, the Supreme Court has emphasised that by publishing a picture of his or her child on *Facebook*, a parent might be violating the right to the private life and data protection of the child.[92]

There has been a court case where the status of a *Twitter* account was evaluated by the Court. The case concerned the Mayor of Riga, who published the pre-election campaign advertisement of a political party he represented on his *Twitter* account one day before the elections of the Parliament. An administrative penalty was applied to him, as the Pre-election Campaign Law prohibited pre-election campaigns and advertisements one day before the elections. Taking into account that the post was made on *Twitter*, the Mayor argued that he had a right to express his opinion on his private profile to the closed group of persons in the form of the particular advertisement. He also argued that it is important to separate private and public online space on the internet. The Court analysed the posts made by the Mayor of Riga and stated that the particular *Twitter* account did not have limited access, therefore, information posted should be considered as publicly posted, irrespective of the fact of how many persons had become acquainted with it.[93]

Conclusions

Freedom of expression was already included in the founding documents of the Latvian state in 1918, but it has been protected at a constitutional level only since 1998. The constitutional protection of the freedom of expression in Latvia follows the tradition in Europe, where this right might be restricted in order to safeguard other human rights, the key principle being the proportionality of limitations. According to the case law of the Constitutional Court and the Supreme Court, freedom of expression has a very wide scope and also includes the notion of "freedom of press" and the right to information in a broad sense – namely,

90 Judgment of Kurzeme regional court of 1 February 2016 in case No. 120030315.
91 Judgment of Daugavpils court of 16 May 2016 in case No. 112014616.
92 Decision of the Administrative Department of the Supreme Court of the Republic of Latvia of 25 June 2015 in case No. SKA-864-15.
93 Judgment of Riga city Ziemeļu district court of 23 December 2014 in case No. 132051114/6.

not only to receive public information provided, but also to actively seek it. It has been established by national courts that cases relating to freedom of expression have to be considered as taking into account the principles and interpretation established by the ECtHR.

The most popular types of media today in Latvia are television and the internet but the most read printed media are weekly magazines. Latvian media law consists of two core legislative acts adopted by Parliament; namely, the Law on the Press and other Mass Media (adopted in 1991) and the Electronic Mass Media Law (adopted in 2010). While the Law on the Press and other Mass Media has a broader scope and its general principles are applicable to all media, including electronic mass media and online media, the Electronic Mass Media Law contains specific legal provisions for electronic mass media.

Latvian courts have faced difficulties with interpreting and correctly applying criteria established by the ECtHR to balance rights provided by Article 8 and Article 10 of the Convention in defamation cases. In many cases, disputed statements were mainly evaluated based on the grammatical interpretation, not the context. Nonetheless, the cases of *Vides Aizsardzības Klubs v Latvia* and *a/s Diena and Ozoliņš v Latvia* have contributed towards greater compliance with the approach used by the ECtHR. Furthermore, the case of *Nagla v Latvia* raised the issue regarding the need to provide stronger legal guarantees in order to ensure the rights of journalists to protect their information sources.

As regards the liability in defamation and privacy cases, the editor is responsible for the content published in the medium and represents the medium in relationship with other persons. However, the claimant's choice against whom to submit a claim in case of breach of privacy or defamation is not restricted. A person may also bear a criminal liability under the Criminal Law for libel. Additionally, self-regulatory bodies may review complaints about journalists' breaches of codes of ethics. Although the legal framework provides the solution for the issue of defamatory comments and comments violating someone's honour and dignity online, the enforcement of the mechanism is often the weak spot for Latvian authorities. According to the Electronic Communications Law and the Civil Procedure Law, a person who has suffered from anonymous comments may require the court to order the disclosure of the identity of the commentator. The courts, however, are often reluctant to apply this mechanism. Nevertheless, if an online media platform does not reveal the identity of the author or does not know the identity, it has to take full liability if the published material is recognised as defamatory.

In recent years, the online environment has been a major source of hate speech. The absolute majority of instances of incitement to hatred have been disseminated through anonymous comments on online news platforms, social media platforms and other online websites. Irrespective of the fact that many online news platforms have not registered as mass media, court practice has acknowledged such platforms as mass media and has applied the Law on the Press and Other Mass Media to the activities carried out by such news platforms.

Traditional rules of criminal liability apply at least to the authors or disseminators of hate speech if there is intent to incite national, ethnic, racial, religious or social hatred or enmity. So far, all criminal proceedings have been instituted against authors or disseminators of such expressions and not against the online media hosting these expressions. Furthermore, according to the specifics of the Latvian Criminal Law, legal persons can only be subject to such forms of punishment as coercive measures. Due to the increasing hate speech content in online comments, the online media themselves have started to monitor the comments sections more carefully and have limited the possibility to comment on the content for some specific articles, topics or on sensitive dates.

8 Human rights law and regulating freedom of expression in new media: Lithuania

Vygantė Milašiūtė

Media environment in Lithuania

According to a recent Eurobarometer survey, 46 per cent of the population in Lithuania trust the media, which is higher than the EU average.[1] Radio is the most trusted media type (66 per cent), followed by television (62 per cent), the written press (53 per cent), the internet (43 per cent) and online social networks (28 per cent).[2] There are 14 national printed dailies published in Lithuania. Newspapers also have their own websites. Due to the development of information technologies, i.e. online media, the circulation of print periodicals as well as the income of the print media from advertising has been shrinking. The Lithuanian radio market is divided between one strong public broadcaster and several private broadcasters. Radio advertising is decreasing.

As regards television, the total number of broadcasters in Lithuania is 28, and they broadcast 37 programmes. Three national commercial channels (broadcasting five programmes) and the public Lithuanian Radio and Television Company compete amongst themselves. The number of internet users has been increasing, but the rate of internet use is still low compared to the EU average. Young people are the most active internet users and they prefer to use online media only.[3] The number of users of certain media websites (e.g. *www.lrytas.lt*, the website of the daily "Lietuvos rytas") can be as high as one million,[4] i.e. slightly more than one third of the whole population of Lithuania. The most popular social network is Facebook, which has around 1,200,000 users.[5] The largest market share in advertising still belongs to television.[6]

---

1 Special Eurobarometer 461, *"Designing Europe's Future"*, April 2017, 14.
2 Standard Eurobarometer 86, *"Public Opinion in the European Union"*, November 2016, T37–T41.
3 A. Nugaraitė, "Media Landscapes. Lithuania", http://ejc.net/media_landscapes/lithuania (last accessed 7 February 2018).
4 "Balandį prie milijono realių vartotojų klubo prisijungė lrytas.lt", 19 May 2016, www.gemius. lt/interneto-ziniasklaidos-naujienos/balandi-prie-milijono-realiu-vartotoju-klubo-prisijunge-lrytaslt-2865.html (last accessed 7 February 2018).
5 R. Balčiūnienė, "'Facebook' – ir lyderis, ir pralaimėtojas", 3 September 2013, http://vz.lt/article/ 20130903/Article/309039877 (last accessed 7 February 2018).
6 *"Žiniasklaidos tyrimų apžvalga 2016"*, KANTAR TNS, 3, www.tns.lt/data/files/Metines_ apzvalgos/Kantar_TNS_Metin%C4%97_%C5%BEiniasklaidos_tyrim%C5%B3_ap%C5%BEvalga_ 2016m.pdf (last accessed 7 February 2018).

Commercial advertising is generally not allowed in the programmes aired by the public broadcasting company (i.e. Lithuanian national radio and television, see Law on the Lithuanian National Radio and Television, Art. 6[7]), but this prohibition does not extend to its internet website. Experts have observed that a self-regulatory Commission of Journalists' and Publishers' Ethics is sufficiently independent, as can be seen from the fact that it found one of the most influential TV companies in Lithuania to be unethical.[8]

Freedom House assesses the press in Lithuania as free, but judging by the score for 2017 it is less free than in the majority of other states in the Nordic-Baltic region.[9] One perceived threat to media pluralism is the presence of a criminal law prohibition of defamation. Experts also indicate that regulation of media in Lithuania is excessively market oriented, self-regulation is close to ineffective, and media diversity is not adequately promoted. The institutions that regulate the media do not deal with business related aspects (e.g. the types of media ownership or competition conditions). There is a lack of healthy media competition, and the media is connected to state advertising, which in many cases can be treated as hidden advertising (paid journalism).[10] Legal restrictions on the dissemination of certain information to minors under the Law on the Protection of Minors against the Detrimental Impact of Public Information,[11] insofar as they can be interpreted as banning information on same-sex family relationships, raised concerns at the UN[12] and EU levels.[13]

Good practice in new media

Admittedly, social networks have contributed to the diversification of the information space. On the downside, new uses of information have resulted in increasing uncertainty about the quality of distributed news.[14] The ongoing discussion on how new media should be treated and a number of initiatives in this area can be seen as examples of good practice.

---

7 Lietuvos Respublikos Lietuvos nacionalinio radijo ir televizijos įstatymas (Žin., 1996, Nr. 102-2319; 2000, Nr. 58-1712; 2005, Nr. 153-5639).

8 M. Lankauskas, S. Zaksaitė, "Teisė į privatumą", in M. Lankauskas et al. (eds.), "*Teisės į privatumą, minties, sąžinės, religijos laisvę ir saviraišką užtikrinimo problemos. Mokslo studija*", Lietuvos teisės institutas, Vilnius, 2013, 21.

9 Freedom of the Press 2017, https://freedomhouse.org/report/freedom-press/freedom-press-2017 (last accessed 7 February 2018).

10 A. Balčytienė, K. Juraitė, A. Nugaraitė, "Media Pluralism Monitor 2015 – Results. Lithuania, 2015", http://monitor.cmpf.eui.eu/mpm2015/results/lithuania/ (last accessed 7 February 2018).

11 Lietuvos Respublikos nepilnamečių apsaugos nuo neigiamo viešosios informacijos poveikio įstatymas (Žin., 2002, Nr. 91-3890; 2009, Nr. 86-3637).

12 UN Human Rights Committee, Concluding observations. Lithuania, 2012, CCPR/C/LTU/CO/3, para. 8.

13 EU Agency for Fundamental Rights, Homophobia, transphobia and discrimination on grounds of sexual orientation and gender identity. 2010 Update. Comparative legal analysis, pp. 33–34.

14 A. Balčytienė, K. Juraitė, "Media Pluralism Monitor 2016 – Results. Lithuania, 2016", http://cmpf.eui.eu/media-pluralism-monitor/mpm-2016-results/lithuania (last accessed 7 February 2018).

Anonymous comments are viewed as a valuable tool of expression by some and as a threat to the quality of online content by others. An initiative by news portal *15min.lt* concerning "internet hygiene"[15] started with the banning of anonymous comments. Two months later, a survey showed that the majority approved of this decision.[16] The news website *delfi.lt* takes a different view and, although it encourages commenting by registered users,[17] it preserves the possibility of anonymous commenting (i.e. a user does not have to indicate their name and email address) which, however, is not fully anonymous, since the IP address of an author is indicated next to a comment.[18] Notwithstanding the difference in the approach towards anonymity, both *15min.lt* and *delfi.lt* have adopted clear rules on commenting and introduced a moderator system for discussions, who can remove inappropriate comments in line with the abovementioned rules.[19] The website *delfi.lt* remains the most visited site, and *15min.lt* is the second among the news websites in Lithuania.[20] Admittedly, *delfi.lt* seems to attract a higher number of comments than *15min.lt*.

In the context of the EU dialogue with major IT companies to fight hate speech,[21] a meeting of Lithuanian authorities, civil society and online media representatives with regional representatives of Facebook and Google was held in the Ministry of Justice of Lithuania in 2017, and further efforts to fight online hate speech were discussed. *Inter alia*, the relationship between hate speech, propaganda and fake news was highlighted, and the need for awareness-raising activities among the public was stressed.

As regards tackling fake news and thus seeking to increase trust in journalism, *delfi.lt* already has a platform called *demaskuok*,[22] where allegedly fake news can be reported and is then investigated by professionals and, if necessary, debunked. A new debunking project by *delfi.lt*, which seeks to create a special platform for investigative journalism to detect fake news and reduce its harmful impact on society, has recently received funding from Google via *The Digital News Initiative*.[23]

---

15 "Interneto higiena", http://internetohigiena.lt/ (last accessed 7 February 2018).
16 "Tyrimas patvirtino: 15min sprendimas dėl komentarų buvo teisingas", 25 July 2018, www.15min.lt/verslas/naujiena/medijos/tyrimas-patvirtino-15min-sprendimas-del-komentaru-buvo-teisingas-921-660011 (last accessed 7 February 2018).
17 "Kas yra DELFI skaitytojų komentarai?", www.delfi.lt/apie/?wid=7271 (last accessed 7 February 2018).
18 *Ibid.*
19 *Ibid.*; "Komentavimo taisyklės", www.15min.lt/komentavimo-taisykles (last accessed 7 February 2018).
20 Gemius, *"Online Publishers Audit"*, http://opa.gemius.lt/ (last accessed 7 February 2018).
21 European Commission – Press Release, *"European Commission and IT Companies announce Code of Conduct on illegal online hate speech"*, Brussels, 31 May 2016, http://europa.eu/rapid/press-release_IP-16-1937_en.htm (last accessed 7 February 2018).
22 "Demaskuok", www.delfi.lt/news/daily/demaskuok/ (last accessed 8 February 2018).
23 Digital News Initiative, https://digitalnewsinitiative.com/dni-projects/debunk-news/ (last accessed 8 February 2018); "DELFI kuriamas kovos prieš melagingas naujienas įrankis gavo 'Google' finansavimą", 6 July 2017, www.delfi.lt/verslas/verslas/delfi-kuriamas-kovos-pries-

Regulation of freedom of expression in Lithuania

Constitutional level

A number of provisions in the Constitution of Lithuania of 1992[24] are relevant for the protection of freedom of speech or expression. Most importantly, Article 25 stipulates that everyone shall have the right to have his own convictions and freely express them; no one must be hindered from seeking, receiving or imparting information and ideas; the freedom to express convictions, as well as to receive and impart information, may not be limited otherwise than by law when this is necessary to protect human health, honour or dignity, private life, or morals, or to defend the constitutional order; the freedom to express convictions and to impart information shall be incompatible with criminal actions – incitement to national, racial, religious, or social hatred, incitement to violence or to discrimination, as well as defamation and disinformation. Notably, this provision is a basis for criminal law provisions restricting freedom of speech. Article 33 contains a provision stating that citizens shall be guaranteed the right to criticise the work of state institutions or their officials and to appeal against their decisions; persecution for criticism shall be prohibited. Article 44 provides that censorship of mass information shall be prohibited; the state, political parties, political or public organisations, or other institutions or persons may not monopolise the mass media.

The Constitutional Court has held that

> [from] Article 25 of the Constitution as well as the other provisions of the Constitution consolidating and guaranteeing the freedom of an individual to seek, obtain and impart information stems the freedom of the media. Under the Constitution, the legislature has a duty to establish the guarantees of the freedom of the media by law.[25]

General media law and specific regulation of online media

The core of the media law in Lithuania is regulated by the Law on Provision of Information to the Public. It establishes the procedure for collecting, producing, publishing and disseminating public information, defines the rights, obligations and liability of the producers, disseminators, journalists and institutions regulating their activities. The Law (Art. 2 para. 87) defines the term journalist as a natural person who, on a professional basis, collects, prepares and presents material

---

melagingas-naujenas-irankis-gavo-google-finansavima.d?id=75155378 (last accessed 8 February 2018).

24 Lietuvos Respublikos Konstitucija (Žin., 1992, Nr. 33-1014).

25 Constitutional Court of the Republic of Lithuania, ruling of 23 October 2002, case no. 36/2000.

to the producer and/or disseminator of public information under a contract with him and/or is a member of a professional journalists' association. Despite the fact that the journalist is involved in specific activities and is granted by law certain rights and duties, the very same law does not demand of the journalist any specific education or qualification requirements, unlike in the case of other professions.[26]

The Law defines the right to receive and disseminate information, express one's ideas and convictions freely and the right of legal or natural persons to protect honour and dignity when the disseminated information is false. Notably, it defines the unpublishable information. Under Article 19, it shall be prohibited to publish information in the media which: (1) incites to change the constitutional order of the Republic of Lithuania through the use of force; (2) instigates attempts against the sovereignty of the Republic of Lithuania, its territorial integrity and political independence; (3) spreads war propaganda, instigates war or hatred, ridicule, humiliation, instigates discrimination, violence, physical violent treatment of a group of people or a person belonging thereto on grounds of age, sex, sexual orientation, ethnic origin, race, nationality, citizenship, language, origin, social status, belief, convictions, views or religion; (4) disseminates, promotes or advertises pornography, also propagates and/or advertises sexual services and paraphilias; (5) promotes and/or advertises addictions and narcotic or psychotropic substances. It shall be prohibited to disseminate disinformation and information which is slanderous and offensive to a person or which degrades his honour and dignity. It shall be prohibited to disseminate information which violates the presumption of innocence and which impedes the impartiality of judicial authorities.

The same article refers to the category of restricted public information by stipulating that the Government shall establish the procedure for the dissemination of press publications, audio, audiovisual works, radio and television programmes, information disseminated in the information society media and other public information assigned to information of an erotic, pornographic or violent nature or other restricted public information. Private information is defined in Article 2 as information about the personal and family life of a person, his personal health, etc., which is not to be published with a view to ensuring the protection of the person's right to privacy.

The Procedure for the Control of Forbidden Information on Public Use Computer Networks and the Distribution of Restricted Public Information adopted by the Government[27] regulates the dissemination of prohibited or restricted information on the internet. Despite a long list of categories of unpublishable and restricted information in Article 19, its application in practice has not resulted

---

26 J. Mažylė, "Professional Journalism and Self-regulation in Lithuania", *International Journal of Art and Commerce*, 3 (8) 2014, 35.

27 Lietuvos Respublikos Vyriausybės 2003 m. kovo 5 d. nutarimas Nr. 290 "Dėl Viešo naudojimo kompiuterių tinkluose neskelbtinos informacijos kontrolės ir ribojamos viešosios informacijos platinimo tvarkos patvirtinimo" (Žin., 2003, Nr. 24-1002).

in much controversy, except with regard to a classic issue of hate speech in the particular context of re-transmitted Russian language TV channels in Lithuania. Measures to restrict the re-transmission raised concerns primarily with respect to the procedural requirements of the Audiovisual Media Services Directive.[28] Moreover, they raised a legally more difficult issue – how to delineate between hate speech and propaganda, from the perspective of national security and public order.[29] This issue may arise again as new decisions to restrict retransmission of Russian language channels, including the availability of access to them on the internet, are adopted.[30] There are no initiatives to shorten the list of prohibited information. The most recent draft amendment to the law[31] submitted by the Ministry of Culture to the Government adds disability as a subject of prohibited hate speech.

In 2005, the Constitutional Court, deciding a question relating to the procedure for the dissemination of information not to be divulged to the public, observed that "the legal regulation established in laws at present is, to a high degree, of a general character, it does not sufficiently take account of the specificity of the Internet as a media for spreading information".[32] The opinion of the Constitutional Court was taken into account by the drafters of the 2006 version of the Law on Provision of Information to the Public, which introduced a new concept of information society media.[33] Nevertheless, researchers still note that media regulation in Lithuania is not internet specific,[34] which can be illustrated by the absence of any references to internet comments in the Law on Provision of

28 Directive 2010/13/EU of the European Parliament and of the Council of 10 March 2010 on the coordination of certain provisions laid down by law, regulation or administrative action in Member States concerning the provision of audiovisual media services, OJ L 95, 15 April 2010, 1-24; European Commission. Ex-post REFIT evaluation of the Audiovisual Media Services Directive 2010/13/EU, SWD(2016) 170 final, p. 26:

> In 2015, Lithuania notified to the Commission measures to restrict the retransmission of a Russian language channel, broadcast from Sweden, on the basis of instances of incitement to hatred. The Directive is silent as regards the procedure to be followed at national level and does not provide many details about the procedure before the Commission. This prompted the need for Lithuania to readopt a national decision and send a supplementary notification to the Commission. In July 2015, the Commission decided that the notified measures are compatible with EU law. C(2015) 4609 final.

29 *Ibid.*, p. 207.
30 See e.g., Lietuvos radijo ir televizijos komisija, Sprendimas dėl televizijos programos "RTR Planeta" laisvo priėmimo laikino sustabdymo, 2016 m. lapkričio 16 d., Nr. KS-200.
31 Lietuvos Respublikos visuomenės informavimo įstatymo Nr. i-1418 17, 19, 22, 24, 341, 49, 50 ir 52 straipsnių pakeitimo įstatymo projektas, 2017-08-14, Nr. 17-9562.
32 Constitutional Court of the Republic of Lithuania, ruling of 19 September 2005, case no. 19/04.
33 L. Ulevičius, "Conceptual Problems of Information Society Media", *Socialinių mokslų studijos/ Social science studies*, 1 (1) 2009, 192.
34 J. Zaleskis, "Country report. Lithuania", in *"Comparative Study on Blocking, Filtering and Take – Down of Illegal Internet Content"*, Swiss Institute of Comparative Law, Lausanne, 2015 (revised in 2016), 410, www.coe.int/en/web/freedom-expression/study-filtering-blocking-and-take-down-of-illegal-content-on-the-internet (last accessed 20 February 2018).

Information to the Public and the resulting lack of clarity regarding liability for this type of the dissemination of information.[35] The answer to the question of how Lithuanian law treats online media can, therefore, be found in the case law developed by the courts and, to some extent, in the practice of other authorities.

Liability

Editorial responsibility

The Law on Provision of Information to the Public defines editorial responsibility as responsibility falling on the producer and/or disseminator of public information, with the exception of the re-broadcaster, for the exercise of control over the production of public information, preparing it for dissemination, as well as exercising control over the selection of programmes and their organisation in a chronological order in a programme schedule and/or over the presentation of programmes in a catalogue (see Art. 2 para. 53). The Law provides for a requirement for every producer of public information or a participant thereof to appoint a person (editor-in-chief, editor, programme host or another person) responsible for the content of the media, and a rule that where the same natural person is both a producer of public information and a participant thereof, he shall have responsibility for the content of his media (Art. 22 para. 10). Consequently, the journalist may be held liable if he publishes information solely under his control, i.e. where there is no higher level responsible above him, e.g. in the case of a blogger.[36] The law also establishes that a producer or disseminator of public information shall be liable for violations of legal rules "regulating the production of public information, also for violating the procedure for dissemination of public information established by law" (Art. 51 para. 1), where "the manager of the information society media shall be liable for the content thereof" (Art. 51 para. 2), and "providers of intermediate information society services shall be liable for the content of the information society media" under the Law on Information Society Services (Art. 51 para. 3 of the Law on Provision of Information to the Public). The notions of the "producer of public information" and the "disseminator of public information", i.e. the two categories of persons who are the bearers of editorial responsibility, *inter alia* include managers of the information society media (Art. 2 paras. 77 and 78) but not providers of intermediate information society services. The law provides for an exemption from editorial responsibility in specified cases (where the producer or disseminator have indicated the source of information, and it has been of a certain type) and stipulates

---

35 L. Meškauskaitė, "*Teisė į privatų gyvenimą*", VĮ Registrų centras, Vilnius, 2015, 267.
36 V. Danilevičiūtė, M. Dapkutė, "Lithuania", in J. Ukrow, G. Iacino (eds.), "*Comparative Study on Investigative Journalism*", European Centre for Press and Media Freedom, Saarbrücken, 2016, 7.

that in those cases liability for the publication of false information shall fall upon those who were the first to publish such information (Art. 54). Such an exemption results in a situation where irrespective of how widely the impermissible (e.g. defamatory or denigrating) information has been disseminated, only the first person who published it would be liable. The Inspector of Journalist Ethics sees it as a failure by the legislator to strengthen an obligation of website managers to control the content and as a limitation of the possibility to defend one's dignity where the information has been published in a number of media outlets.[37]

As regards the liability scope that falls on managers of the information society media and, more specifically, the liability of managers of internet websites for comments made by its users, including in discussion fora,[38] in the context of protection of honour and dignity, the Civil Code[39] specifies that:

> [t]he mass medium, which publicised erroneous data abasing person's reputation shall have to redress property and non-pecuniary damage incurred on the person only in those cases, when it knew or had to know that the data were erroneous as well as in those cases when the data were made public by its employees or the data was made public anonymously and the mass medium refuses to name the person who supplied the said data.
>
> (Civil Code, Art. 2.24 para. 5)

The general provisions of the Civil Code regarding the duty to compensate for damage caused by another person in cases established by the law ("In cases established by laws, a person shall also be liable to compensation for damage caused by the actions of another person or by the action of things in his custody" – see Art. 6.263 para. 3) and the right of counterclaim may also be relevant in this context:

> A person who has compensated the damage caused by another person shall have the right of recourse (the right of counterclaim) against the person by whom the damage was caused in the amount equal to the paid compensation unless a different amount is established by the law.
>
> (Civil Code, Art. 6.280)

---

37 Žurnalistų etikos inspektoriaus 2010 m. veiklos ataskaita, www.lrs.lt/apps3/1/2433_HKZ-RVEXM.PDF (last accessed 8 February 2018), 49–50.

38 For a discussion of liability for comments, especially as regards the necessary attitude of the portals, see J. Mažylė, "The Issue of Responsibility for Online Comments (the Lithuanian Case)", *International Journal of Art and Commerce*, 4 (2) 2015, 64–76; for a discussion of the legal liability of the website founders and managers for users' comments, see R. Burbulienė, "Interneto tinklalapio įkūrėjo (valdytojo) atsakomybė už forumo dalyvių komentarus", 31 October 2012, www.visasverslas.lt/portal/categories/15/1/0/1/article/5130/interneto-tinklalapio-ikurejo-valdytojo-atsakomybe-uz-forumo-dalyviu-komentarus (last accessed 8 February 2018).

39 Lietuvos Respublikos civilinis kodeksas (Žin., 2000, Nr. 74-2262; 200).

Liability of intermediary service providers

The EU Directive on E-Commerce[40] was transposed into Lithuanian law by the Law on Information Society Services.[41] The fact that the Directive was written when intermediary service providers were mainly passive, and the resulting lack of clarity as to what the legal position of active intermediaries was under the Directive,[42] was apparently not given much thought in the process of its transposition, and the question remained unresolved in the above law. This law provides for exceptions from liability for providers of intermediate information society services (Arts. 12–14). Notably, the host is not liable for the information hosted on behalf of the customer as long as: (1) it does not have actual knowledge of illegal activity or information and, as regards claims for damages, is not aware of the facts or circumstances which prove the existence of illegal activity or information; (2) upon obtaining such knowledge or awareness, acts expeditiously to remove or to disable access to the information (Art. 14).

As can be seen from the above provision, removal of stored information is not required. Lithuania belongs to the group of EU Member States that provides for a special obligation on the part of intermediaries to communicate illegal activities or information on their services.[43] In particular, all providers of information society services have an obligation to inform the Information Society Development Committee of any suspected illegal activity of a service recipient or of the fact of the possibly illegal nature of the acquisition, production or modification of information provided by the service recipient (Art. 15 para. 1). They must provide the above Committee, upon its request, with data identifying the service recipients (Art. 15 para. 2). Persons whose rights are violated by the activities of intermediary service providers (e.g. transmitting, storing data) may apply to the court with a request to obligate the provider to terminate or prevent a violation even though the intermediaries are not liable for that violation (Art. 15 para. 3).

The optional notice and take down procedure implementing the Law on Information Society Services as regards the hosts (Art. 14 para. 3) is codified in the Government regulation on the Description of the Procedure for Blocking Access to the Unlawfully Acquired, Produced, Modified or Used Information.[44]

---

40 Directive 2000/31/EC of the European Parliament and of the Council of 8 June 2000 on certain legal aspects of information society services, in particular electronic commerce, in the Internal Market, OJ L 178, 17 July 2000, 1–16.

41 Lietuvos Respublikos informacinės visuomenės paslaugų įstatymas (Žin., 2006, Nr. 65-2380).

42 B. van der Sloot, "Welcome to the Jungle: the Liability of Internet Intermediaries for Privacy violations in Europe", *Journal of Intellectual Property, Information Technology and Electronic Commerce Law*, 6 2015, 212-213 paras. 3–5, www.jipitec.eu/issues/jipitec-6-3-2015/4318/ van der sloot (3).pdf (last accessed 7 February 2018).

43 See Study on the Liability of Internet Intermediaries, Markt/2006/09/E (Service Contract ETD/2006/IM/E2/69), 2007, p. 72.

44 Lietuvos Respublikos Vyriausybės 2007 m. rugpjūčio 22 d. nutarimas Nr. 881 "Dėl Galimybės pasiekti neteisėtu būdu įgytą, sukurtą, pakeistą ar naudojamą informaciją panaikinimo tvarkos aprašo patvirtinimo" (Žin., 2007, Nr. 94-3784).

The Government regulation on the Procedure for the Control of Forbidden Information on Public Use Computer Networks and the Distribution of Restricted Public Information[45] delineates the responsibility of the founder and the manager of an internet website by specifying (para. 11) that where the founder and the manager is not the same person, the manager of the website shall be responsible for the content of the website.

Types of legal liability

In the context of online media, legal liability in Lithuania for transgressing the limits of freedom of expression comprises civil, administrative and criminal liability. Infringements of personal rights, such as the right to privacy, can form a basis for bringing a civil action. As regards administrative liability, the following examples from the Code on Administrative Infringements[46] are illustrative. Publishing information detrimental to minors can result in a warning or the imposition of a fine (Art. 79). Violation of the honour or dignity of a politician, state official, civil servant or a public administrator can result in a fine (Art. 507), while violation of the Law on Information Society Services can result in a fine for service providers (Art. 478). Refusal to provide information to representatives of media or obstruction of journalist activities can lead to a fine (Art. 547), while expression of hate towards a person shall be an aggravating circumstance (Art. 36 para. 1 (7)). The gravest violations relating to the unlawful exercise of one's freedom of expression can result in criminal liability foreseen in the Criminal Code,[47] notably in the case of defamation (Art. 154), incitement against any national, racial, ethnic, religious or other group of persons (Art. 170) and public condoning, denial or gross trivialisation of international crimes and crimes of the USSR or Nazi Germany against the Republic of Lithuania or its inhabitants (Art. 170–172). Insult was decriminalised in 2015.

Supervisory authorities, self-regulatory bodies and codes of ethics

Authorities

The most relevant authorities and self-regulatory bodies for online media are listed in the Law on Provision of Information to the Public and comprise the

---

45 Lietuvos Respublikos Vyriausybės 2003 m. kovo 5 d. nutarimas Nr. 290 "Dėl Viešo naudojimo kompiuterių tinkluose neskelbtinos informacijos kontrolės ir ribojamos viešosios informacijos platinimo tvarkos patvirtinimo" (Žin., 2003, Nr. 24-1002).
46 Lietuvos Respublikos administracinių nusižengimų kodeksas (TAR, 2015-07-10, Nr. 2015-11216).
47 Lietuvos Respublikos baudžiamasis kodeksas (Žin., 2000, Nr. 89-2741).

institution authorised by the Government – the Association of Ethics in the Provision of Information to the Public, the Radio and Television Commission of Lithuania and the Inspector of Journalist Ethics (Arts. 45–50).

The Ministry of Culture, as the institution authorised by the Government, is in charge of the implementation of the state media policy (Art. 45).

The Radio and Television Commission of Lithuania (Arts. 47–48), an independent body accountable to the Parliament, regulates and controls the activities of broadcasters of radio and/or television programmes and providers of on-demand audiovisual media services falling under the jurisdiction of Lithuania. It also supervises the activities of re-broadcasters operating within the territory of Lithuania and other persons, providing the users of Lithuania with the service of the dissemination of television programmes and/or individual programmes via the internet and, notably, issues licences and controls compliance with the requirements of legal acts with regard to the content of public information. It may impose penalties and revoke licences as well as apply to the court regarding the temporary suspension or termination of internet based broadcasting or dissemination activities.

The Inspector of Journalist Ethics (Art. 49) is a state official appointed by the Parliament, who supervises the application of the Law on Provision of Information to the Public and the Law on Protection of Minors against the Detrimental Impact of Public Information. As of 2010, the Inspector has a mandate to evaluate, following the conclusions of expert groups (experts), whether public information released in the media may be inciting discord based on gender, sexual orientation, race, nationality, language, origin, social status, religion, beliefs or opinions. This function was transferred to the Inspector from the Journalists and Publishers Ethics Commission,[48] a self-regulatory body and the predecessor to the abovementioned Association of Ethics in the Provision of Information to the Public. The legal position of the Inspector within the Lithuanian legal system is similar to that of Ombudspersons.

Self-regulatory bodies

The Association of Ethics in the Provision of Information to the Public (Art. 46) is a self-regulatory body. It consists of organisations uniting public information producers, disseminators and journalists with the norms of the Code, applying to the activities of the members of organisations such as the Lithuanian Journalists' Union, the Society of Lithuanian Journalists, the Association of Internet Media, the Lithuanian Radio and Television Association, the Association of Regional Television, the Lithuanian Cable Television Association and the National Regional and City Publishers Association (Art. 46 para. 2). It has the task of

48 The status of this Commission as a self-regulatory authority, which does not perform public administration, was confirmed in the case law of Lithuanian courts. See, e.g., Supreme Administrative Court of Lithuania, ruling of 21 March 2011, administrative case no. A^{444}-777/2011.

ensuring compliance with the principles of ethics (Art. 46 para. 1). The decisions of the Association are taken by its collegial body, the Commission of Ethics in the Provision of Information to the Public (Art. 46 para. 1).

Codes of ethics

The Commission of Ethics in the Provision of Information to the Public applies the Code of Ethics of the Provision of Information to the Public,[49] adopted in a meeting between the producers and disseminators of public information, as well as members of the Association of Ethics in the Provision of Information to the Public in 2016. This Code replaced the Ethics Code of Journalists and Publishers, which had been adopted in 2005 and was void of any references to the online dimension.[50] The new Code specifically mentions the internet in the context of the require-ment to verify and indicate the sources of information (including the information obtained using the internet, see Art. 54) and to correct the information (where the information was corrected on the internet, it is required to indicate that the publication was amended or supplemented, see Art. 17). The Code also stipulates that it does not prohibit using other codes of professional ethics or conduct, which would envisage more detailed or stricter professional obligations (Art. 66). The Law on Provision of Information to the Public also provides (Art. 23 para. 1) that the producer of public information must have rules of procedure and/or an inter-nal code of ethics. At least one of these documents approved by the producer of public information must establish the rights, duties and responsibilities and official relations of journalists, as well as the protection of journalists against the possible restrictions of their rights. The Law on Information Society Services stipulates that the Information Society Development Committee under the Ministry of Transport and Communications (Art. 16 para. 5) shall promote the elaboration of codes of conduct regarding the protection of minors and human dignity. The Inspector of Journalist Ethics notes that the latter provision of the law has been dormant.[51]

Online media issues in Article 10 cases at the ECtHR against Lithuania

Of all Article 10 cases against Lithuania decided by the European Court of Human Rights (ECtHR),[52] one is of interest for the purposes of this paper. In

---

49 Lietuvos visuomenės informavimo etikos kodeksas, 2016, www.etikoskomisija.lt/teisine-infor-macija/etikos-kodeksas/item/69-lietuvos-visuomenes-informavimo-etikos-kodeksas (last accessed 8 February 2018).

50 Lietuvos žurnalistų ir leidėjų etikos kodeksas, 2005, www.lrs.lt/apps3/1/2386_fdqouedy.pdf (last accessed 8 February 2018).

51 Žurnalistų etikos inspektoriaus tarnybos 2015 m. veiklos ataskaita, 2016, www.lrs.lt/apps3/1/5122_ZEIT%202015%20M.%20VEIKLOS%20ATASKAITA.pdf (last accessed 8 February 2018), 34.

52 *Jankovskis v. Lithuania*, ECtHR judgment of 17 January 2017, app. no. 21575/08; *Balsytė-Lideikienė v. Lithuania*, ECtHR judgment of 04 November 2008, app. no. 72596/01; *Lietuvos*

Jankovskis v. Lithuania,[53] the applicant complained that he had not had internet access in prison and was, therefore, prevented from receiving educationrelated information published on a website belonging to the Ministry of Education and Science. Having noted that Article 10 cannot be interpreted as imposing a general obligation to provide access to the internet or to specific internet sites, for prisoners the ECtHR nevertheless found a violation of Article 10 in the specific circumstances of the case. Importantly, access to information relating to education is granted under Lithuanian law, the Ministry referred the applicant to a specific internet site in reply to his request to provide information, and the Lithuanian authorities did not even consider the possibility of granting the applicant limited or controlled internet access to this particular website administered by a state institution, which could have hardly posed a security risk, such as telephone fraud, indicated by the Government. The interference with the applicant's right to receive information was, therefore, not sufficiently justified by the Government. Notwithstanding the finding of a violation, it remains true that the ECtHR accepts the legitimacy of certain restrictions on prisoners' access to online media, which is important for the scope of the right both to receive and to impart information online.

Overview of Lithuanian case law

Cases reviewed in this section were chosen based on the criterion of online media as a subject matter and international human rights law as an argument that influenced the outcome of the case.

Legal status of the author of information posted online

The phenomenon of online expression raises the question of which part of it should be qualified as essentially analogous to the traditional mass media, whose function is to provide information to the public. Notably, the status of the author of information posted online may be to some extent comparable to that of the journalist.

As regards the status of bloggers, the Supreme Administrative Court of Lithuania in 2009 clarified that the former can have the status of a media outlet and the latter of a journalist. Specifically, the Court held that in certain cases, in particular when used for professionally preparing and disseminating public information, blogs can be considered a means of provision of information to the public (in particular, information society media) within the meaning of the Law on the Provision of Information to the Public, which essentially regulates the

---

nacionalinis radijas ir televizija and Tapinas ir partneriai v. Lithuania, ECtHR decision of 06 July 2010, app. no. 27930/05; *Biriuk v. Lithuania*, ECtHR judgment of 25 November 2008, app. no. 23373/03; *Armonienė v. Lithuania*, ECtHR judgment of 25 November 2008, app. no. 36919/02.

53 *Jankovskis v. Lithuania, ibid.*

work of mass media. Furthermore, bloggers can have the same status as journalists. This seems to be in line with the Council of Europe's recommendation that

> [a]s regards in particular new media, codes of conduct or ethical standards for bloggers have already been accepted by at least part of the online journalism community. Nonetheless, bloggers should only be considered media if they fulfil the criteria to a sufficient degree.[54]

In the case examined by the Supreme Administrative Court, a blogger was complaining about the fact that he was refused accreditation as a journalist at the Parliament of Lithuania. The Court decided that when he professionally collects, prepares and publishes information a blogger is a journalist and the Registry of the Parliament was obliged to issue accreditation to him. In the same case, the Court explained that although the Law on Provision of Information to the Public is silent on the subject, a journalist and a producer of public information can be the same person.[55] Bearing in mind that with the development of online media anyone can disseminate essentially unedited information,[56] the latter conclusion by the Court implies that bloggers are themselves responsible for the content they post. A difficult question remains – to what extent can the same conclusion be applied to a broader category of persons contributing to the content of online media, including authors of comments.

Legal status of persons other than authors of online media

Following the amendments of the Law on Provision of Information to the Public in 2010, editorial responsibility was limited so that responsibility for internet comments under this Law lies solely on the authors of the comments rather than on the disseminators of public information.[57] A manager of a website is, however, liable under the Law on Information Society Services (see Arts. 14 para. 1(2), 15 para. 2) if he refuses to remove a particular comment and (or) to provide the data allowing the identification of the author. Lithuanian courts have decided a number of cases regarding the failure of website managers to remove comments upon notification by the injured party.

A large proportion of these cases concern the internet website *www.skundai. lt* that provides a platform for complaints. Persons and companies that regarded the complaints posted on the website as harmful to their honour, dignity or

---

54 Council of Europe, Recommendation of the Committee of Ministers to member states on a new notion of media, CM/Rec(2011)7, para. 41.
55 Supreme Administrative Court of Lithuania, decision of 20 April 2009, administrative case no. A^{444}-70/2009.
56 A. Šindeikis, "Žodžio laisvė ir jos ribų kaita per du atkurtos nepriklausomybės dešimtmečius", *Jurisprudencija*, 20 (3) 2013, 1054.
57 See Periodic report of Lithuania under CERD, 2014, UN doc. No. CERD/C/LTU/6-8, para. 198.

reputation sued the manager of the website, demanding the removal of those comments and an award of compensation for the damage suffered. The courts had to address an argument by the manager of the website, in which he claimed that he had the status of a web hosting provider, i.e. an intermediary to whom exceptions from liability applied under the EU Directive on E-Commerce and the Lithuanian law transposing this Directive (i.e. the Law on Information Society Services). The courts held that the manager of that website was a provider of information society services under the Law on Information Society Services, however, due to his active role in checking the posted comments and authorising their public display, he could not be considered as merely a host, i.e. he was not a passive intermediary service provider to whom exceptions of liability applied. Because of his status as a provider of information services, the manager of a website is the correct respondent in the case of a requirement to stop a violation (i.e. to remove impermissible information from the website) to be filed in accordance with the Law on Information Society Services, even though the manager is not responsible for the violation itself.[58]

The request to remove access to the information on the website is independent from the request to award non-pecuniary damage (i.e. to apply civil liability), which can be proven by establishing fewer circumstances and can be granted irrespective of whether civil liability for damages was applied.[59] As the manager of the website is bound by the Law on Information Society Services and is not exempted from liability under it because he is not a passive intermediary, theoretically it is possible that the manager of the website could be liable for the harm caused by failure to remove certain materials from the website. However, where this issue was raised, the court of appeals rejected the request to award compensation. It noted that the manager of the information society media outlet did not know and did not have to know that the data published were not truthful. It also held that due to modern technologies it is not always possible to identify the author of the comments, which does not lead to the conclusion that damage done by dissemination of data has to be compensated by the media outlet.[60] This part of the decision was not appealed, and the Supreme Court did not have a chance to rule on it.[61] The courts also held that while being an information society service provider under the Law on Information Society Services, the manager of the portal was also a manager of information society media under the Law on Provision of Information to the Public.[62] The courts did not elaborate on the issue of the extent to which intermediaries, either passive or active, are bound by the obligations of the above laws or are entitled to rights provided therein and in the related European acts,

58 Supreme Court of Lithuania, ruling of 13 November 2012, civil case no. 3K-3-479/2012.
59 Supreme Court of Lithuania, ruling of 13 November 2012, civil case no. 3K-3-586/2012.
60 Kaunas Regional Court, ruling of 24 May 2012, civil case no. 2A-852-324/2012.
61 Supreme Court of Lithuania, ruling of 27 February 2013, civil case no. 3K-3-50/2013.
62 Kaunas Regional Court, ruling of 24 May 2012, civil case no. 2A-852-324/2012.

namely the EU Directive on E-Commerce and Art. 10 of the European Convention on Human Rights (ECHR).[63]

A certain change in the reasoning of the Supreme Court occurred in reaction to the ECtHR chamber judgment in *Delfi v. Estonia*.[64] In examining the situation of the same website for complaints, *skundai.lt*, and the request to block access to certain materials published on it, the Supreme Court extensively referred to the ECtHR case law, *inter alia* the above judgment in *Delfi*. The Supreme Court noted that the same criteria that applied in *Delfi* for assessing the reasonableness of civil liability applied to the internet website for comments by other persons. Even though the Supreme Court in that case was not asked to consider the question of the damage inflicted by disseminating information via the website, it specifically mentioned that the ECtHR arguments in *Delfi* related to the specificity of the internet. It then concluded that, by allowing the unregistered users to post comments, the provider of information society services (i.e. the manager of the complaints website) assumed a certain responsibility for those comments.

The Supreme Court also seems to have paid more attention than in previous cases to the issue of the freedom of expression of the internet website, in addition to the freedom of expression of the authors of comments. It defined the question to be examined as that of the limits of the freedom of expression and noted the importance of balancing the rights of the company whose reputation was at issue and the disseminators of information, notably the authors of comments and the internet website. Then, applying the *Axel Springer*[65] criteria for assessing to what extent the public debate contributed to the general interest, it examined the limits of allowed criticism in debates of various types. It concluded that because of the nature of the website (i.e. its dedication to complaints) and the fact that comments might create a greater risk for harming the reputation of business, both the authors of comments and the person storing these data had a duty of broader care.[66] Notably, the obligations of the authors and the website were examined together, which may have implications for future cases where questions of harm produced by failure to fulfil those obligations may be raised. Thus, a hypothetical future finding under the Lithuanian law that websites may have to compensate for the harm done by disseminating impermissible information and the failure to remove it before any request to do so seems to have become more likely. There is still a lack of guidance from the Supreme Court on how the question of whether the liability of the actual authors of the comments could

---

63 For a useful analysis of how the legal status, notably the scope of the duty of care, of an active intermediary differs depending on whether it is analysed in the context of obligations under the Directive on E-Commerce or rights under Art. 10 ECHR, see van der Sloot, n. 42, para. 32.

64 *Delfi v. Estonia*, ECtHR judgment of 10 October 2013, app. no. 64569/09.

65 *Axel Springer AG v. Germany*, ECtHR Grand Chamber judgment of 07 February 2012, app. no. 39954/08.

66 Supreme Court of Lithuania, ruling of 19 February 2014, civil case no. 3K-3-30/2014.

serve as a sensible alternative to the liability of the internet news website[67] and how it might be decided in the context of Lithuanian law. In particular, to what extent the possibility of the author's liability would rule out the liability of the website remains unclear. It is clear that in determining this, Lithuanian courts would have to follow the ECtHR case law, however, given the current content of Lithuanian laws, its impact on this issue may be limited.

As regards the scope of obligations of intermediary providers of information society services, the Law on Information Society Services imposes the same obligation to remove impermissible comments upon notification on all providers of information society services, including intermediaries. Thus, in a case where both a blogger and a web hosting provider was sued in civil proceedings after a text infringing on the honour and dignity of a person was posted on that blog, the courts found the blogger responsible for posting and the host responsible for failure to react to a notification requesting the removal of that text.[68] The Supreme Court observed that information society services are diverse, and the persons involved in these activities have different rights and obligations depending on the nature of their activities and functions, which has a bearing on the legal effects of a violation of other persons' rights and lawful interests. In classifying the respondent company as an intermediary and defining the scope of its obligations, the Supreme Court *inter alia* relied on the Directive on E-Commerce as interpreted by the Court of Justice of the European Union and the ruling of the Constitutional Court of 19 September 2005.[69] The Directive (Art. 15 para. 1) does not impose on intermediaries either a general obligation to monitor the information they transmit or store, or a general obligation to actively seek facts or circumstances indicating illegal activity. The Constitutional Court, having noted the technical functions of a host, concluded that everyone has a duty not to disseminate impermissible information prohibited by laws. Whoever finds out that they participate in or contribute to disseminating such information must immediately cease such activities.

The latter finding of the Constitutional Court would also apply to active information society service intermediary providers, such as internet website managers who exercise a substantial degree of control over the comments published on their sites.[70] Based on the ruling of the Constitutional Court, the person who contributes to disseminating impermissible information by way of providing a platform for comments would be required to cease those activities upon becoming aware of the impermissible content of comments. On the issue of classifying

---

67   i.e. the "liability of the author of the comments" criterion, see *Delfi v. Estonia*, ECtHR Grand Chamber judgment of 16 June 2015, app. no. 64569/09, paras. 147–151; *Magyar Tartalomszolgáltatók Egyesülete and Index.hu Zrt v. Hungary*, ECtHR judgment of 02 May 2016, app. no. 22947/13, paras. 78–79.

68   Supreme Court of Lithuania, ruling of 27 February 2013, civil case no. 3K-3-49/2013.

69   Case no. 19/04, n. 32.

70   They are in that respect in a situation analogous to *Delfi AS* examined by the ECtHR – see *Delfi v. Estonia*, n. 67, para. 153.

an internet website as an entity participating in or contributing to the dissemination of information and the absence of a legal basis for its liability under the law regulating journalistic activities (i.e. the Law on Provision of Information to the Public), it is worth recalling that in *Delfi v. Estonia* the ECtHR held that the conduct of the applicants in providing a platform for third parties to exercise their freedom of expression by posting comments is a journalistic activity of a particular nature.[71] Furthermore, the ECtHR in *MTE v. Hungary* frowned upon the domestic courts in Hungary qualifying the applicants' conduct of providing a platform for comments as "disseminating" defamatory statements but conceded in that particular case to analyse the above conduct on this premise.[72]

In light of this, the Lithuanian classification of internet websites for the purposes of liability for internet comments as information society service providers contributing to dissemination rather than providers of public information may seem somewhat questionable. On the other hand, the fact that it is accepted in the domestic case law that website managers are both information society service providers (who have obligations under the Law on Information Society Services) and disseminators of public information (who have obligations under the Law of Provision of Information to the Public) points towards a conclusion that Lithuanian law sufficiently takes into account the journalistic nature of the activity of offering a platform for internet comments.

Copyright issues

In one case, the owner of the internet news site *15min.lt* was sued and found in breach of copyright for reproducing articles or summaries of articles published in the biggest daily *Lietuvos rytas* and its internet website *lrytas.lt*. The Court rejected the argument by the respondent that the exchange of information was common practice among the mass media and that the internet news sites in particular include the news on events published in either paper or internet sources, indicating the original source and, thus, both spreading the news and inviting people to look for further information in the original. The respondent also alleged that original information is not an object of copyright, as those are merely items of information and not original works.[73] When the Court found in favour of the applicant, holding that the original items amounted to copyright protected works, the respondent *15min.lt* sued *lrytas.lt* in a separate case for the fact that the latter had reproduced a number of items originally published in *15min.lt* with very insignificant changes. The Supreme Court found that the lower courts had not properly examined the nature of the original items, i.e. if they were original works or mere news items and referred the case back for further examina-

---

71 See *ibid.*, paras. 112–113.
72 *Magyar Tartalomszolgáltatók Egyesülete and Index.hu Zrt v. Hungary*, n. 67, para. 79: "Even accepting the domestic courts' qualification of the applicants' conduct as 'disseminating' defamatory statements, [...]".
73 Vilnius Regional Court, ruling of 18 April 2014, civil case no. 2A-680-565/2014.

tion.[74] Vilnius Regional Court then found that the majority of items originally published in *15min.lt* and reproduced in *lrytas.lt* were mere items of information to which copyright did not apply. In the one case, where the item had certain features of a copyright protected work, the similarity between the article published in *15min.lt* and *lrytas.lt* could be caused by the fact that both articles relied on the same information published by the person, whose story was presented in the article, on her website and accessible to everyone who requested it.[75]

Notably, the courts in this context, especially at the highest instance, rely on the ECHR and take into account the ECtHR case law. In the case discussed above, the Supreme Court,[76] relying on *Ashby Donald v. France*,[77] noted the importance of Article 10 of the ECHR when limiting freedom of expression in order to comply with copyright requirements.[78] In a case where the internet network provider was sued alleging that its user used "peer 2 peer" to send copies of a computer game without the consent of the copyright holder, the Supreme Court was confronted with an issue of whether the network provider was obliged to provide the copyright holder with the IP address of the user. The Court relied on the ECtHR *Pirate Bay*[79] case to show that copyright violations may justify restrictions on freedom of speech. It also noted that under the ECHR there is a need to strike an equilibrium between the right to intellectual property and privacy. In the circumstances of the case, the claim of the copyright holder addressed to the company was not satisfied on procedural grounds.[80] The case is, nevertheless, important as it highlighted the courts' approach in civil cases to the issue of the scope of the obligations of information service providers with regard to the protection of personal data of their users and could potentially be used in the context of the managers of the internet websites that provide platforms for anonymous comments.

Freedom of expression online and offline

In addition to what has already been said on this issue above, the following should be noted.

In principle, the position of Lithuanian courts is that as regards information disseminated by means of mass media, the protection of rights of persons has to be ensured irrespective of the genre of information or the manner in which it was submitted.[81] This implies that any specificity of online media, which is

---

74 Supreme Court of Lithuania, ruling of 12 June 2015, civil case no. 3K-3-388-313/2015 (S).
75 Vilnius Regional Court, ruling of 14 March 2016, civil case no. e2A-320-262/2016.
76 Case no. 3K-3-388-313/2015 (S), n. 74.
77 *Ashby Donald v. France*, ECtHR judgment of 10 January 2013, app. no. 36769/08.
78 Case no. 3K-3-388-313/2015 (S), n. 74.
79 *Neij and Sunde Kolmisoppi v. Sweden*, ECtHR decision of 19 February 2013, app. no. 40397/12.
80 Supreme Court of Lithuania, ruling of 06 January 2016, civil case no. e3K-3-52-687/2016.
81 Supreme Administrative Court of Lithuania, ruling of 24 September 2012, administrative case no. A-502-1700/2012.

not explicitly reflected in the law, is not considered to require adaptation of the general rules on the obligations of the providers of public information. Thus, the Supreme Administrative Court has held that limitations foreseen in the Law on the Control of Alcohol for the advertising of alcohol apply online just as they do offline. This is irrespective of the fact that the by-law on the control of information not to be posted on public computer networks and on the procedure for dissemination of restricted information does not explicitly prohibit or restrict the advertising of alcohol.[82] The Inspector of Journalist Ethics has taken essentially the same approach and consistently held that the sphere where the journalists' ethics standards apply is the sphere of provision of information to the public, irrespective of whether information is provided via traditional media or by other means.[83]

At the same time, arguments on the specificity of online media are raised, and to some extent accepted by both the courts and other authorities. For example, the Inspector of Journalist Ethics in 2012 assessed Lithuanian legal regulation as more favourable to the internet than to the traditional media, notably newspapers. In her opinion, internet media benefit from more favourable legal regulation regarding advertisements, including political advertisements, as well as more lenient liability rules. Internet media classified as unethical are under no risk of losing tax benefits even though all types of media, if classified unethical, lose one source of income, namely public procurement advertisements. The only area in which traditional media enjoys better legal conditions than online media is in the system of state support for cultural and educational projects, where online media is allocated a smaller proportion of funds.[84] Presumably, the assessment regarding the leniency of liability rules needs to be reconsidered in light of the changes of the case law of the ECtHR and, as a corollary, that of the domestic courts. The example of how *Delfi v. Estonia* influenced the reasoning of Lithuanian courts shows a growing understanding of the responsibilities attached to online media activities. Importantly, the specificity of the internet, while not ruling out liability for violating the limits on freedom of expression, requires redefining the classical notions such as the journalist to avoid uncertainty regarding the rights and responsibilities of bloggers and other persons contributing to content online. This work is in progress in Lithuania, and international human rights law is a factor taken into account as the example of the blogger status case discussed above shows. Bloggers are granted the same status as journalists but only if they meet certain conditions. Another point to

82 Supreme Administrative Court of Lithuania, decision of 27 January 2011, administrative case no. A^{822}-37/2011.
83 Žurnalistų etikos inspektoriaus 2012 metų veiklos ataskaita, 2013, www.lrs.lt/apps3/1/2428_tqtwwtxs.pdf (last accessed 8 February 2018), 34.
84 Žurnalistų etikos inspektorius, "Kas galima internetui, negalima laikraščiui" (santrauka iš Žurnalistų etikos inspektoriaus 2012 metų veiklos ataskaitos ir 2011-2012 metų analitinės apžvalgos "Demokratinės visuomenės informavimo kultūros plėtros gairės"), www.lrs.lt/apps3/1/2922_2011_2012_inter%20laikr%20_2_.pdf (last accessed 8 February 2018).

note in this regard is that even though Lithuanian courts admittedly, in examining the freedom of expression cases, follow the ECHR and generally apply the tests developed by the ECtHR,[85] other factors may outweigh the factor of the specificity of the internet. Thus, although in one hate speech case[86] the Supreme Court of Lithuania specifically quoted the ECtHR Grand Chamber judgment in *Delfi v. Estonia*, on the point of the impact of the information disseminated via the internet as contrasted with traditional mass media, it acquitted the author of internet comments relying on the *ultima ratio* principle, according to which criminal law is applied only where the objectives of protection of legal values cannot be achieved by using milder means.

85 See Šindeikis, n. 56, 1057.
86 Supreme Court of Lithuania, judgment of 1 March 2016, criminal case no. 2K-86-648/2016.

9 Regulation of online media in Norway

Ellen Lexerød Hovlid

Introduction

This article will focus on the regulation of online media in Norway. The presentation will start with a description of the Norwegian media landscape. Then it will be shown how freedom of speech is regulated in Norwegian legislation, before the relationship between Norwegian and international law is described. Cases involving media law that have gone against Norway in the European Court of Human Rights will also be presented.

Following the introduction, the article will deal with the regulation of the content of online media, i.e. the rules that set limits for the types of content that may legally be published in such media. Then the focus will be on the regulation of the placement of responsibility in online media, meaning the rules that decide who is going to be held responsible when the legal limits have been transgressed.

In this presentation, the main question is whether the rules that apply to the so-called traditional media, such as print newspapers, radio and television; also apply to the new online media. In the Norwegian debate, this is referred to as the question of whether the rules should be neutral with regard to technology or platforms.[1] In addition, the article also tries to answer questions which are of great relevance when it comes to online media: are there rules that apply to journalism and do not apply to other publication activities, and how is journalism distinguished from other publication activities?

The Norwegian media environment

Norway saw its first newspaper published around 1760,[2] but it took almost 100 years before reading newspapers became a frequent activity amongst ordinary people. Today there are between 220 and 230 newspapers in Norway.[3]

---

1 See, for example, NOU 2011:12, p. 24.
2 H. Grue Bastiansen and H.F. Dahl, *Norsk mediehistorie* [*A Norwegian history of media*], 2nd ed., Oslo, Universitetsforlaget 2008, p. 48.
3 Antall aviser og samlet opplag, www.medienorge.uib.no/statistikk/medium/avis/361 (last accessed 9 February 2018).

Norwegians are known as a newspaper-reading people. Even so, the percentage of Norwegians who read print newspapers on a regular basis has declined considerably in recent years. In 1991, 84 per cent of the population read newspapers on an average day. By 2015, that percentage had sunk to 42.[4]

Broadcasting was inaugurated in Norway in 1924. Since 1933, there has been a state-owned broadcasting company called the Norwegian Broadcasting Corporation (NRK). The operations of NRK are almost exclusively financed through a licence fee paid by the viewers. There have been suggestions that NRK ought to be sold to private investors, but this has not been politically acceptable. The NRK still retains a dominant position in the Norwegian media landscape.

The share of Norwegians who listen to the radio in the course of an average day was 59 per cent in 2015. The share of Norwegians who watch television on an average day stayed fairly stable for a long time at slightly over 80 per cent. In recent years, however, there has been a decline, and by 2015 that share had fallen to 67 per cent.

The internet plays a huge role in Norway. Ninety-six per cent of the population have access to the internet, and 87 per cent report that they have used the internet on an average day. More Norwegians read online newspapers than their printed counterparts. Fifty-one per cent read newspapers online on an average day.

Social media has become very popular in Norway. The average Norwegian is a member of 2.6 social networks online.[5] Even if social media is popular among all age groups, it is the twenty-somethings who use it most extensively. In the 15–29 age group cohort, as many as 97 per cent are members of one or more social networks. At the top of the list of the most popular social networks in Norway, we find Facebook. In Norway, interest in this new network grew dramatically from 2007 onwards, and in 2015 69 per cent of Norway's internet users visited Facebook daily. This makes Facebook indisputably the most popular social network in Norway. Facebook is followed by the photo application Snapchat, which was visited daily by 33 per cent. In third place, we find Instagram with 22 per cent, and in fourth place Twitter with 7 per cent.

These observations reveal that Norway enjoys a wide variety of media, and that Norwegians use the media, including online media, quite extensively. The legal regulation of online media is, therefore, of great importance for many people.

National legislation regarding freedom of speech

The freedom of speech doctrine in Norway

The Norwegian Constitution was written in 1814, when the Danish-Norwegian union was dissolved. Very few human rights were included in the Constitution

---

4 Norsk mediebarometer, 2015, www.ssb.no/kultur-og-fritid/statistikker/medie/aar/2016-04-14 (last accessed 9 February 2018).
5 TNS Gallup, InterBuss Q2 2015—Norway's most comprehensive research into people's Internet habits.

from the beginning, but the freedom of the press acquired its own provision in Article 100. The provision included in Article 100 remained unchanged for almost 200 years. However, at the turn of the millennium this provision was extensively revised. The need for such a revision was justified because the provision was now seen as outdated.[6] It was pointed out that there had been, and still was, a rapid development in areas of importance for freedom of expression. It was particularly emphasised that "the situation is characterised by new media, an ever-growing, increasingly comprehensive, offer of information channels—and by the internationalisation of these channels of information".

The revised provision entered into force in 2004. This revision of Article 100 of the Constitution constitutes a milestone in the history of Norwegian freedom of expression. The new provision strengthened people's freedom of expression. In this particular context, it is especially important to point out that the revision took the principle of technological neutrality[7] as its starting point. This principle was justified by the fact that modern digital developments create convergence and nullify the boundaries between technologies that have traditionally been separate.

The goal of technological neutrality manifested itself in the replacement of the formulation "liberty of the Press" in the old provision with "freedom of expression" in the new. In the first subsection of Article 100, it now says that "there shall be freedom of expression".[8] The new provision provides protection for expressions through any kind of medium, not just printed ones.[9] It is thus made clear that utterances expressed on the internet are covered by the Constitutional protections of today.

Even if the revision of Article 100 took as its starting point that freedom of expression is a fundamental condition of a democracy,[10] it was recognised that this freedom cannot be absolute. The old provision had been criticised for being unclear with regards to how the limits of freedom of expression should be drawn and for giving too much leeway for those who wanted to restrict this freedom. In the new provision, the right to limit freedom of expression is defined in subsection 2, which runs as follows:

> No one may be held liable in law for having imparted or received information, ideas or messages unless this can be justified in relation to the grounds for freedom of expression, which are the seeking of truth, the promotion of democracy and the individual's freedom to form opinions. Such legal liability shall be prescribed by law.

---

6 See NOU 1999:27, p. 15.
7 See, for instance, NOU 1999:27, pp. 179–181 and St.meld. No. 26 (2003–2004), p. 26.
8 Translation taken from www.stortinget.no/globalassets/pdf/english/constitutionenglish.pdf (last accessed 9 February 2018).
9 Cf. St.meld. No. 26 (2003–2004), p. 26.
10 Cf. NOU 1999:27, p. 15.

The new provision thus specifies two conditions for holding anyone legally responsible for his/her statements. In addition to the fact that the responsibility must be "prescribed by law", it is also a requirement that this responsibility "can be justified", seen in relation to the considerations on which the freedom of expression is based. This means that the infringement's purpose has to be weighed against the damage or disturbance that such an infringement may cause to the considerations underlying the freedom of expression principle.[11] The fundamental considerations underlying the freedom of expression are formulated as "the seeking of truth, the promotion of democracy and the individual's freedom to form opinions".

It was also emphasised in the new provision that the expression of political opinions should enjoy particularly strong protections. The possibility of restricting such opinions is regulated in subsection 3:

> Everyone shall be free to speak their mind frankly on the administration of the State and on any other subject whatsoever. Clearly defined limitations to this right may only be imposed when particularly weighty considerations so justify in relation to the grounds for freedom of expression.

In the case of expressing political opinions, it is thus not sufficient that the responsibility "can be justified" against the concerns underlying freedom of expression. There must be "particularly weighty considerations" present to make any such infringement justifiable.

During the revision of the Constitution, the application of the provision was also extended, so that it now comprises not just the freedom to impart information (also called "classic" freedom of expression or freedom of utterance) and receive information. In addition, the new provision includes two positive requirements: namely, the demand for access to information from all public bodies in subsection 5 (also known as the principle of public access) and the demand that the Government should promote an open and well-informed public discourse on subsection 6 (also called the infrastructure requirement).

It should be obvious from these considerations that the constitutional protection of the principle of freedom of expression is strong in Norway. This constitutional protection will also apply to utterances on the internet.

When the Constitution was revised, one of the purposes of this revision was to create a genuine barrier for legislators, courts and all other legal instances. The old constitutional provision was criticised for being so unclear that it did not function as such a barrier. However, the goal of the new provision has not really been fulfilled.[12] Article 100 of the Constitution is only rarely referred to in

---

11 Cf. St.meld. No. 26 (2003–2004), p. 183.
12 Cf. A. Kierulf, "Hvilken rolle spiller Grunnloven § 100 i Høyesteretts ytringsfrihetspraksis?" ["What Role Does § 100 of the Constitution Play in the Supreme Court's Practice in Freedom of Expression Cases"], *Lov og Rett*, 2012, pp. 131–150 (p. 149).

the Supreme Court's arguments in freedom of expression cases. Instead, the Supreme Court tends to relate its argumentation to the European Convention on Human Rights (ECHR) and the European Court of Human Rights (ECtHR). In a later section, this article will present Norway's relationship to the ECHR.

Regulations of freedom of speech in ordinary legislation

There are several legal provisions in Norwegian law that set limits for freedom of speech. Examples of this are defamation provisions (the Compensatory Damages Act § 3-6a), protection of the right to private life (the Criminal Code § 267 and the Compensatory Damages Act § 3-6), the right to your own picture (the Copyright Act § 45c, cf. §§ 54 and 55), presentation of court cases (the Courts of Justice Act Chapter 7), discriminating and hateful utterances (the Criminal Code § 185), threats (the Criminal Code §§ 263 and 264), incitement to criminal acts (the Criminal Code § 183), the circulation of descriptions of violent acts (the Criminal Code § 236) and the distribution of pornographic material (the Criminal Code § 317).

Non-judicial regulations

In Norway, media that is engaged in journalistic activities is regulated by both a judicial and a non-judicial system. The non-judicial system has been created by the Norwegian Press Association and is completely without any formal influence from state authorities. It is, in other words, purely an internal journalistic affair. The structure is technologically neutral and includes newspapers, TV, radio and online publications.

This kind of self-policing consists of an organ for complaints, called the Norwegian Press Complaints Commission (the Norwegian name is Pressens Faglige Utvalg—PFU), which registers complaints and passes judgments based on the guidelines for journalistic ethics contained in the Code of Ethics of the Norwegian Press (Vær Varsom-plakaten).[13] If a certain media outlet is convicted by the PFU, the outlet has to print the verdict in a conspicuous place or air it at an appropriate time. Beyond this, the PFU has no other sanctions to impose.

The Norwegian system of self-policing functions well in the sense that it is widely accepted among Norwegian journalists and is considered to play an important role when it comes to increasing awareness of the need for accountability in the journalistic media.[14] The press is highly motivated to sustain a well-functioning system of press ethics, in order to avoid more extensive state regulation of its activities.

---

13 Code of Ethics of the Norwegian Press, http://presse.no/pfu/etiske-regler/vaer-varsom-plakaten/
   vvpl-engelsk/ (last accessed 9 February 2018).
14 See, for instance, NOU 2011:12, p. 35.

The Code of Ethics of the Norwegian Press has over the course of time acquired a few points that specifically deal with online publication, for instance, a point about links (point 4.16) and a point that deals with digital exchanges of opinions (point 4.17).

The PFU has experienced a large increase in the number of complaints in recent years. In 2015, the Commission received 500 complaints.[15] It can be assumed that this, among other things, is due to the fact that an ever-increasing percentage of journalistic products will remain on the internet "forever". This probably motivates more people to try their cases. Many of today's complaints involve publication on several platforms, for instance, on paper and online, or on radio programmes that can also be found on the internet. In such cases, the PFU appears to treat online media in the same way as other media.

In addition to the journalists' own self-policing, in 2001, a set of "Ethical Rules for the Internet" was adopted, which was intended to be administered by a board for internet publication. This board was supposed to be financed by the media itself, and the ethics rules were meant to govern the activities of everyone who had accepted them. However, this internet board never acquired any central importance for the online media, and after a few years, the financing disappeared and the board was dissolved. A number of people thought this was unfortunate,[16] but still nothing has been done to revive such an institution. In 2009, the government-appointed Right of Privacy Commission suggested the creation of a state-financed internet board to be organised under public law.[17] Two years later, a Media Responsibility Committee was appointed to study the question of the allocation of responsibility in the media. This Committee was of the opinion that a system with a special internet board was difficult to combine with the already existing system of supervision in this area.[18] After this attempt, no internet board has been created.

Instead of an internet board, a service called slettmeg.no ("deleteme.no") has been inaugurated. This is a service that helps people who experience violations of their rights of privacy on the internet. The service is founded in public law, but does not itself exercise such legal authority. It does not itself have a mandate to delete or to demand that anything be deleted from the internet, but it helps people to establish contact with those who have uploaded the information or with the service where the information can be found. Slettmeg.no can also provide technical assistance and give advice on the best strategy for getting the offending information removed. The service has been a great success. In 2015,

---

15 Pressens Faglige Utvalg Statistikk, http://presse.no/pfu/statistikk/ (last accessed 9 February 2018).

16 See, for instance, J. Bing, *Ansvar for ytringer på net: særlig om formidlerens ansvar* [*Responsibility for online utterances: especially about the responsibility of intermediaries*], Oslo, Universitetsforlaget 2008, p. 255.

17 NOU 2009:1, pp. 122–123.

18 NOU 2011:12, p. 50.

it handled 7826 cases, and the website was accessed by 334,000 users.[19] The types of cases that are registered at slettmeg.no concern the deletion of profiles, questions about search engines and deletion of one's listing there, pictures and video entries, registration in online catalogues, deletion of false profiles, handling of dead people's profiles, loss of access to one's own profile, hacked profiles or self-published content.

This means that in Norway there are non-judicial arrangements both for journalistic and other types of online publication activities that function well and also relieve the legal system. The rest of this presentation will deal with the legal regulation of online media.

Attitudes toward transnational protection of human rights in Norway

Norway joined the ECHR as early as in 1952, and in 1999 the ECHR became incorporated into Norwegian law with the Human Rights Act.[20] The law stipulates that the ECHR should be given precedence in cases where there is a conflict between the provisions of the Convention and other parts of Norwegian legislation (Article 3). Today the ECHR and the practice of the ECtHR play a central role in the Supreme Court's decisions in cases involving freedom of expression. Norway has also been involved in a number of important cases relating to freedom of expression in the ECtHR and has been convicted on several occasions. These decisions will be discussed in the following section.

Norway is not a member of the European Union (EU), but is associated with the Union through its membership in the European Economic Area (EEA). Legislative acts from the EU, which the EEA Committee considers to be relevant, are incorporated into the EEA agreement and thus implemented in Norwegian law. There are many examples of media-relevant EU directives that have become implemented in Norwegian legislation, such as the Audiovisual Media Services Directive (mainly implemented through the Broadcasting Act),[21] the Copyright Directive (implemented through the Copyright Act),[22] the Right of Privacy Directive (implemented through the Personal Data Act)[23] and the Directive on Electronic Commerce (implemented through the E-Commerce Act).[24] EEA law is founded on the principle of homogeneity, which means that EEA provisions

---

19 Slettmeg årsrapport 2015, https://slettmeg.no/wp-content/uploads/sites/3/2016/05/Slettmeg-no-årsrapport-2015-digital.pdf (last accessed 9 February 2018).
20 Act of 21 May 1999 relating to the strengthening of the status of human rights in Norwegian law. An English translation can be found at http://app.uio.no/ub/ujur/oversatte-lover/data/lov-19990521-030-eng.pdf (last accessed 9 February 2018).
21 *Official Journal of the European Union* L 95, 15.4.2010, pp. 1–24.
22 *Official Journal of the European Union* L 167, 22.6.2001, pp. 10–19.
23 *Official Journal of the European Union* L 281, 23.11.1995, pp. 31–50.
24 *Official Journal of the European Union* L 178, 17.7.2000, pp. 1–16.

that are equal to the legal provisions of the EU must be interpreted and implemented in such a way that the state of the law is the same within the EEA as in
the EU. This means that decisions from the EU Court should be attached great
significance in Norway. For instance, the Norwegian Data Protection Authority
has based its decisions on the Google Spain case.[25] Norway has not yet been
involved in cases that deal with the media-related legal regulations of the EU.

Landmark cases from ECtHR and the influence of these cases

The increased focus on the ECHR in Norway in the 1990s led to a situation
where the ECtHR filed a complaint against the Norwegian state in three cases
involving defamation. In Norway, defamation cases had been treated according
to criminal laws and regulations that put quite strict demands on the press.

The first case where the ECtHR filed a complaint against Norway involved
a newspaper that had communicated accusations against a crew of sealers. The
crew were accused of having used illegal methods to catch the seals. It was a
sealing inspector who had made these accusations in an unpublished report. The
Norwegian courts found that the accusations were likely to offend the sealers'
honour, and that they had not been proven correct, so the paper was convicted.
The ECtHR concluded that Norway had been in violation of Article 10 of the
ECHR. This judgment, *Bladet Tromsø vs. Norway*,[26] was taken to mean that
the ECtHR attaches great weight to the important role played by the press as a
communicator of information of general public interest.[27]

Just six months later, the ECtHR announced another judgment that went
against Norway. This time the case concerned critical statements made against
a professor during a debate about police violence. The Supreme Court had
stressed that the freedom of expression has its limits, even in the context of a
public debate. The Court considered the critical statements about the professor
to be factual utterances that could be judged to be true or false.[28] The Court
believed that such required evidence had not been presented. The ECtHR, on
the contrary, based its decision in the case of *Nilsen and Johnsen vs. Norway* on
its opinion that many of the relevant statements were value judgments that could
not be proven true or false.[29] Thus, Norway was again found to be in violation
of Article 10 of the ECHR. The decision was interpreted to mean that it takes
a great deal for characterisations and value judgments not to be protected by
Article 10.[30]

---

25 Cf. PVN-2015-06 Google.
26 Bladet Tromsø vs. Norway, no. 21980/93, ECtHR 1999.
27 Cf. K. Eggen, *Ytringsfrihet: Vernet om ytringsfriheten i norsk rett* [*Freedom of Expression: The
    Protection of the Freedom of Expression in Norwegian Law*], Oslo, Cappelen 2002, p. 887.
28 Rt. [Norwegian Law Reports – collection of decisions from the Supreme Court], 1993, p. 537
    (p. 544).
29 *Nilsen and Johnsen vs. Norway* [GC], no. 23118/93, ECtHR 1999.
30 Cf. Eggen 2002 (see note 26), pp. 944–945.

Another six months later, the ECtHR handed down its judgment in the case of *Bergens Tidende and others vs. Norway*.[31] This case concerned the communication in a newspaper of serious criticism against a plastic surgeon. The Supreme Court had interpreted the criticism from the doctor's patients as accusations of a lack of surgical competence, something that the Court found had not been substantiated.[32] Again, the ECHR, with reference to *Bladet Tromsø vs. Norway*, took as its starting point the fact that the case commanded great general interest. For the third time in less than a year, Norway was convicted of failing to respect Article 10 of the ECHR in a libel case.

These three cases led to what has been called "a paradigm shift" in Norwegian libel law.[33] From then on, the Supreme Court took the decisions of the ECtHR as their real starting point. Freedom of expression was henceforth given more attention in the application of the law, and the Supreme Court adopted the same basic reasoning in the evaluation as the ECtHR had done.

Even so, the ECtHR again had to "correct" the Supreme Court in 2007 in a fourth libel case, *Tønsbergs Blad AS and Haukom vs. Norway*.[34] Here the Supreme Court had convicted a newspaper of printing allegations that a well-known businessman was registered on an internal municipal list of people who were in violation of their duty to occupy their beachfront properties.[35] The judgment of the ECtHR was taken to imply that the press was allowed to use identifiable people as "illustrative material" in reporting cases of general importance to society to a greater extent than what had been usual in Norwegian courts.[36]

In one libel case, Norway has been found in violation of Article 8 of the ECHR. This was the decision reached in *A. vs. Norway*,[37] concerning the identification of an innocent man who had been an object of suspicion in a police investigation of a rape and murder of two girls. The man was described as a possible perpetrator and believed to be guilty by many people. He did not win his case in the Supreme Court.[38] The ECtHR's conclusion that Article 8 had been violated has been cited in support of the opinion that the ECtHR has been willing to keep pictures of private individuals off limits from publication to a greater extent than what has earlier been the practice in Norwegian courts.[39] This impression is supported by the case of *Egeland and Hanseid vs. Norway*.[40] In this

---

31 *Bergens Tidende and others vs. Norway*, no. 26132/95, ECtHR 2000.

32 Rt. 1994, p. 348.

33 More information on this development can be found in J. Wessel-Aas, "Utviklingen fra ytrings-frihetskommisjonen i 1999 til status i 2014", in *Status for ytringsfriheten i Norge [The Status of Freedom of Expression in Norway]*, Oslo, Institutt for samfunnsforskning 2014 (p. 23 onwards).

34 *Tønsbergs Blad AS and Haukom vs. Norway*, no. 510/04, ECtHR 2007.

35 Rt. 2003, p. 928.

36 Cf. Wessel-Aas 2014 (see note 32), p. 27.

37 *A. vs. Norway*, no. 28070/06, ECtHR 2009.

38 Rt. 2005, p. 1677.

39 Cf. Wessel-Aas 2014 (see note 32), p. 30.

40 *Egeland and Hanseid vs. Norway*, no. 34438/04, ECtHR 2009.

case, two editors sued the state because they had been found guilty of publishing pictures of a convicted murderer as he was being led out of the courtroom.[41] In this case, the judgment in the ECtHR went against the editors, as Norway was not found to be in violation of Article 10.

Norway has also been convicted in the ECtHR for being in breach of Article 10 in a case that concerned advertising for a small political party on a Norwegian TV channel (TV-West). The channel was fined for having failed to respect the prohibition against political advertising on TV. The case was appealed all the way up to the Supreme Court, which found that Article 10 of the ECHR was not a hindrance for the imposition of the fine.[42] In the decision on the case of *TV-Vest AS and Rogaland Pensjonistparti vs. Norway*,[43] however, the ECtHR reached the opposite conclusion. Norway was here again found to have violated Article 10 of the ECtHR.

In the matter of the invasion of private life, a complaint was filed against Norway in the ECtHR for violation of Article 8 of the ECHR in the case of *Lillo-Stenberg and Sæther vs. Norway*.[44] This case concerned a presentation of the wedding of two Norwegian celebrities in a weekly magazine. The magazine had been acquitted by the Supreme Court.[45] Here, the ECtHR found that this did not represent any breach of Norway's positive obligations according to Article 8.

We have seen, then, that as far as media law is concerned, it is particularly the practice of Norwegian courts in libel cases that has been the subject of convictions in the ECtHR. The decisions of the Court in this field have led to significant adjustments in Norwegian libel law. Freedom of expression and the important role played by the press are given more attention than before.

Content regulation in online media

The neutral legal provisions

General observations

As shown earlier, the principle of technological neutrality was the basis of the revision of the Constitution in 2004. The Norwegian Constitution will thus, as a starting point, resist regulations that are not technologically neutral—also called vertical law-making.[46] The reasoning behind the desire to have technologically neutral laws has recently been more extensively elaborated in the following manner:

---

41 Rt. 2004, p. 510.
42 Rt. 2004, p. 1737.
43 *TV-Vest AS and Rogaland Pensjonistparti vs. Norway*, no. 21132/05, ECtHR 2008.
44 *Lillo-Stenberg and Sæther vs. Norway*, no. 13258/09, ECtHR 2014.
45 Rt. 2008, p. 1089.
46 Cf. NOU 2011:12, p. 24.

There are several concerns that constitute the basis of this principle. The most important one is that the freedom of expression applies to everyone, and the regulation of the activities of the media should be linked to content, not to form. [...] An additional concern is that the laws should not favour specific technologies and thereby distort competition. At the same time, there is a risk that legislation that is not media neutral, may create unforeseen effects.[47]

When it comes to regulating media content, the obvious main rule in Norwegian legislation is in keeping with this principle. The general rule is that the provisions that regulate content are technologically neutral.[48] This applies to all the provisions that were mentioned above under the heading "Regulations of freedom of speech in ordinary legislation". This means that the provisions are directed at publication on all technological platforms, and that the material conditions for responsibility are the same for all types of technology. The same conditions that are identified for holding the traditional media responsible are also applicable to publication on the internet.

The same conditions are also the rule for utterances that are a part of journalistic publishing and utterances that are not. In other words, the provisions are fundamentally neutral with regard to what type of publication activity the utterances are a part of.

However, several of the provisions mentioned require that the utterances are made "publicly". Within the Criminal Code, this requirement previously excluded online publication. The Criminal Code, in fact, contained a legal definition, which implied that the internet had to be considered as a "printed text" to fulfil the "public" requirement in the law. In 2012, the Appeals Committee of the Supreme Court reached a decision saying that the internet cannot be considered "printed text", the way it was defined in the Criminal Code.[49] The principle of legality made such an interpretation problematic. In other words, the definition of the "public" condition meant that the relevant provisions were not entirely technologically neutral after all.

The decision from the Appeals Committee of the Supreme Court quickly led to a change in the Criminal Code. Today the legal definition states that an utterance is "public" when it has been made "in such a way as to make it suitable for reaching a large number of people" (§ 10, subsection 2).[50] More than 20–30 people is seen as "a large number of people".[51] This new alternative is technologically neutral, i.e. it includes all types of media, for instance, radio, TV, the internet and posters.[52]

47 NOU 2011:12, p. 24.
48 Cf. NOU 2011:12, p. 15.
49 Rt. 2012, p. 1211.
50 Act of 20 May 2005, translation not found, therefore my own translation.
51 Prop. 53 L (2012–2013).
52 For more information about the definition of a "public" utterance, see E. Lexerød Hovlid, "Straffelovens legaldefinisjon av en 'offentlig handling'" ["The definition of a 'public act' in the Criminal Code"], *Tidsskrift for Strafferett*, 2016, pp. 161–181.

The provisions referred to above are enforced by the regular courts. The legal practice relating to these provisions is dominated by decisions against the media that are engaged in journalistic activities, which here means the traditional media, such as print newspapers, radio and television.

It is likely that a great many Norwegians do not know that these rules apply not only to journalistic media, but also to ordinary people who register their opinions on the internet. People's infringements of the rules are probably very common.[53] As shown earlier, the slettmeg.no service receives a great many complaints about violations on the internet. Studies have shown that online bullying is widespread in Norway.[54] For most people who feel offended online, a relatively high threshold must be surmounted before they choose to make a formal complaint or file charges. Even so, there has been an increase in the number of complaints and lawsuits in this area.

Emphasis on technology and publication form in legal assessments

Even if the conditions in most of the provisions about illegal utterances are neutral with regard to technology and form of publication, one may ask if these factors are still of importance when it comes to legal judgments of whether limits have been transgressed. Often there will be a balancing of broad interests at the heart of such judgments, and in this balancing of interests it is possible to emphasise many different factors.

Technologically specific concerns are generally given little weight in Norwegian legal practice. However, one can find examples of courts that have emphasised the immediate effect of TV.[55] One can also find examples of courts emphasising the scaleability of the public and the danger of endless dissemination on the internet.[56] In light of the case law of the ECtHR, one may ask whether the courts should take into account the specific characteristics of the technology used in their assessments more often.

Norwegian courts have also tended to stress the central democratic role of the press and of journalism in their assessments.[57] In other words, the courts make a point of identifying the form of publication activity that the utterances are a part of. The attention paid to the types of publication activities raises the question of how these different types ought to be delimited. What is journalism and who is a journalist today? In Norwegian legal literature, like in much of international literature, it has been pointed out that since almost everybody

---

53 Cf. NOU 2011:12, p. 41.
54 Cf. E. Staksrud, *Digital mobbing: hvem, hvor, hvordan, hvorfor – og hva kan voksne gjøre?* [*Digital bullying: who, where, how, why – and what can adults do?*], Oslo, Kommuneforlaget 2013.
55 LB-1999-1336 (Court of Appeal).
56 See Rt. 2003, p. 1091, paragraphs 15–17, referred to by Bing 2008 (see note 16), p. 49.
57 See, for instance, Rt. 2015, p. 746, paragraph 65.

today is a kind of online publicist, these questions have become more difficult to answer than before.[58]

Specific legal provisions

Technology-specific legal provisions

There are certain exceptions from the main rule of technologically neutral legal regulations of media content. One exception is expressed in the provisions of the Broadcasting Act.[59] Broadcasting is here defined as "the transmission of speech, music, images and the like via electronic communication networks, intended or suitable for direct and simultaneous reception by the public" (§ 1-1, letter a). Broadcasting thus requires the use of a certain technology, i.e. "electronic communication networks".

Beyond this area, the Broadcasting Act is on the whole technologically neutral. It applies to all forms of "electronic communication networks". The internet is one such electronic network, and online publication can be covered by the Broadcasting Law. But much of online publication will not fulfil the requirement of being "simultaneous" in the definition of broadcasting. This requirement was added in 2002 as a consequence of a wish to differentiate between broadcasting and interactive services.[60] Interactive services on the internet, where the receiver him/herself initiates the transmission, are not covered by this law.[61]

The Broadcasting Act does not contain many rules and regulations that establish limitations on what kinds of content may be published. The general rules mentioned above are the ones that create most of the boundaries for the expression of content in the broadcast media. However, the law contains certain special regulations for advertising in broadcasting. Advertising directed at children is not allowed (§ 3-1, subsection 2), and hidden advertising and other forms of concealed marketing are forbidden (§ 3-3). The law also contains certain specific rules that only apply to television. It is not allowed to advertise religious or philosophical convictions or political views on TV (§ 3-1, subsection 3), and advertisements should mainly appear in blocks between programmes (§ 3-2).

The Broadcasting Law is enforced by the Norwegian Media Authority. Its decisions can be appealed to the Board of Complaints for Media Cases. Possible

---

58 E. Lexerød Hovlid, "Krenkelser ved offentliggjøring av private opplysninger og bilder på sosiale medier" ["Violations through sharing of private information and photos on social media"], *Tidsskrift for Rettsvitenskap*, 2016, pp. 138–175 (p. 162).

59 Act of 4 December 1992 relating to broadcasting and audio-visual on-demand services. An unofficial translation can be found at www.medietilsynet.no/globalassets/engelsk/act-relating-to-broadcasting-and-audiovisual-on-demand-services.pdf (last accessed 9 February 2018).

60 Cf. Ot. Prp. (official proposition) No. 107 (2001–2002).

61 Cf. Bing 2008 (see note 16), pp. 132–134.

lawsuits must be directed at the state through the above-mentioned Board of Complaints. The Media Authority also has other tasks, such as setting age limits for movies shown in cinemas. It also monitors the compliance with the rules of the Act Relating to the Protection of Minors against Harmful Audiovisual Programmes.[62] According to this law, a visual programme cannot be made available without having been given an age limit (§ 3).

For online publication that cannot be subsumed under the Broadcasting Law, the ordinary rules of advertising found in the Marketing Control Act will apply.[63]

Another exception from the main rule of technologically neutral legal provisions is the Copyright Act.[64] This Act regulates violations of immaterial rights. The starting point is a situation where the law gives the author a generally formulated monopoly that is technologically neutral. In other words, the same principles will be applied regardless of what kind of technological platform is used to publish the work.

The Copyright Act is not completely technologically neutral, however. For example, according to the current rules of contractual licence for the authorisation of audiovisual content, it makes a difference whether the transmission uses wire or is wireless, and if the transmission can be characterised as broadcasting or forwarding (§§ 30, 32 and 34). The rules for quoting rights and reproducing works are not quite technologically neutral either (§§ 22-25). For example, the right to reproduce a work in reports only applies to broadcasting and film (§ 25).

At the moment, work is in progress to revise and simplify the Copyright Act, because it is relatively inaccessible today after many earlier minor revisions. The new proposal replaces the current provisions for contractual licences and opens up the use of such licences independently of how the material is made accessible.[65] It has also been proposed that the provision for reproduction of a work in reports should be made technologically neutral.[66]

Specific legal provisions for journalistic publication activities

There are also a few exceptions to the main rule, which say that legal provisions are neutral with regard to what kind of publication activity the relevant utterances are a part of. One such exception is the Personal Data Act.[67] This law

---

62 Act of 6 February 2015, translation can be found at www.medietilsynet.no/globalassets/engelsk/act-relating-to-the-protection-of-minors-against-harmful-audiovisual-programmes-norway-unofficial-translation-february-2015.pdf (last accessed 9 February 2018).

63 Act of 9 January 2009, No 2, relating to the Control of Marketing and Contract Terms and Conditions, etc. A translation can be found at https://forbrukerombudet.no/english/the-marketing-control-act (last accessed 9 February 2018).

64 Act of 12 May 1961, no official translation found.

65 Prop. 104 L (2016–2017), p. 10 and 190 onwards.

66 Ibid., p. 16 and 147 onwards.

67 Act of 14 April 2000, No. 31, relating to the processing of personal data. A translation can be found at www.datatilsynet.no/en/regulations-and-tools/regulations-and-decisions/norwegian-privacy-law/personal-data-act/ (last accessed 9 February 2018).

regulates the treatment of personal data. The law is enforced by the Norwegian Data Protection Authority, whose decisions may be appealed to the Privacy Appeals Board. Lawsuits that question the validity of the decisions of the Privacy Appeals Board should be filed against the state.

Apart from a chapter on camera surveillance (Chapter 7), the Personal Data Act is technologically neutral. It also applies, in other words, to the handling of personal information on the internet.

However, the Personal Data Act makes exceptions for handling personal information that has certain kinds of purposes, and these exceptions are relevant for online publication. Large parts of the Act do not apply to the handling of information that has "exclusively personal or other private purposes" (§ 3, subsection 2), nor to handling "exclusively for artistic, literary or journalistic purposes" (§ 7). The Act is, therefore, not neutral with regard to what kind of publication activity the utterance is a part of. Whether a publication has "artistic, literary or journalistic purpose" depends on the nature of the publication activity and not on the formal status of the publisher.[68]

Another act, which is not neutral with regard to the form of publication activity, is the Media Freedom Act.[69] This Act does not set content boundaries for online media, but regulates who should make decisions when it comes to content. The law was passed in 2008 and establishes the principle that it is the editor who should lead all journalistic activities and have the final say in editorial matters (§ 4, subsection 1).

The Media Freedom Act is technologically neutral. It applies to publication on all technological platforms, including the internet. Still, the law does not apply to all types of online publishing. This is a consequence of the scope of the law, which in § 2 has been defined as follows:

1   Daily newspapers and other periodical publications that are engaged in journalistic production and communication of news, features and public debate,
2   broadcasters, cf. the Broadcasting Act § 1-1, subsection 3, and
3   electronic mass media that have equivalent purposes and functions as the media mentioned under nos. 1 and 2.

It is specified that the law does not apply to "media which have as their main purpose to engage in advertising or marketing, or which are mainly directed towards members or employees in certain organisations, associations or societies" (§ 2, subsection 2).

This definition raises several questions of interpretation: how much activity must there be in order for a publication to be regarded as "periodical"? And

---

68 Cf. Ot. Prp. No. 92 (1998–1999), s. 107.
69 Act of 13 June 2008, translation not found, therefore my own translation.

again: what is "journalistic production and communication"? The decisive factor for this assessment is, like under the Personal Data Act, the nature of the publication activity in question.[70]

This definition in the Media Freedom Act has been used as a basis in later legal discussions. We will come back to that below.

Regulation of liability placement in online media

The natural liability system

The question then becomes who should be held liable when the limits of legal utterances in online media have been transgressed.

In the Norwegian debate about freedom of expression and rules of liability, a fundamental dividing line is drawn between two types of systems of liability: a "natural liability system", based on the legal system's ordinary rules concerning illegal utterances that are directed at all citizens, and an "artificial liability system", which is often also called an objective liability system.[71]

The starting point in Norway is a natural liability system. It is, in other words, the ordinary rules about illegal utterances that primarily decide who can be held liable.

Whether a person can be held liable according to these ordinary rules is dependent on a concrete assessment of whether the person has shown the kind of subjective guilt that the relevant legal provision requires. The ordinary guilt requirements in Norwegian courts are intent and negligence. In criminal law, the main rule is to require intent (Criminal Code § 21). In order to impose an obligation to pay for damages and vindication, negligence is sufficient (the Compensatory Damages Act §§ 3-6 and 3-6a).

This starting point is technologically neutral in the sense that the natural liability system applies to publishing on all platforms, including the internet, paper, TV and radio. It also applies to both journalistic publication and other types of publication activities.

The main rule in the natural liability system is that the person who is responsible for making the utterance, the so-called original author, is the one held liable. In the journalistic media, this is normally the journalist who has composed the illegal article or report. A person who contributes to the making of illegal utterances can also be held liable. This implies that it is not just the original author who can be held liable, but also a number of other individuals. For example, both editors and other journalists may be a target, if the condition of guilt is fulfilled.

However, the liability system in Norway is not a purely natural system. It is modified by several provisions that imply both extensions and reductions

---

70 Ot. Prp. No. 19 (2007–2008), s. 22.
71 Cf. NOU 2011:12, p. 16.

compared to the natural liability system. The most important liability extension is the special editorial liability. This will be further described under the next point below. In addition, the responsibility for media activities also represents an extension in comparison with the natural liability system. For the media's technical contributors, on the other hand, one can find that liability reductions are in order. This is also discussed below.

The special editorial liability

In the Criminal Code, the following formulation can be found (§ 269, subsection 1):

> The person who makes decisions about the content of a printed text or a broadcast transmission, is criminally liable if there is published something that would have made the editor liable according to any other legal provision if he had known this content.

According to this provision, the editor's liability is described as "objective", because the editor must be judged as if he or she had known the content of the relevant utterances. However, the criminal liability of editors in Norway is not completely objective. According to subsection 3, the editor cannot be held liable if he "can prove that he cannot be blamed for lack of control of the relevant content or supervision or inspection or information for his deputy, co-workers or subordinates". The exception is meant to be understood as a strict liability for negligence.[72]

An important question in connection with the editorial liability is who can be legitimately considered to be an "editor". In the Criminal Code, it says that the "editor" is "the person who makes the decisions about the content in a printed text" (§ 270, subsection 4). The principle of editorial liability is thus framed in a functional way.[73] It is the way the person functions, not his job description or other formal features, that will decide whether he/she will be considered to be the editor. There is no official directory of editors in Norway.

This editorial liability principle only applies to "printed text" and "broadcast transmission". When the internet became widely available, the question was raised whether "printed text" should also include the internet. In the old Criminal Code, "printed text" was defined in a way which excluded the internet.[74] In the new Criminal Code, however, the strict definition of "printed text" is removed. Still, it is assumed that the principle of editorial liability does not apply to the internet. The preparatory works for the new Criminal Code serve as an argument for this. The Justice Department declared that

---

72 Cf. NOU 2011:12, p. 64, with special reference to Rt. 1950, p. 1027.
73 Cf. H. Manshaus, "Ansvar for ytringer på Internett" [«Liability for utterances on Internet»], *Lov og data*, 2012, pp. 21–23.
74 Rt. 2012, p. 1211.

a technologically neutral editorial liability rule "will entail a significant extension of the rule's area of application, especially since publications on the Internet will be covered by this provision".[75] The Department pointed out, in particular, that even private individuals with a personal homepage where other people than themselves are allowed to post information might be held criminally liable. Against this background, a broader evaluation of the question was requested. In 2009, the Media Liability Committee was appointed and asked, among other things, to consider the question of introducing a technologically neutral editorial liability rule.

The Media Liability Committee split into a majority and a minority faction. The majority suggested that the provision on editorial liability in the Criminal Code should be abolished. They pointed out that it would be difficult to define the role of the editor on the internet.[76] The Committee majority discussed the possibility of instituting a registration system for editors. Further on, the majority discussed the possibility of limiting editorial liability to media that are covered by the Media Freedom Law. This will mean that the editorial liability online will apply to publications that have corresponding aims and functions to those of daily newspapers and other periodical publications "that are engaged in journalistic production and dissemination of news, current events features and public debate". The majority believed that it would be unfortunate to limit the reach of the editors' liability to such media.

The proposals of the majority for abolishing the provision on editorial liability have not been followed up politically. Instead, the Parliament has recently asked the Government for a report on the need for a technologically neutral Media Liability Act.[77] Today, Norway has no Media Liability Act.

This report shall include the question about the editor's liability for utterances made in online debates. In Norwegian law today, this is regulated by the natural liability system described above. In more recent judicial literature, the editorial staff are given the following advice, on the basis of the ECtHR's decisions in the cases *Delfi AS vs. Estonia*[78] and *Magyar Tartalomszolgáltatók Egyesülete and Index.hu Zrt vs. Hungary:*[79] They ought to, in addition to having automatic filters that through algorithms flag certain specific comments, have in place a system for manual control of the comments sections.[80]

---

75 Cf. Ot. Prp. No. 22 (2008–2009), p. 155.
76 NOU 2011:12, p. 69 onwards.
77 Innst. 155 S (2016–2017).
78 *Delfi AS vs. Estonia* [GC], no. 64569/09, ECtHR 2015.
79 *Magyar Tartalomszolgáltatók Egyesülete and Index.hu Zrt vs. Hungary*, no. 18030/11, ECtHR 2016.
80 J. Wessel-Aas, *Opphavsrett, fotorett og personbilder i nettjournalistikk [Copyright, photoright and photos of persons in online journalism]*, Oslo, Cappelen 2016, p. 86.

The liability of media concerns

Even media concerns can be held liable in certain situations. According to the protection of people's private life in civil law, "the owner or publisher of a mass medium" can be held liable in cases where someone, who has acted on their behalf, has been guilty of invasion of private life (the Compensatory Damages Act § 3-6a, subsection 3). The same rule applies to defamation of character. The liability of the owner and publisher here does not presume guilt, it is a liability based on identification.

Earlier this liability was only applicable to "printed text". This expression has now been replaced by "mass medium" to make the provision technologically neutral. In other words, this liability also applies to the internet.

The criminal law equivalent to the identification liability in civil law is the corporate liability provision of the Criminal Code (§ 27). This corporate liability means that when a penal provision has been transgressed by someone who has acted on behalf of the corporation it is liable to punishment. The rules of corporate liability involving the media in the Criminal Code are also technologically neutral. Such punishment has only been imposed in one case.[81] This case involved handing over press photographs to the police.[82] The Media Liability Committee held the opinion that the main rule should still be that this kind of punishment should not be used against the media.[83] The majority in this regard were also concerned about the problems of delimitation. It is difficult to make laws that in a precise and accurate way can distinguish between media operations that should not receive punishment and those that one might want to react against.

Limitations of liability for the media's technical support staff

As mentioned above, a person who contributes to the expression of an illegal utterance may be held responsible. When it comes to statements that violate a person's right to private life, there are exceptions made in the Criminal Code for "a person who has just contributed through technical support or distribution of a newspaper or magazine produced in the realm" (§ 267, subsection 2). Arguments for this provision refer to the conviction that liability should not be spread too widely to too many liability subjects.[84] The exception clause means that a person who engages in lay-out, stands behind a camera or works as a lighting technician or newspaper boy cannot be held liable.

---

81 Cf. N. E. Øy, *Medierett for journalister* [*Media Law for Journalists*], Oslo, Cappelen 2013, p. 283.
82 Rt. 1996, p. 1375.
83 NOU 2011:12, p. 119.
84 Ibid., p. 102.

The provision of the Criminal Code only applies to "newspapers or magazines". The civil law provision that safeguards a person's right to private life is given a technologically neutral formulation. Here it says that liability does not apply to "a person who has only participated in technical production or dissemination of the utterance" (Compensatory Damages Act § 3-6, subsection 2). The same rules apply to libellous statements (Compensatory Damages Act § 3-6a, subsection 3). The Media Liability Committee suggested that the Criminal Code should be given the same wording.[85] However, so far this suggestion has not been followed up either.

In recent years, Norway has also implemented supplementary rules for certain groups of technical personnel through the E-Commerce Act.[86] The rules in this law are particularly geared towards electronic publication.

Summary

In the previous pages, it has been shown that Norwegians are very active users of media, including online media, and that freedom of expression has a strong position in the Norwegian Constitution after the revisions of 2004. Even so, Norway has been found guilty by the ECtHR in several cases involving freedom of expression, especially in the field of defamation. These judgments from the ECtHR have had an important influence on Norwegian legal practice.

It has also been pointed out that there are non-judicial arrangements in Norway for online publishing that are well-functioning and can relieve the legal system. The service called slettmeg.no ("deleteme.no") in particular has been a great success. The service has gained interest from other countries as well, for example, Sweden.

When it comes to the legal regulations, it has been shown that a number of provisions can be found in Norwegian law that set limits for what kinds of content can be published in online media and regulate the placing of liability when these limits have been transgressed.

By way of introduction to this article, it was mentioned that one question would be given particular attention in the description of these regulations: whether the rules that apply to the so-called traditional media, namely print newspapers, radio and TV, also apply to the new online media. After what has been said above, one should generally be able to answer this question in the affirmative. The Norwegian Constitution is based on the principle of technological neutrality, and most of the provisions that limit the freedom of expression are technologically neutral. Several provisions that used to be technologically specific have recently been made technologically neutral. However, technologically specific concerns are not irrelevant when it comes to these provisions. Technological concerns can

---

85 Ibid., p. 103.
86 Act of 23 May 2003, translation not found.

be given weight in the balancing exercise that these provisions demand. In light of the case law of the ECtHR, this seems to be a good practice.

However, examples of provisions that apply to traditional media, but not to online publishing, can still be found. The criminal editorial liability provision is an important example of this. It is a point of active discussion today whether these provisions should also be made technologically neutral.

The article has also shown that there are several special rules for journalistic publication activities in Norway. Furthermore, whether the utterances are part of a journalistic publication is taken into account in the balancing exercise when the courts apply the general rules. Whether the publication in question may be qualified as a form of journalism or not depends on the nature of the publication activity.

10 Internet, freedom of expression and the right to privacy in Sweden

Victoria Enkvist and Sverker Scheutz

Media climate in Sweden

In Sweden, approximately 95% of the population has access to the internet and about 80% have smart phones. Even though traditional media such as TV, radio, books and newspapers are still the most popular media form, they are now being consumed on the internet and not through traditional fora. This development can be called a media convergence.[1]

The agency for press, radio and TV, the Swedish Press and Broadcasting Authority, has investigated the development in media in Sweden. The investigation shows that in 1997 Swedes spent approximately 340 minutes daily on consuming media. This is the exact same amount of time as today. During these years, a new category of media called social media emerged. The use of traditional media platforms such as TV, radio and newspapers declined due to the internet. Today, social media takes 46 minutes of the 340 minutes that previously were spent on traditional media. The remaining time is focused on traditional internet media and video clips.[2] The average Swede still devotes 77 minutes to traditional media. Even though the media landscape has changed radically and new mobile and digital technologies have emerged, media habits still change relatively slowly.[3]

There are approximately 160 newspapers in Sweden. Many of them can be found on the internet and some of them only exist on the internet. Even though a few actors own a disproportionate number of the newspapers, there is still market competition.

Today the radio and TV market is relatively free and the possibilities to broadcast on the internet have eliminated most of the barriers that applied to broadcasting before the internet revolution.

Public broadcasting services are funded by fees, and other forms of radio and TV are settled by advertising and funding from the users.

---

1 SOU 2016:58, Ändrade mediegrundlagar, pp. 177–179 et passim.
2 For example, YouTube.
3 *Medieutveckling 2017 – Mediekonsumtion*, Myndigheten för press, radio och tv, p. 4. Also see www.mprt.se

Background

In Sweden, there is a long tradition of constitutional protection of freedom of expression. The constitutional law regarding freedom of expression can be traced as far back as 1766. These traditions are based on a combination of enlightenment ideas concerning free speech and a free political environment. During the 18th century, the Parliament had political power in Sweden for the first time, and new ideas about freedom of speech flourished in the new climate.[4]

The principles of freedom of the press and the right to free access to public documents were first established in the fundamental law from 1766 (the Press Act). The above-mentioned rights and principles where strengthened in 1809 and 1812, when two fundamental laws in addition to the Press Act were adopted: the Instrument of Government (IoG) and the Freedom of the Press Act (the Press Act).[5] The latter contains regulations about the right to express oneself in magazines, newspapers, books, fliers, etc. Both of these fundamental laws protected freedom of speech and expression, though the latter specifically concerned printed matters.

An additional Fundamental Law on Freedom of Expression was enacted in 1991. The legislation from 1991 protects expressions made in modern media, such as, for example, radio, TV, film and video.[6] Through the establishment of the Fundamental Law on Freedom of Expression, some new forms of media became protected.

Freedom of expression in the Constitution – a general and a special protection

As mentioned in the introduction, we have no less than three fundamental laws that protect freedom of speech in Sweden. The protection of freedom of expression in the IoG is called the general protection in this text. The Press Act and the Fundamental Law on Freedom of Expression stipulate special protection. The extent of the general and the special protection will be elaborated further in the following chapter.

One feature of the special protection in the Press Act and the Fundamental Law on Freedom of Expression is that the laws protect certain kinds of forums rather than specific expressions. The protection is related to the forum, not to the content. This is in order to avoid a demarcation problem, such as what kind of expression should be protected and which should not.

---

4 Axberger, H-G, Yttrandefrihetsgrundlagarna, 3 uppl., Wolters Kluwer, Stockholm, pp. 17–28.
5 The IoG was adopted in 1809 and the Press Act in 1812. Axberger, H-G, Constitutional Responsibility for the free flow of Information and Ideas in the Internet Age in *Information and Law in Transition: Freedom of Speech, the Internet, Privacy and Democracy in the 21st Century*, Lind, A-S, Reichel, J & Österdahl, I (eds.), 1. ed., Liber, Stockholm, 2015, p. 43.
6 Axberger (see note 4), pp. 25–28.

The relationship between the three fundamental laws is not always easy to understand, and there are no clear definitions of what situations fall within the IoG, the Press Act and the Fundamental Law on Freedom of Expression. The basic idea is that certain kinds of public expression shall be more protected than the protection given in the IoG. The important feature is the *form* of the expression and whether the expression is public.

One of the most difficult questions to answer is what kind of expressions are protected by the IoG and where is the line drawn for expressions that are protected by the Press Act or the Fundamental Law on Freedom of Expression. To some extent, the courts and the Chancellor of Justice have clarified this through case law.

The fact that the forum of the expression decides which law is implicated can result in situations that are similar to each other, however, the legal outcome can differ due to the form of the expression. For example, expressions that are performed at a theatre performance or at an art exhibit between individuals or in a smaller gathering are protected by the IoG. The same legislation protects expressions that are made in public meetings that are not broadcasted on radio or TV.[7] If the same expressions are made on TV, they are most likely protected by the Press Act or the Fundamental Law on Freedom of Expression.

Expressions that are made during public meetings are also protected by the right to freedom of assembly in the IoG. Freedom of religion is another human right that can be implicated simultaneously to freedom of expression. This can create some problems when it comes to the possibilities to limit the manifestation of the specific freedom.

As a consequence, in such cases the conditions for limiting both freedom of expression and freedom of assembly or freedom of religion must be met in order to be a lawful limitation.[8] Freedom of religion, in chapter 2 article 1 p. 6, is an absolute right that cannot be restricted according to the chapter 2 article 20 *e contrario*.

The scope of the general protection

Much can be said about the scope of freedom of expression in Swedish legislation, but we can establish that the right can be understood as a right to convey messages to other people in different ways without the interference of the state. This can be illustrated in the following way:

The case law surrounding the article about freedom of expression is of great importance because the constructions of the regulations are quite wide and possible to interpret in different ways.

---

7 See Nergelius J, Svensk statsrätt, 3 uppl., Studentlitteratur, Lund, 2014, p. 133.
8 Ibid., p. 134.

Freedom of expression

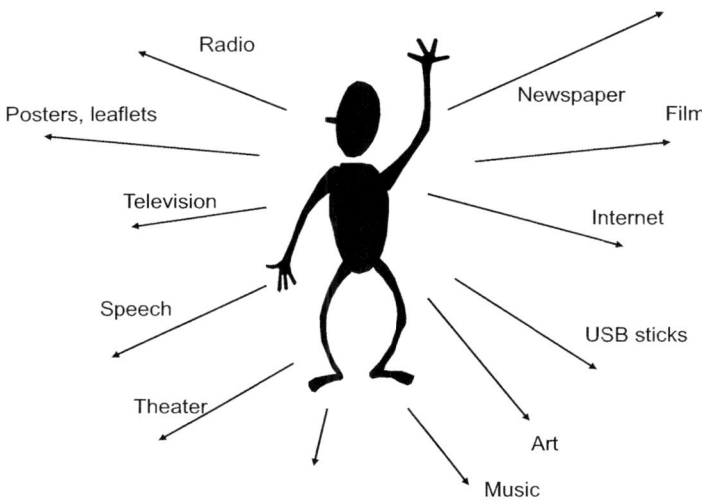

In Swedish law, there is a difference, both in theory and in practice, between freedom of expression and freedom of information. Freedom of expression can be seen as a way to express, relay or broadcast different kinds of messages.

Freedom of information in the IoG can be seen as the right to receive these messages and to collect information. Freedom of information can be illustrated in the following way:

Freedom of information

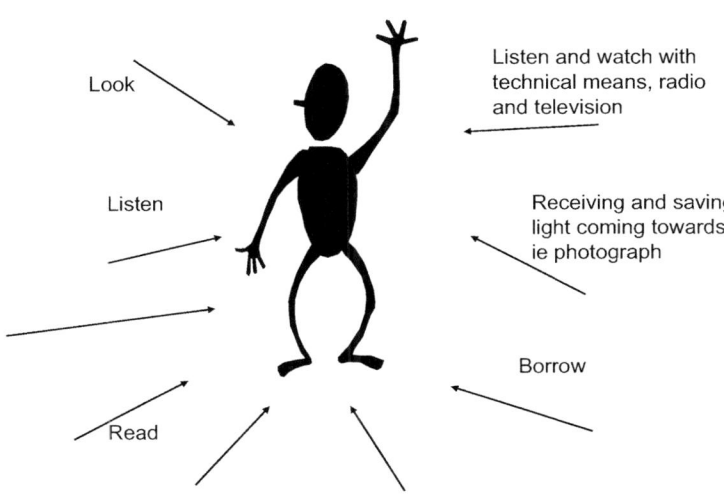

This distinction is not made in, for example, the European Convention on Human Rights (ECHR), where both freedom of speech and the right to gain information are protected in article 10.

The scope and limitations of the freedom of expression in national constitutional doctrine

As mentioned earlier, the protection of freedom of expression can be found in three different constitutional laws in Sweden, which indicates its importance.

The Press Act and the Fundamental Law on Freedom of Expression constitutes the special protection that will be explained further in this text. In the following passage, we will present the so-called general protection.

In some situations, it is hard to draw a definitive line between freedom of expression and freedom of information. The following discussion will not focus on this distinction, but it is interesting that this distinction is made in the Swedish system.

This text is mainly focused on freedom of expression and limitations to freedom of expression. The scope of freedom of speech in chapter 2 article 1 in the IoG is partly limited in the way the right is formulated and partly by ordinary legislation. The right is formulated in the following way:

> Everyone shall be guaranteed the following rights and freedoms in his or her relations with the public institutions; the freedom of expression: that is, the freedom to communicate information and express thoughts, opinions and sentiments, whether orally, pictorially, in writing, or in any other way.

As can be seen, freedom of expression is broadly formulated and can be interpreted in several ways. The broad formulation can be explained by the fact that when the chapter on human rights in the IoG was enacted, it was a compromise between the political parties in Sweden that had different opinions on the significance of human rights and what role rights should have in the parliamentary system.

The wide formulation has resulted in an extensive case law that cannot be presented in this text, but the general idea is that freedom of expression is fundamental for Swedish society and limitations to the right should be made cautiously.

Conditions for limiting freedom of expression in the IoG

Most of the rights that are protected in chapter 2 article 1 of the IoG are relative rights, which mean that they can be restricted. When the Swedish Parliament enacts ordinary legislation that sets limits to, for example, freedom of speech, it must follow a certain procedure. The conditions that the Assembly must follow can be found in chapter 2 articles 20–24 of the IoG.

In chapter 2 article 20, it is stated that to the extent provided for in articles 21 to 24, the following rights and freedoms may be limited in law: 1. freedom of expression, freedom of information, freedom of assembly, freedom to demonstrate and freedom of association (article 1, points 1 to 5). Point 6, freedom of religion can *e contrario* not be restricted.

Article 21 states the condition that limitations may be imposed only to satisfy a purpose acceptable in a democratic society. What is acceptable in a democratic society is a political decision, and the arguments concerning what is acceptable have changed over time. Another prerequisite is that a limitation must never go beyond what is necessary with regard to the purpose which occasioned it. This sentence is an expression of the proportionality principle. Nor may the limitation be carried so far as to constitute a threat to the free shaping of opinion as one of the fundaments of democracy. No limitation may be imposed solely on the grounds of a political, religious, cultural or other such opinion.

In addition to article 21, article 23 sets the conditions for limiting freedom of expression. Freedom of expression and freedom of information may be limited with regard to the security of the realm, the national supply of goods, public order and public safety, the good repute of the individual, the sanctity of private life and the prevention and prosecution of crime. Freedom of expression may also be limited in business activities. Freedom of expression and freedom of information may otherwise be limited only where particularly important grounds so warrant.

The last condition is quite broad, and the opportunities to limit the right are extensive. But the article also states that when judging what limitations may be allowed, particular attention shall be paid to the importance of the widest possible freedom of expression and freedom of information in political, religious, professional, scientific and cultural matters. The adoption of provisions which regulate in more detail a particular manner of disseminating or receiving information, without regard to its content, shall not be deemed a limitation of the freedom of expression or the freedom of information.

In other words, this means that the scope of freedom of expression in the IoG is partly determined by the rules concerning the possibilities to limit the right. The rules regarding limitations in the IoG offer strong protection to expressions that are political, religious and cultural in content, with lesser protection extended to other forms of expression, which are presumed to be subject to regulation. More specific protection of the freedom of expression can be found for the specially protected forums in the Press Act and the Fundamental Law on Freedom of Expression.

Two different pieces of legislation constitute the *general protection* of freedom of speech: the IoG and the ECHR. Sweden has had the obligation to comply with the ECHR since the beginning of 1950. In 1994, the ECHR became part of Sweden's statutory law through *lag* (1194:1219) *om den europeiska konventionen angående skydd för de mänskliga rättigheterna och grundläggande friheterna*. Effectively, all agencies in Sweden are covered by the Convention, which means that they have to apply Swedish law in a way that does not violate the ECHR. At the same time as the Convention became law, a new provision of the IoG was adopted in chapter 2 article 19. The regulation gives the ECHR a special protection in the Constitution, stating that no regulation that comes into conflict with the ECHR can be adopted in Sweden.

In a couple of judgments, the European Court of Human Rights (ECtHR) evaluated the Swedish protection of freedom of expression and its accordance with the ECHR. One famous case is Vejdeland v. Sweden.[9] The circumstances of the case involved a group of Nazis, who visited a public school in Sweden and distributed fliers with a content that constituted hate speech against homosexuals according to Swedish law.[10] The ECtHR found that, although the legislation was considered a limitation of article 10 in the ECHR, the Swedish legislation on hate speech was justified and in accordance with the ECHR. The main reason for the judgment was that the distribution of the fliers occurred at a school and it was difficult for the pupils to ignore.

The Charter of Fundamental Rights of the European Union[11] works in a similar way in situations where it is applicable.

The protection in the Press Act and the Fundamental Law on Freedom of Expression constitute the *special protection*. This protection is not related to content in the same way as protection in the general area.

The scope of the special protection

Some forms of expression have been protected for a long time in Sweden. The first Freedom of Press Act was, as already mentioned, established in 1766. In 2016, the Press Act turned 250 years old.[12] The current Press Act was founded after World War II and was developed as a response to experiences from the war era. After the War, the need for formal regulations concerning human rights was extensive. In 1949, the new constitutional Press Act was enacted. In many ways, freedom of expression regarding printed media was strengthened after the War because it was considered to be vital for a democratic society and the protection of minorities.

The protection of freedom of expression has expanded over time. For example, in 1976, the Assembly amended the law to also cover photocopied published works. But at the same time, extensive limitations have been made to the same right. One example is the widening of the hate speech legislation to protect sexual orientation.

In 1991, the Assembly adopted a new law of constitutional stature – the Fundamental Law on Freedom of Expression. This law, which remains in effect today, both protects and regulates freedom of speech in broadcasting media, databases, and even websites and "technical recordings" (USB-sticks, DVD and

---

9   Vejdeland and others v. Sweden, Application no. 1813/07, 09 May 2012.
10 Hets mot folkgrupp chapter 16 article 8 in the Criminal Code (1962:700).
11 Charter of Fundamental Rights of the European Union 2012/C 326/02
12 Introduction in *Transparency in the Future – Swedish Openness 250 Years*, Lind, A-S, Reichel, J & Österdahl, I (eds.), 1 ed., Tallin, Ragulka Press, 2017, p. 9.

CD). Everyone has the right to broadcast programmes through wire transmissions. The right to written publications and technical recordings is also a part of the special protection.

Personal or private websites on the internet, even those not controlled by mass media companies, are presumptively entitled to receive potential protection by the Fundamental Law on Freedom of Expression in some circumstances.[13] This legislation is the most important legislation when it comes to new media. Even though it covers several different forums, it can be criticised as obsolete.

As mentioned before, the Press Act and the Fundamental Law on Freedom of Expression together establish a special protection of freedom of expression in Sweden. The relation between the general and the special protection of freedom of speech can be illustrated as follows:

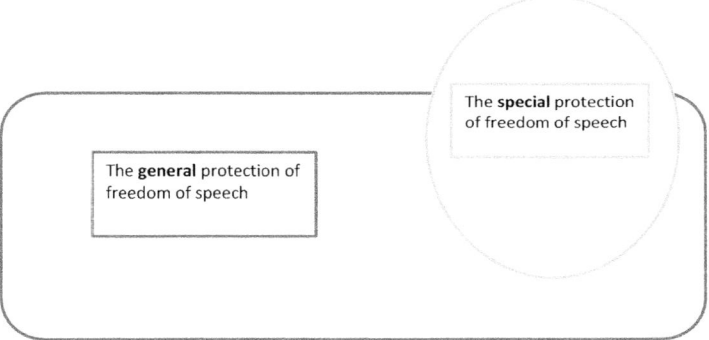

In the area of the special protection, certain concrete protections of both freedom of expression and freedom of information can be found. The Fundamental Law on Freedom of Expression, for example, contains a protection for freedom of information by recognising the right in the context of several media formats, *inter alia*, by recognising that everyone has the right to possess radio sets, televisions and apparatus used for databases and homepages. In the current Constitutional Press Act, five principles remain from the ordinary legislation concerning the free press from 1766. These principles are considered to be important principles for freedom of expression, and they are: the prohibition against censorship, the principle of legality or rule of law, the principle of exclusivity, the chain of responsibility and, last but not least, the rule that decisions must be made by courts.[14]

---

13 Warnling-Nerep, W, Bernitz, H, *En orientering i tryckfrihet och yttrandefrihet*, 5., [rev.] uppl., Jure, Stockholm, 2013, p. 102.

14 Hirschfelt, J, Free Access to Public Documents – a heritage from 1766 in *Transparency in the Future – Swedish Openness 250 Years*, Lind, A-S, Reichel, J & Österdahl, I (eds.), Tallin, Ragulka Press, 2017, p. 24.

Prohibition against censorship

Both the Press Act and the Fundamental Law on Freedom of Expression contain prohibitions against censorship. Both also set forth unconditional rights to produce publications, programmes and technical recordings. The content in the above-mentioned publications can only be punishable if the content is criminalised in either the Press Act or in the Fundamental Law on Freedom of Expression.

The Press Act and the Fundamental Law on Freedom of Expression also include a prohibition against censorship prior to publication. Restrictive measures can only be taken after the content has already been distributed. Thus, a publication punishable due to its content cannot become illegal until it is distributed. This prohibition is crucial for the transparency of state affairs.

The right to anonymity when using the right to convey messages to the press is another general principal and rule in the special protection. Related to this rule is the prohibition for the public sector to investigate who submitted information. Nor can the person who has submitted information be punished in any way.

Responsibility of presumed intent and liability for damages

A feature of the special protection is the individual responsibility regarding the content of the publication, application, database or recording. For books, it is normally the author alone (and not publishers, printers, spreaders, etc.) who has criminal liability. The civil liability for damages is assigned by the publisher. For newspapers and other mass media, it is typically the publisher who has criminal liability. In some cases, liability is shared with the owner of the media.

A jury system and the instruction

Another feature in the special protection of the freedom of expression in the Press Act is the special trial procedure. Briefly, the Chancellor of Justice is sole prosecutor, and the process takes place in two steps. The first step is a jury trial. If the jury acquits the defendant, a criminal conviction cannot be pronounced. If the jury finds the defendant guilty, the case continues in an ordinary court. The ordinary court is not bound by the jury's conviction.

In the Press Act and the Fundamental Law on Freedom of Expression, you can find the so-called instruction. This is another feature of the special protection. It is addressed to those who decide cases concerning freedom of speech when the Press Act and the Fundamental Law on Freedom of Expression are applied. The instruction can be found in chapter 1 article 5 of the Fundamental Law on Expression and in chapter 1 article 4 of the Press Act. The instruction expresses that in cases concerning freedom of speech the Court shall give the benefit of the doubt.

The rules that here have been called special protection have a special position in the Swedish legislation because the legislator considers them to be fundamental for a democratic society.

Exemptions in the special protection

In both the Fundamental Law on Freedom of Expression and the Press Act, it is stated that certain criminal activities are excluded from protection. These expressions fall within the general protection in the IoG. According to the IoG, it is possible to limit certain kinds of expression through legislation that the Assembly adopts. Child pornography, which is criminally punishable, is one example. Other regulated activities permit restrictions on the content and use, particularly, of copyrighted materials, alcohol and tobacco advertisements, credit information and certain advertisements that concern health and the environment.

It is an undisputed fact that freedom of speech and freedom of expression are rights with great fundamental value in Sweden. Even so, the rights can be restricted in order to uphold other rights and freedoms. The Press Act and the ECHR can in some cases come into conflict. In these cases, the Press Act has higher judicial value because it is a fundamental law. The consequence in these cases is that Sweden does not fulfil the obligations set out in the ECHR. One example in which such a situation can arise is when the protection for privacy in article 8 collides with the rights in the Press Act.

Freedom of expression – a cornerstone in Swedish society

In the IoG, freedom of expression, freedom of assembly, freedom of information, freedom of meeting, freedom of demonstration and freedom of religion are regulated in chapter 2 article 1. These freedoms are all considered important for an open democratic society and the formation of opinion. The most important is freedom of expression.

The Press Act and the Fundamental Law on Freedom of Expression are unique as fundamental laws in that they are detailed and include both procedural and criminal regulations.[15]

The special protection for freedom of expression covers a wide range of situations and subjects – for example, journalists' sources are protected. Providers of information and journalists have a right to be anonymous. Those who provide information cannot be punished if the aim of the broadcasted information is publication. Of course, there are some limitations; these are found in special legislation concerning confidentiality, the *Sekretesslagen*, OSL (2009:400).

The right to access public documents

A special feature in the Swedish regulation is the right to access public documents. In 1766, the principle of free access to public documents was introduced

---

15 For a more elaborated discussion about these rules, see Lind, A-S, Freedom of the Press Act – from then to now in *Transparency in the Future*, ibid., p. 53 et passim.

to Sweden in the first law on freedom of press. This law was an ordinary law and not a constitutional law. In 1809, the right to access public documents became constitutionally protected so the right of citizens to have access to public documents has a long tradition in Swedish society.[16] The right to access public documents can also be seen as a part of the freedom of information within the same act, see chapter 2 of the Press Act. All actions of authorities must be transparent, and anyone who wants to read the authorities´ official documents has the right to do so. The principle of public access is a cornerstone of Swedish society, and limitations to this right are only allowed in certain circumstances.[17] Confidentiality rules exist to protect private and public interests. For example, there is confidentiality concerning international cooperation, the protection of the state, preliminary investigations by the police, information concerning individuals within health care, social services and education.

This construction of freedom of expression and freedom of information is unique to Sweden. Due to Sweden's membership in the European Union, the principle of transparency has influenced the system in the European Union and made it more transparent.

Limitations in freedom of expression

One method of limiting rights is to interpret the right narrowly. Formally speaking, printed text is generally protected by the Press Act, but exemptions can be found in the legislation for certain kinds of expressions that fall outside of the area that the legislator wants to protect, for example, falsifications that are made in a press. It cannot be excluded that similar exemptions will be made in the future regarding the general protected sphere of speech, as well as the expressions protected by the Fundamental Law on Freedom of Expression.

"Non-limitations" as limitations

As already mentioned, there are several ways to limit freedoms. Some of them are only mentioned briefly in this text, while others will be discussed in more detail. One limitation that has been actualised and discussed is the protection of personal integrity. Due to the strong protection for freedom of expression and the unwillingness to limit freedom of expression, the protection of personal integrity has been weak in Sweden until recently. Protection of integrity postulates limitations in freedom of expression, which means that it is possible that a conflict arises between two rights. In the following passage, we will focus on the protection of personal integrity and the limitations to freedom of expression that have been made in order to uphold the protection of personal integrity.

16 Hirschfeldt, J, Free Access to public documents – a heritage from 1766 in *Transparency in the Future*, ibid., p. 21.
17 SOU 2016:41, Hur står det till med den personliga integriteten, p. 128.

Limitations in freedom of expression of importance for the right to personal integrity

In this text, only limitations to freedom of expression that are connected to personal integrity will be presented.

It is not an easy task to briefly summarise and explain the judicial term "personal integrity". It is not possible to give a short or clear cut answer to what is included in personal privacy. It is often described as the individual being surrounded by a sphere that is worthy of protection in various ways. In the investigation "*Hur står det till med den personliga integriteten*" it is said that:

> It is difficult to define such a concept with a clearer delimitation than what normally appears urgent when it comes to protecting the private subject, who shall be ensured a private and preserved zone.[18]

It is possible to say that all penal regulations that protect private subjects are part of the protection of personal integrity.[19] Even though these definitions of personal integrity aren't clear, they fit the purpose of this text.

In 2010, the Assembly amended the IoG to encompass a general protection regarding personal integrity in chapter 2 article 6 paragraph 2. The aim was to strengthen the protection of personal integrity from public interferences. As with other rights in the IoG, the regulation is a relative right, which means that the Assembly can limit it according to the prerequisites in 2:20–25§§.

Moreover, the construction of the text in 2:6 of the IoG is vague, and the interpretation has been criticised for being weak, so the right is not generally considered to provide particularly strong protection.[20]

> Art. 6. [...] everyone shall be protected in their relations with the public institutions against significant invasions of their personal privacy, if these occur without their consent and involve the surveillance or systematic monitoring of the individual's personal circumstances.

General area

Within the area for the general protection of freedom of expression, there are several crimes in the Criminal Code that are related to and aim at protecting personal integrity. Defamation, insult, hate speech, threats and sexual harassment are examples of such crimes. Some expressions can be prohibited without being criminally punishable or subject to public prosecution. An injured party, in some

---

18 SOU 2016:41, Hur står det till med den personliga integriteten, p. 147 (authors' translation).
19 SOU 2016:7, Integritet och straffskydd, chapter 3.
20 Holmberg, E, m fl, Grundlagarna: regeringsformen, successionsordningen, riksdagsordningen, 3., [rev.] uppl., Norstedts juridik, Stockholm, 2012, pp. 115–117.

cases, can sue for compensation of damages. Examples of such legislation are those that provide for protections of privacy or integrity in general, as well as through specific legislation, such as anti-discrimination law and education law. All of these prohibitions effectively narrow the scope of the general sphere of protection of freedom of speech.

The limitations mentioned above are important parts of the protection of the right to personal integrity. One regulation of importance is article 8 in the ECHR.

These sources of law each protect the freedom of expression, freedom of speech and the right to personal integrity, although in different ways. It is not yet clear how a conflict between the other rights in the Charter or the ECHR can be resolved, respecting both the general and special spheres of protection.

Today Swedish fundamental law trumps the ECHR, but the future will tell how other conflicts are solved. If Sweden interprets the IoG in a way that does not protect freedom of expression, the interpretation violates the ECHR. Sweden has no authority over the ECHR or how the ECtHR enforces the rights in the Convention. And because the margin of appreciation regarding free speech is narrow, the ECtHR and its rulings regarding free speech become even more important. When Swedish constitutional law is in conflict with the ECHR, the Swedish provisions will be applied. Of course, this opens up Sweden to liability under international law, and maybe Sweden will be forced to pay damages fines if the ECHtR finds it in violation of human rights.

The most obvious protection of privacy in Swedish legislation can be found in *Personuppgiftslagen* (PUL) (1999:1229). It was enacted in the 1990s in order to incorporate an EU directive on data protection.[21]

The PUL stipulates that all systematic treatment of personal data must be permitted. The aim of the Directive is to protect the privacy of the individual.

A proposal for new legislation has been made, which implies that the distribution of offensive pictures or other information about a person's sex life, health, nude pictures and the violation of integrity is a criminal offence.[22]

Special area

Within the special protected area, only a few limitations to freedom of expression exist. These specific limitations are stipulated in the Press Act and in the Fundamental Law on Freedom of Expression. The catalogue of crimes in both pieces of legislation contains, amongst others, slander, defamation and hate speech. The crimes enumerated in the Press Act and the Fundamental Law on Freedom of Expression must be regulated in the fundamental laws and the Criminal Code.[23]

---

21 Directive 95/46/EC of the European Parliament and of the Council of 24 October 1995 on the protection of individuals with regard to the processing of personal data and on the free movement of such data.
22 Proposition 2016/2017:222.
23 Axberger (see note 4), p. 99.

Compared to the general protection area in the IoG, for example, sexual harassment cannot be found in the special protection area in the Press Act and the Fundamental Law on Freedom of Expression. Nor are there prohibitions that are sanctioned solely with damages within the special protection area.[24]

It is not possible to apply the PUL when the Press Act or the Fundamental Law of Freedom of Expression is applicable. This is a consequence of the so-called principle of exclusivity, which means that when the Press Act or the Fundamental Law of Freedom of Expression is applicable, no other legislation can be used.

The practical possibilities to use the PUL are rather narrow because of article 7. In the article, it is stated that exemptions from the PUL can be made if the aim of the data is journalistic, artistic or literary. One case that shows the PUL's limited scope is NJA 2001 s. 409, which indicates that the PUL cannot be used to protect integrity if the aim of the expression is to inform, criticise or initiate a debate.[25]

Another landmark case is the so-called Google case from the European Court of Justice. This case clarified that individuals can demand that private actors such as Google erase the personal data of the users in order to protect freedom of integrity. On the other hand, this case limits freedom of information.[26]

One case that has influenced the Swedish legislation concerning protection is Söderman v. Sweden.[27] The circumstances of the case involved a stepfather, who tried to take nude photos of his 15 year old stepdaughter in the bathroom. Because of the fact that Sweden didn't have any regulations that prohibited him from taking the photos, he was acquitted. Sweden adopted new legislation after the case was tried in the ECtHR. Today it is illegal to photograph in secret in houses and in spaces like bathrooms, toilets and locker rooms.[28] After the ruling from the ECtHR, Sweden changed the Criminal Code so it became compatible with the protection for integrity in article 8 of the ECHR.

Something about freedom of expression for the media

As mentioned earlier, the media is regulated either through the Press Act or the Fundamental Law on Freedom of Expression, depending on the type of media. These two laws together constitute the special protection. The special protection includes a detailed protection for press, radio, TV and internet based media. For public service radio and TV, there are special rules and regulations that require objectivity.

---

24 This can be seen in chapter 1 article 3 in the Press Act and in chapter 1 article 5 in the Fundamental Law on Freedom of Expression.
25 For further comments on the case, see Axberger (see note 4), p. 128.
26 C-131/12 Google Spain SL and others v. Agencia Española de Protección de Datos, CJEU judgment of 13 May 2014.
27 Söderman v. Sweden, Application no. 5786/08, 12 November 2013.
28 Penal Code chapter 4 article 6a § (Brottsbalken).

Permission is not required to own, create or distribute mass media. Ground based Swedish radio or TV broadcasts require permission mostly due to the fact that the frequencies must be shared.

Mass media is also covered by a voluntary regulation that first and foremost aims to protect individuals against publications that infringe upon personal integrity. The mass media that participate in this system, which is the majority, have accepted the press ethics rules and agree to a ruling system where those who break the rules and are found "guilty" must pay a fee to the association that upholds this protection.

Those who want to publish blogs on the internet without being covered by the regulations concerning mass media can get protection through the special protection of freedom of speech if certain conditions are fulfilled. One condition is that it has to be a specific person that is responsible for the blog or website. That person has sole responsibility for the content on the website. No one else shall have the right to change, erase or add information, as outlined in chapter 1 article 9 of the Fundamental Law on Freedom of Expression.

As mentioned before, it is difficult to draw a line between which expressions are protected by the fundamental laws and which fall outside the protected sphere. Publications on the internet have been considered to fall outside the scope of the special protection. There are, however, two exemptions from this general principle and they concern live broadcasting on the internet, handled in chapter 1 article 6 of the Fundamental Law on Freedom of Expression. The other article of interest is one that regulates the content on websites – chapter 1 article 9 of the Fundamental Law on Freedom of Expression.

The scope of chapter 1 article 9 of the Fundamental Law on Freedom of Expression is quite comprehensive and due to the increasing use of social media includes stipulations for broadcasting live. Everyone who broadcasts live on, for example, Facebook is protected by the fundamental law. This was probably not the intent of the legislator.[29] Case B 4377-17[30] concerned a rape that was filmed and broadcasted live on Facebook. The Court found that the prosecuted was guilty of slander. Surprisingly, there was an ordinary trial in this case. In similar cases, there is normally a special trial order with the Chancellor of Justice as prosecutor and a jury.

Another law that concerns publications on the internet is the Lag om ansvar för elektroniska anslagstavlor (1998:112). This law contains rules about the responsibility for electronic noticeboards. It mainly concerns those situations that are not covered by the special protection for freedom of expression. The legislation obliges the liable person to monitor their website regularly and erase certain kinds of comments.

In Sweden, there is no special legislation concerning children and mass media. There are, however, laws that prohibit the circulation of certain kinds of content to children, among them pornography and violent depictions.

---

29 For a thorough discussion about this, see Ruotsi, M, *Webbsidor, hemsidor och oönskat grundlagsskydd* I SvJT, pp. 673–683, 2017.
30 Judgement B 4377-17 from Svea Hovrätt the 28th of June 2017.

The most important agency formally involved with guarding freedom of speech within the special protected area is the Chancellor of Justice (JK). It is possible for JK to launch a preliminary investigation and indictment for crimes violating the Press Act and the Fundamental Law on Freedom of Expression. A special feature in such a process is that it is a trial with a jury.

Along with JK and the court, the organisation of the voluntary ethical protection of mass media has had a big influence.

The general rules for crimes against freedom of expression can be found in the Press Act and in the Fundamental Law on Freedom of Expression. As is stated in the Fundamental Law on Freedom of Expression, it is possible to enact further laws concerning radio and TV. This has been done, the result of which is called the Radio and Television Act.[31]

The programmes on TV and radio must follow the principles of a democratic society and the principle that all people are equal. The programmes must also take into account that all individuals are free and possess human dignity. This means that the programmes and broadcasts cannot be anti-democratic. The broadcasting company has to take into account that TV and radio has a great impact and must ensure that the privacy of individuals is respected.

The Chancellor of Justice supervises the observance of the rules of the press that are stated in the Press Act, the Fundamental Law on Freedom of Expression and the rules in the Radio and Television Act concerning violence and pornography.

The remaining rules in the Radio and Television Act are supervised by the *Granskningsnämnden* for radio and TV. The board controls programmes in hindsight, and if the board decides that the content of a programme is in conflict with the legislation, the broadcasting company can be fined. The broadcasting company can also lose its broadcasting license.[32]

Sanctions in criminal law

As mentioned above, it is possible to be punished for several crimes both within the special and general protection areas. The general area contains more criminal sanctions than the special area. All crimes within the special area can be found within the general area, while certain types of expression are solely criminal if the expression falls outside the special protection area.

Criminal expressions can often be sanctioned according to regulations concerning damages.

Another piece of legislation worth mentioning in this context is the law on electronic noticeboards, which stipulates that the individual who is responsible for a website is obliged to monitor the website and remove criminal expressions.[33]

The regulation assigns personal liability to a designated individual. The responsibility is an artificial one-man responsibility that builds upon presumed

31 Radio- och tv-lag (2010:696) kap 4 och 16.
32 Axberger (see note 4), p. 152 ff.
33 Warnling-Nerep, Bernitz (see note 12), p. 133.

intent. Authors of books or the publishing company, the responsible editors for press, radio, TV and other technical recordings have sole responsibility in a strict chain of command.

Criminal liability is only an option if the crime is enumerated in both the fundamental law and the Criminal Code. The most important crimes are defamation, hate speech and crimes against the security of the state.

One "new" technology is the internet, which is sometimes described as a new arena for threats and different forms of harassment. The rise of different forms of online attacks on personal integrity and privacy represents a significant risk to the privacy of an individual and is a growing problem in Sweden and elsewhere around the world. This phenomenon is called internet hate.[34]

It is more common for women to face harassment online than men. In the long run, this can lead to self-censorship and limitations on the freedom of expression.[35] Internet hate can also be carried out by organisations, for example, against journalists in attempts to force journalistic scrutiny to stop.[36]

In cases when attacks are carried out, sometimes two constitutional and human rights may come into conflict, namely the right to freedom of speech and the right to personal integrity. Those who "attack" the personal integrity of others may be exercising (or abusing) their freedom of speech, while those who feel that they are under attack are in some cases protected by regulations concerning personal integrity. The latter protections are often constructed as limitations to freedom of speech and freedom of information.[37]

To sum up, one can say that general rules regarding the right to integrity and privacy can be found in the ECHR, the EU Charter and the IoG.

The ECHR is a law in Sweden (adopted by the Assembly), but it has a unique status because the ECHR is protected in the IoG chapter 2 article 19, which states that no regulations can be adopted by the Assembly if they come into conflict with the rights and freedoms in the ECHR.

When it comes to the special protection area of freedom of speech, it is evident that in this area there are less limitations of freedom of speech than in the general protection area. For example, the privacy protection law is not applicable in the special protection area. It is important to remember though that the mass media has created a system on a voluntary basis with fees as a penalty when "breaches" against the system occur.

Conclusion and summary

In sum, in Sweden personal integrity online is protected by:

- The general protection (ECHR and the Charter)
- The IoG chapter 2 article 6 para 2

---

34 SOU 2016:41, Hur står det till med den personliga integriteten, p. 127.
35 See SOU 2016:7 and SOU 2016:41, Hur står det till med den personliga integriteten, p. 127.
36 SOU 2016:41, Hur står det till med den personliga integriteten, p. 127.
37 The conflict is analysed in SOU 2016:7, Integritet och Straffskydd, chapter 4.

- The ECHR as law in Sweden
- Criminal limitations of freedom of speech
- Limitations of freedom of speech made in private law.

One possibility is to extend this regulation in a way that is suggested in SOU 2016:7. The report suggests that a new crime called an unlawful integrity breach should be adopted in the penal law.[38]

The Personal Data Act (1998:204) is the Swedish implementation of Directive 95/46/EG.[39] The Personal Data Act exempts expressions that are protected by the special protection area. This exemption has been used as an "opportunity" to spread information about individuals' financial situations, addresses and so on. The fact that the Personal Data Act cannot be applied to mass media and databases with a publication license means that, for example, Lexbase.se can publish all penal sentences in Sweden. Another example of a database to which the rules of the Personal Data Act cannot be applied is Birthday.se. This database publishes the Swedish civil register on the internet. There are databases that contain information about incomes, debts and so on. One suggestion that could raise the protection for integrity on the internet is to apply the Personal Data Act to all databases with the exception of databases controlled by mass media corporations.

The development of the internet has dramatically changed the media landscape in the world and, of course, also in Sweden. According to the Swedish legislation, it is the form of the message that decides which of the fundamental laws, if any, is applicable. One consequence of this technical development, as with others, is that none of the above-mentioned laws can be applied in situations concerning new technologies.[40]

In Sweden, it is the forum not the content that is protected. One benefit of such an approach is that the protection of freedom of expression is quite strong in Sweden.

In article 86 of the constitutional laws regarding free press from 1809, it was stipulated that

> The freedom of the press is understood to mean the right of every Swedish citizen to publish written matter without any of the public power pre-laid obstacles and not to be prosecuted thereafter on grounds of its content than before a lawful court or punished therefore other than because the content contravenes an express provision of law, enacted to preserve public order without suppressing information to the public.

This quote still illuminates the core meaning behind the main principles of freedom of expression and especially the scope of freedom of press in Sweden. The

38 SOU 2016:7, pp. 22–24 and chapter 10.
39 Directive 95/46/EC of the European Parliament and of the Council of 24 October 1995 on the protection of individuals with regard to the processing of personal data and on the free movement of such data.
40 Lind, Reichel, & Österdahl (see note 5), p. 13.

quote concludes the principles that we have discussed in our text, and they are considered necessary for a free debate and a free society.

A special feature in the Swedish protection of freedom of expression is the detailed protection in the Press Act and the Fundamental Law of Freedom of Expression. In Sweden, the protection of freedom of expression is quite extensive if the expression is made in a forum that is protected in one of the fundamental laws. The protection of certain kinds of forums is different from the forums that are not covered by the Press Act and the Fundamental Law of Freedom of Expression.

A third special feature concerning freedom of expression in Sweden is the openness that applies to the public authorities in Sweden. The principle of public access to official records is a very important principle in Swedish society and it benefits the free word and an open debate. On the other hand, it does not benefit freedom of integrity, but it gives the representatives of the media a huge amount of material when they review the authorities.

When it comes to the protection of personal integrity, Sweden has relatively weak protection. One explanation is the strong protection of freedom of expression. There is an existing protection for personal integrity but it is not comprehensive. At the moment, some suggestions have been made to increase the general protection of personal integrity within the sphere of the general protection of freedom of expression in Swedish legislation.

Balancing freedom of expression and the right to privacy is a delicate matter, however, it is necessary in today's society with its rapid media development and the increasing use of social media. The questions that remain to be answered include whether freedom of expression should be limited and, if so, what kind of limitations are legitimate? What kind of material is considered to be dangerous and offensive? The right to privacy is on one side of the scale, and on the other side of the scale lies the freedom of expression. Although we need to consider the privacy of individuals, we have to remember that "Even in Sweden, freedom of expression is a rather recent phenomenon, and you can never take it for granted. It is a fragile phenomenon, most vulnerable when most needed".[41]

---

41 Kumlien, M, Transparency, tradition och transfer in Lind, Reichel, & Österdahl (see note 5), p. 13.

11 Comparative analysis of the Nordic/Baltic approaches and standards

Mart Susi and Eiríkur Jónsson

Introduction

In this article, a broad comparative overview will be given of the approaches and standards in the Nordic and Baltic region with regard to human rights law and regulating freedom of expression in new media.

The coverage, which is built on the country articles in chapters 3 to 10 of this collection, is divided into four parts. First, a brief general overview will be given of the media environment in the region. Second, an introduction will be given to the freedom of expression doctrines in the region. Third, the influence of supranational human rights instruments will be covered. Finally, media law in the region will be discussed. That includes an overview of how new media is regulated in the region and of liability issues. It is beyond debate that the principle of horizontal governance on the internet and obligation of online portals to safeguard human rights in user-generated content is a novel principle in the global human rights landscape.

Media environment in the region

The media environment in the region is influenced by the fact that most of the countries are small in terms of inhabitants but, nevertheless, have their own language. This means that each country has its own media market, which is rather small. In the Baltic countries, the markets are even smaller due to different ethnicities and languages. For example, in Latvia the Latvian-speaking audience is around 60% of the population and the Russian-speaking audience is around 40% of the population, and these two groups demand different media products. Another feature of the media environment, which probably follows to some extent from the small market size, seems to be rather big and strong public broadcasting companies, at least in the Nordic countries.

Despite its small size, the media environment in the region can be seen as rather diverse and multiform. The media market in each country thus generally includes television and radio stations, some generally run by a public broadcasting company and some by private companies, newspapers, magazines and, to an ever-increasing extent, online media. The region enjoys a highly powerful and diverse media market, highlighted by the fact that there are between 220 and 230 newspapers published in Norway alone, for example.

Internet usage is common in the region, and in the Nordic countries it is well above average in Europe. The Baltic countries are closer to average in Europe, with the exception of Lithuania, where the numbers on internet usage are somewhat lower than average numbers in Europe.[1] As mostly elsewhere, the media landscape has been moving more and more towards the internet. Traditional media have established online versions and a range of media is online only. Many, if not most of them, provide some kind of commenting system where users can comment on the articles or material that is published. The usage of social media is fairly common in the region. In fact, the percentage of individuals who use the internet for participation in social networking is well above the European average in the Nordic countries and somewhat above average in Estonia and Latvia, whereas the number is below average in Lithuania.[2] Although the online media environment has increased, it generally receives rather little of the money spent on advertising, for example, around 19% in Estonia, 15% in Iceland and 8% in Finland.

The countries in the region generally do well in the Reporters Without Borders' World Press Freedom Index, especially the Nordic countries. In fact, in the 2017 ranking, Norway, Sweden, Finland and Denmark dominate the first four places, whereas Iceland is number 10 and Estonia number 12. Latvia is ranked number 28 and Lithuania number 36.[3]

Freedom of expression doctrines in the region

All the countries in the region have constitutional provisions proclaiming freedom of expression. The concept of such protection dates back to the 18th and 19th centuries in the Nordic countries, which have a strong tradition of free speech protection. Most of the operative provisions in the region are, however, fairly new, with the exception of Denmark, where the provision dates back to 1849. Thus, the constitutional provision in Norway was revised in 2004, in Iceland in 1995, and the Fundamental Law on Freedom of Expression was passed in Sweden in 1991.[4] The current provisions in the Baltic countries are likewise new, i.e. were enacted after the Soviet era.

In a general way, these provisions declare that everyone has the right to freedom of expression. Most of these provisions specifically proscribe censorship and other preventive measures, while allowing measures taken after publication under certain circumstances. It varies how detailed the described requirements for interferences are. In fact, the Danish provision mentions no such requirements

---

1 See further http://ec.europa.eu/eurostat/statistics-explained/index.php/Internet_access_ and_use_statistics_-_households_and_individuals (last accessed 12 February 2018).
2 See further http://ec.europa.eu/eurostat/statistics-explained/index.php/Digital_economy_ and_society_statistics_-_households_and_individuals (last accessed 12 February 2018).
3 See https://rsf.org/en/ranking (last accessed 12 February 2018).
4 The Swedish Freedom of the Press Act and the fundamental laws on Instrument of Government are, however, much older, as described in the country article on Sweden in Chapter 10.

and, therefore, does not prevent the legislator from implementing restrictions according to political will.[5] Other provisions, e.g. the Icelandic and Lithuanian one, include requirements similar to article 10 (2) of the European Convention on Human Rights (ECHR). Sweden stands out compared to the other countries since it has highly detailed provisions on freedom of expression. This is due to the fact that the Fundamental Law on Freedom of Expression, which together with three other fundamental laws makes up the Swedish Constitution, is in fact an act of more than 60 articles. Two other examples of these fundamental laws also have provisions on freedom of speech and expression, i.e. the Instrument of Government and the Freedom of the Press Act.

All the countries in the region are members to the ECHR. The status of the Convention in national law differs somewhat, but in some countries, e.g. in Iceland and Latvia, the Convention and the judgments from the European Court of Human Rights (ECtHR) have an influence on the interpretation of the constitutional provisions.

The constitutional provisions on freedom of expression in the region generally apply to online expression, just as expression elsewhere, at least as a point of departure.

Influence of supranational human rights instruments

Introduction

We will review the influence of supranational instruments upon the Nordic new media landscape from the perspective of courts' jurisprudence and normative regulation – both within the meaning of positive and soft law, as well as various policy documents relating to new media.

The European Convention on Human Rights

The jurisprudence of the ECtHR is without doubt the single most important supranational source influencing the conceptualisation and protection of freedom of expression in all Nordic and Baltic countries. All eight countries have lost cases in the ECtHR relating to the protection of freedom of expression under article 10 of the ECHR. Finland has the highest number of article 10 related cases at 28, the number of cases for other countries is below 10. These are cases relating primarily to the protection of freedom of expression in traditional media. The impact of the judgments can be divided into the following three categories:

1   Four countries have changed domestic legislation as a direct result of the Strasbourg jurisprudence. Iceland has changed rules on the defamation of public servants. It has also changed liability rules. Finland has amended

---

5   As described in the country article on Denmark in Chapter 3, the Danish legislator has however been reasonably protective of freedom of speech.

its Penal Code on definitions of defamation, now allowing the balancing of conflicting rights at stake and has abolished the possibility of imprisonment. Denmark's legislature is now giving more weight to journalistic freedom. Sweden changed its domestic legislation so that taking photos of people at home in private places is no longer permissible. In these countries, the courts are also relying on the Strasbourg standards in their domestic case law.

2   In two countries, the Strasbourg jurisprudence has not led to changes in domestic legislation, but the ECtHR principles are taken as the main source to adjudicate freedom of expression issues. A "paradigm shift" occurred in Norwegian libel law due to the defeats in Strasbourg. Norwegian courts take ECtHR case law as a starting point, and also the lower level courts are giving more attention to the important role of the press. In Latvia, the ECtHR case law is cited in almost all domestic judgments dealing with freedom of expression.

3   In reference to two countries, the authors in the present collection report no influence of the Strasbourg jurisprudence on freedom of expression case law. These are Lithuania and Estonia. The explanation may be that there simply are no respective cases at the level of supreme courts, nor is there comprehensive data available about the lower level cases.

National cases in front of the Strasbourg Court relating to new media from the Nordic countries are scarce.[6] This is not surprising due to the novelty of issues concerning the new media and freedom of expression. There is one case from Estonia – *Delfi vs Estonia*[7] and one from Finland – *Satakunnan Markkinapörssi OY vs Finland*,[8] which deal precisely with new media issues.[9] A careful reader has noticed that the *Delfi* case is mentioned in almost all articles in the present collection, leading to conclude the current significance of this judgment in conceptualising online media liability for the content. Indeed, several country articles report that this case has led to the development of online media regulation (Norway and Lithuania). Before the *Delfi* case, Latvia had already introduced ideas on how to manage harmful online comments on a national level, and the Strasbourg position merely provided confirmation. Iceland concurs that the Delfi findings could have been reached under the national Media Act, but the problems for small non-commercial websites remain.

---

6 There is one case from Lithuania – *Jankovskis vs Lithuania*, judgment of 17 January 2017, no 21575/08 – and one from Estonia – *Kalda vs Estonia*, judgment of 19 January 2016, no 17429/10 – dealing with prisoners' access to the internet, but these remain outside the scope of the present analysis.

7 *Delfi vs Estonia*, judgment of 16 June 2015 (Grand Chamber), no 64569/09.

8 *Satakunnan Markkinapörssi OY and Satamedia OY vs Finland*, judgment of 27 June 2017 (Grand Chamber), no 931/13.

9 For details, please see the country articles on Estonia and Finland in chapters 4 and 5 respectively.

Interestingly, no country article reports that the *Delfi* case has led to any changes in the practice of online portals. This raises the question of reasons. One can argue that the *Delfi* judgment was not specific enough for the online portals to clearly understand their concrete obligations – indeed, the judgment of an international court is not intended to be a practice directive. This position suggests that the judgment provided constitutional level understanding of the horizontal protection of human rights in the digital realm. Another argument can be that, rhetorically, the online portals simply do not care, or less rhetorically, at a time when the responsibility of online portals towards assessing online content has not been clearly justified, it takes more than one judgment of a reputable international court to lead to a change in practice.[10]

It has to be concluded, however, that the *Delfi* judgment has become a part of the national human rights domain in all Nordic countries. Even if it has not led to legislative changes, or changes in the practice of the courts or online portals, it has shined a spotlight on the emerging responsibility and liability of private online portals for user-generated content.

EU law

There seems to be little influence in this area of international courts other than the ECtHR, with the exception of one case towards Finland – the judgment of the Grand Chamber of the Court of Justice of the European Union (CJEU) in *Tietosuojavaltuutettu vs Satakunnan Markkinapörssi Oy and Satamedia Oy*.[11] The *Google* judgment[12] remains in the background of academic and occasional public discussion regarding the responsibilities of new media enterprises, but has not materialised as a point of reference in concrete legislative or judicial developments in any of the Nordic countries. The Member States of the EU (eight countries in the collection, except Norway and Iceland) are bound by the European Charter of Fundamental Rights.[13] Its influence is implied rather than specifically discussed in the country articles. Some authors mention the

10 We also refer to the ongoing debate about the fundamental question of whether the responsibility of online portals to assess content can be justified. There are conflicting positions, the other side to the ECtHR and the CJEU in the *Google* judgment – both advocating that the online companies are well placed to assess online content, is represented, among many, by Frank La Rue in the capacity of the UN Special Rapporteur on the Internet, stating that censorship measures should never be delegated to a private entity – see Report of the Special Rapporteur on the promotion and protection of the right to freedom of opinion and expression, Frank La Rue, adopted by the UN Human Rights Council on 16 May 2011, para 43.

11 Case C-73/07 *Tietosuojavaltuutettu vs Satakunnan Markkinapörssi Oy and Satamedia Oy* (Grand Chamber) CJEU judgment of 06 December 2008. In paras 60–62 the Court explained the meaning of "journalistic activity" and left it for the national authorities to decide whether certain activity falls under the definition.

12 C -131/12 *Google Spain SL and others vs Agencia Española de Protección de Datos*, CJEU judgment of 13 May 2014.

13 *Charter of Fundamental Rights of the European Union*, OJ 2012/C 326/02, 26.10.2012, pp. 391–407

reliance on domestic legislative activity upon other European level legal acts, such as the E-Commerce Directive[14], the General Data Protection Regulation, the Copyright Directive[15] and the International Covenant on Civil and Political Rights (ICCPR). It appears though that the national courts primarily refer to the ECHR and occasionally to a few EU legal acts.

Not surprisingly, the courts of other Nordic countries, the EU or the Council of Europe Member States have not had any influence or any effect on the conceptualisation and realisation of the right to freedom of expression in these eight countries.

Remarks

We now formulate the question: taking into account the existence of dozens of various policy documents and standards, originating from formal policy organs, the civil sector and the online stakeholders either in isolation or in co-operation with policy organs, why have these remained dormant in the Nordic human rights landscape relating to new media? The abundance of various initiatives to formulate guidelines and principles for the protection of human rights in the new media is evidenced by the international policy organs – Recommendations issued by the Committee of Ministers of the Council of Europe,[16] the United Nations – see, for example, the UN General Assembly Resolution "The promotion, protection and enjoyment of human rights on the Internet",[17] or the EU – see, for example, the EU Code of Conduct on countering illegal hate speech online.[18] One has to add to this "table" of standards and guidelines the work by non-governmental or private-public forums – the UN Internet Governance Forum,[19] the Global Network Initiative,[20] or the Manila Principles[21] – just to name a few. None of these initiatives are reflected or perhaps even noticed in the Nordic human rights landscape, if we were to judge by the legislative activity or the courts' jurisprudence.

14 Directive 2000/31/EC of the European Parliament and of the Council of 8 June 2000 on certain legal aspects of information society services, in particular electronic commerce, in the Internal Market ('Directive on electronic commerce'), OJ L 178, 17.7.2000, pp. 1–16
15 Directive 2001/29/EC of the European Parliament and of the Council of 22 May 2001 on the harmonisation of certain aspects of copyright and related rights in the information society, OJ L 167, 22.06.2001, pp. 10–19
16 See for example, among many, Appendix to Recommendation CM/Rec(2016)1 of the Committee of Ministers to member States on protecting and promoting the right to freedom of expression and the right to private life with regard to network neutrality, adopted by the Committee of Ministers on 13 January 2016, at the 124th meeting of the Ministers' Deputies.
17 UN Human Rights Council Resolution A/HRC/32/L.20, adopted at the 43rd meeting on 01 July 2016.
18 Adopted on 31 May 2016 by the EU Commission and Facebook, Microsoft, Twitter and YouTube.
19 See its website at www.intgovforum.org – it is a multistakeholder platform to facilitate discussion of public policy issues pertaining to the internet, existing under the authority of the UN.
20 Microsoft, Yahoo!, Google, Linkedin and Facebook participate from the large companies.
21 While the Global Network Initiative involves US stakeholders primarily, the Manila Principles involve many from Europe and the Arab countries.

Generalising on the trends of the practice of domestic European courts, Pollicino and Romeo write:

> [D]omestic courts are increasingly distancing themselves from Strasbourg case law, recognizing the need to contextualize the speech in the specific medium of the internet and arguing for a higher threshold of harm that should be required to limit the exercise of the freedom of (digital) expression. Once again, where the internet phenomenon is concerned, framing activity plays an important role in judicial outcomes.[22]

This statement does not apply in the Nordic countries. The jurisprudence of the courts in the Nordic countries in relation to freedom of expression cases is embedded into the Strasbourg jurisprudence. This conclusion is confirmed by the absence of any dialogue between the highest national courts and the ECtHR on matters relating to the protection of freedom of expression.[23] Apart from this observation, one can ask whether the Nordic human rights landscape is distancing itself from the soft law and policy documents originating from the international public and private sector The reply is negative, since distancing can occur as a consequence of closeness. There is no evidence to suggest that the aforementioned soft law and policy documents are or have been part of the judicial or public discourse regarding freedom of expression. Consequently, there is no closeness to distance from. Too many standards and guidelines, often conflicting, mean no standards and guidelines – at least from the practitioner's perspective. We conclude that despite the absence of a significant influence of supranational instruments on the protection of freedom of expression in the Nordic countries, relative compliance with this fundamental right remains consistently high. Perhaps it is exactly because of the absence of such influence, since legal uncertainty created by conflicting conceptual positions, standards and legal obligations can easily lead to conflicting interpretation by administrative and judicial organs.

Media law in the region

Is there specific new media legislation?

This book rests on the assumption that the Nordic countries form a region where the level of freedom of expression is high. Can it be assumed that the

---

22 Oreste Pollicino and Graziella Romeo, *Concluding remarks: internet law, protection of fundamental rights and the role of constitutional adjudication*, 234–251, at 244 in The Internet and Constitutional Law: The protection of fundamental rights and constitutional adjudication in Europe (Oreste Pollicino and Graziella Romeo, editors), Routledge Research in Constitutional Law, 2016.
23 This is despite the suggestion in the Finnish article that the Finnish Supreme Court has entered into dialogue with the Strasbourg Court in relation to the protection of article 10 rights in the traditional media. The careful analysis by an international court of the judgments of the highest national court and finding that there is no reason to intervene may mean nothing else than concurrence with the way in which the Strasbourg standards were applied.

relatively comparable commitment to freedom of expression originates from similar domestic legal regulation of media? Indeed, the pattern is rather clear.

First, there is a group of countries where media and new media are regulated by general legislation and no specific media law exists. Lithuania does not have specific media laws, which led the Supreme Court to observe as early as 2005 that the general legislation does not take into account the specificity of the internet. Denmark has no specific media law and general law also applies to new media. Therefore, issues often emerge in relation to the implementation of general legislation in the new media environment (lack of knowledge of law by media representatives, prosecution problems and jurisdiction matters). Sweden has no specific media law either, and freedom of expression is protected under three fundamental laws, including the Fundamental Law on Freedom of Expression. There is the Press Act, adopted after World War II, but it does not meet the requirements of present-day modern society. Nor does Estonia have any media laws and the courts have difficulties in applying general liability legislation to the task of balancing conflicting rights apparent in media.

Second, there is a group of countries that have passed special legislation to deal with media issues, but not specifically with new media. Norway has the Media Freedom Act, which stipulates that the editor is the one who has to lead all journalistic activities. Iceland has had the Media Act from 2011, which relates to all media forms. It does apply to online media, but not to personal conversations on social media. Finland passed the Freedom of Expression in Mass Media Act in 2003, which is based on a horizontal protection of mass media.

Only Latvia has special legislation regulating new media. In 2010, it passed the Electronic Mass Media Law, which has specific provisions for electronic mass media.

The pattern is, thus, the absence of specific legislation for new media. Authors report that new media and the internet remain mostly unregulated, and the general legislation is not capable of addressing all new media specific issues. This conclusion is not surprising. The regulatory framework is generically dependent upon the social context, which for new media and the internet is global. Faced with the overwhelming impact of policy documents and guidelines originating from transnational sources, domestic policy organs may simply accept the inevitable and not aspire to generate domestic regulation, which can either copy transnational standards or introduce country-specific guidelines, which have the risk of running counter to the former.

Self-regulation

The relative vacuum of new media legal regulation originating from transnational or domestic sources is compensated to some extent by media self-regulation. This is generally media specific and not focusing specifically on new media. Norway has a non-judicial system created by the Norwegian Press Association. This "self-policing" is based on the Code of Ethics and functions well. Lithuania's Association of Ethics in the Provision of Information to the Public is based on a new code of ethics, which specifically mentions the need to verify the accuracy of information on the internet. Latvia has established a National Electronic Mass Media Council. Estonia's self-regulatory framework operates well and its decisions are not usually subject to appeals. Finland's Mass Media Council's rulings are implemented broadly and efficiently. Similarly to Estonia, the rulings are usually complied with. Case law is scarce. In Denmark, new media organisations have an option to subject their activities to the scrutiny of the Press Council.

Some countries have attempted to set up new media specific self-regulation, which has not led to efficient systems extending such regulation to new media relationships. Norway attempted to create an internet "watchdog" at the start of the 2000s, which failed. Lithuania's Law on Information Society required the promotion of codes of conduct to protect minors and human dignity, which has remained dormant. Therefore, it can be concluded that in none of the Nordic countries have the media self-regulatory frameworks resulted in a consistent and efficient system compensating for the lack of new media specific normative regulation.

Origin of standards

The discussion about standards is led by courts, stakeholders and academia. The discussions reflect similar debates in European and global human rights discourse. The discussions are given in the following sections.

Same rights online and offline

Norwegian protection of freedom of expression in the new media environment is based on the principle of technological neutrality. This manifests the idea that freedom of expression needs to be protected for everyone, not linked to the form of expression but to that of the content. At the same time, the question remains whether the idea of technical neutrality should be provided by specific new media regulation. Similar debates about source neutrality are ongoing in Lithuania. Latvia is following the standard of sameness of rules online and offline, originating from European human rights approaches. This means that the same factors need to be analysed when assessing new media content as with traditional media. For example, the Latvian Supreme Court stipulated in 2012 that online news platforms are mass media.

Editorial responsibility and who is a journalist?

These debates are ongoing in several countries, such as Norway, Lithuania and Finland. Iceland's Supreme Court is advocating a doctrine of duty to supervise online media content. Latvia's Supreme Court has stipulated the responsibility of bloggers for their content. The overarching consensus stipulating the editorial responsibility for online content has remained doctrinal and has not led to specific regulation, either as a policy measure or a norm.

Anything new?

The only new concept that has emerged from the Nordic countries is terminological – the concept of information society media developed by the Lithuanian Supreme Court. It can be concluded that the Nordic countries have not contributed significantly to European-wide debate relating to freedom of expression in new media. The only exception seems to be Estonia, which initiated the Tallinn Agenda for Freedom Online, adopted in Tallinn on 28 April 2014.[24] This document includes the following introductory statement, "… the same rights that people have offline must also be protected online …"[25] This agenda has remained largely unnoticed in the international arena – there are no referrals to this agenda in literature or in policy documents. Be as it may, the agenda is mirroring the doctrine of sameness of fundamental rights, which has emerged outside of the Nordic countries.

Generalisation of liability rules

Following the logic of legal media regulation, the liability for the infringement of freedom of speech is specific to general (traditional) media and not to new media. The focus in reference to new media is on the expansion of editorial liability to the author of the information, and/or establishing liability of the online portal.

The Norwegian regime enables both the author and those who contribute to be held liable. It is assumed that editorial liability does not apply to the internet. The Lithuanian Law on Provisions of Information to the Public specifies editorial liability. The producer or disseminator of information could, in principle, be exempted from liability. After the *Delfi* judgment, the law is now understood in a way that online service providers and disseminators both have obligations regarding the content. Latvian regulation originates from 1991 and stipulates the editor's liability. A private person may bear criminal liability for libel. In Iceland, the author of statements under his name can be held liable. Doubts regarding liability have to be resolved on the basis of general rules. Likewise, in Denmark and Estonia general rules apply to determine liability in online cases.

The lesson from the above is that the Nordic countries have not hurried to change legislation with the purpose of establishing specific liability regulation for online content. We will reflect on the reasons in the next section.

Conclusions

The media environment in the Nordic/Baltic countries is rather diverse and multiform. Internet usage is common and the media landscape has been moving

---

24 Tallinn Agenda for Freedom Online Recommendations, www.freedomonline.ee/foc-recommen dations (last accessed 12 February 2018).
25 Ibid.

more and more towards the internet. The percentage of individuals who use the internet for participation in social networking is well above the European average. The countries generally do well in the Reporters Without Borders' World Press Freedom Index. There is a strong tradition of free speech protection in the Nordic countries. The concept of such protection dates back to the 18th and 19th century, and this strong tradition is of importance in ensuring a high level of free speech protection. All the countries in the region have constitutional provisions proclaiming freedom of expression. These provisions generally apply to online expression, just as expression elsewhere, at least as a point of departure.

The dominant supranational instrument influencing the human rights landscape in the region regarding (new) media is the jurisprudence of the ECtHR. The jurisprudence of other international and national courts, as well as various European and international policy documents, and soft and positive law instruments has little or no significant importance for adjudication and law-making.

With the exception of Latvia, none of the countries have specific laws regulating new media. This is explainable by the nature of new media, where the protection of human rights is influenced by global human rights law and domestic regulation is incapable of competing with the overwhelming nature of transnational instruments. In other words, supranational instruments do not influence the domestic human rights architecture in protecting freedom of expression in the new media, nor are there counterbalancing domestic regulations. The lesson from the Nordic countries is that the level of freedom of expression, which as assessed by indexing and public perception, is relatively high in all these countries, is not dependent on the influence of supranational instruments upon domestic human rights law, or on the adoption of domestic specific new media legislation. As a conclusion applicable to the wider context of freedom of expression protection in the new media, it almost appears as if there were two realms related to the protection of freedom of expression in the new media. One realm belongs to the stakeholders and end users, which operate outside of the direct influence of supranational concepts and without new media specific legislation. Another belongs to the academia, policy-makers and European legislators, who are concerned with norm and policy development. These two realms exist independently from one another.

Our final reflection relates to the development of new principles in human rights law. How is a novel human right or principle claim gaining universal recognition? The principle of horizontal governance on the internet and the obligation of online portals to safeguard human rights in user-generated content are novel principles in the global human rights landscape and have emerged due to the incapability of the "traditional" principles governing freedom of expression protection in media to provide comparable protection in the digital realm. Human rights theory has no consensual understanding of how a novel right or principle claim has reached a status of being part of the established human rights or principles family. On the one hand, there is Alston's quality control (appellation contrôlée) test,[26] which states that a claim of a new human right becomes an established human right only if the UN General Assembly says so. Nowadays in the European context this may mean a clear acceptance by relevant EU or Council of Europe organs. Against the background of the role and significance of various new human rights protection instruments, this test seems extreme. On the other hand, a novel human right or principle claim can serve as a mobilising instrument of various social groups or advance an important societal cause. In our view, a new human rights norm or principle is derived from or implied by a recognised human rights norm or principle because of the incapability of this recognised right or principle to provide a comparable level of protection usually associated with it in responding to challenges emerging from a shift in political climate, a push by the civil society or special interest group, and technological or intellectual developments. This derivation or implication may lead to the emergence of a new autonomous human right or principle, or to the expansion of the scope of an existing human right or principle, based on the degree of this incapability. Is the universe of human rights and principles ever-expanding, or is there, senso strictu, a closed circle of human rights and we can only speak of more detailed articulation of long-standing rights? None of these propositions seem correct. Although in certain instances the emergence of a new human right or principle claim can be justified, turning in time to a recognised human rights norm or principle, this is more an exception for which weighty reasons are expected.

The Nordic countries exhibit restraint in incorporating the new principle of horizontal governance and the authority of private online portals to assess user content into national human rights regulation, be it as a novel human rights norm or principle. The lesson from the observation above is that this principle, despite overwhelming rhetorical discussion, remains in a state of contestation and is not yet a generally accepted principle in the European and global human rights landscape.

---

26 Philip Alston, Conjuring up New Human Rights: A Proposal for Quality Control, *The American Journal of International Law*, vol 78, No 3 (July 1984) pp. 607–621, at 614.

12 Updating freedom of expression doctrines in the new media cases: lessons from Strasbourg and other international treaty bodies

Artūrs Kučs and Jukka Viljanen

Clarification of rules

The new media continuum in the Strasbourg case law has been rapidly evolving in the past decade and is still under construction. Even after the landmark case of *Delfi AS v. Estonia* (16.6.2015), it does not fully answer all questions that have been surfacing in the academic discourse. The early case law in the field of freedom of expression has laid down the main principles. Ever since the *Handyside* case, the understanding of the limitation clauses under Article 10 of the ECHR is setting a standard, with freedom of expression constituting one of the essential foundations of a democratic society. Subject to paragraph 2 of Article 10, it is applicable not only to "information" or "ideas" that are favourably received or regarded as inoffensive or as a matter of indifference, but also to those that offend, shock or disturb. Such are the demands of pluralism, tolerance and broadmindedness without which there is no "democratic society".[1] As set forth in Article 10, freedom of expression is subject to exceptions, which must, however, be construed strictly, and the need for any restrictions must be established convincingly. The European Court of Human Rights has emphasised the essential role played by the press in a democratic society. Not only does the press have the task of imparting such information and ideas; the public also has a right to receive them. Were it otherwise, the press would be unable to play its vital role of "public watchdog".[2]

In the case of *Editorial Board of Pravoye and Shtekel v. Ukraine* (5.5.2011),[3] the Court acknowledged the different role of the internet as a communication tool compared to print media.

> 63. It is true that the Internet is an information and communication tool particularly distinct from the printed media, in particular as regards the capacity to store and transmit information. The electronic network serving billions of users worldwide is not and potentially cannot be subject to the

---

1 Handyside v. the United Kingdom, 7.12.1976, para. 49.
2 *Axel Springer AG v. Germany*, 7.2.2012, paras. 78–79.
3 *Editorial Board of Pravoye and Shtekel v. Ukraine*, 5.5.2011, para 63.

same regulations and control. The risk of harm posed by content and communications on the Internet to the exercise and enjoyment of human rights and freedoms, particularly the right to respect for private life, is certainly higher than that posed by the press. Therefore, the policies governing reproduction of material from the printed media and the Internet may differ. The latter undeniably have to be adjusted according to the technology's specific features in order to secure the protection and promotion of the rights and freedoms concerned.[4]

In the recent *Arnarson* case (13.6.2017), it was confirmed that the Court had addressed the distinction between the internet, as an information and communication tool, and the printed media, referring to a number of cases in addition to *Delfi*.[5] Interpretation of other new technologies is still surfacing, but most recent cases have been related to the right to private life and the secrecy of communications.[6]

While the key cases previously focused on the responsibility of journalists and editors in cases relating to defamation—in cases like Sunday Times II (26.11.1991), Observer and Guardian (26.11.1991), or Fressoz and Roire (21.1.1991)[7]—the logic of the internet has changed the focus towards those who are providing platforms for different forms of speech (*Delfi AS v. Estonia*). The role of internet service providers is relevant in a number recent cases. One of the key elements in the new media continuum has been the question of liability and, especially, the liability of the intermediaries. This was elucidated in the *Delfi AS* case and the Hungarian case of *Magyar T.E. and Index.hu Zrt.*[8] These new elements in the liability regime have been described comprehensively in the article written by Judge Robert Spano in chapter 2.

---

4 See also similar reference in *Węgrzynowski and Smolczewski v. Poland*, no. 33846/07, 16 July 2013, para. 58. This point was also made in *Delfi AS v. Estonia*, Grand Chamber, 16.6.2015 the Joint Dissenting Opinion of Judges Sajo and Tsotsoria, para 21. They consider it to be an important benchmark when something is considered to be reasonably foreseeable for the applicant company.

5 Arnarson v. Iceland, 13.6.2017, para 32. See e.g. *Węgrzynowski and Smolczewski v. Poland*, ibid., § 58; *Editorial Board of Pravoye Delo and Shtekel v. Ukraine*, no. 33014/05, § 63, ECHR 2011 (extracts); and *Times Newspapers Ltd v. the United Kingdom (nos. 1 and 2)*, nos. 3002/03 and 23676/03, § 27, ECHR 2009.

6 See e.g. *Bărbulescu v. Romania*, GC, 5.9.2017, where the Grand Chamber overturned the previous Chamber's judgment in relation to using Yahoo Messenger, an online chat service offering real-time text transmission over the internet. The monitoring by the employer and the dismissal of the applicant was in breach of Article 8. The Court considered that the domestic authorities did not afford adequate protection of the applicant's right to respect for his private life and correspondence, and that they consequently failed to strike a fair balance between the interests at stake.

7 See Sunday Times v. the United Kingdom (No. 2), 26.11.1991, Observer and Guardian v. the United Kingdom, 26.11.1991, Fressoz and Roire v. France, 21.1.1999.

8 *Magyar Tartalomszolgáltatók Egyesülete and Index.hu Zrt v. Hungary*, 2.2.2016.

New elements that have been raised in the European and global discourse, such as cyberbullying, have not been tested in case law. Previous case law suggests that certain types of restrictions are justified in relation to bullying[9] or there might even be a need to take positive measures to protect freedom of expression from actions and threats made by other individuals.[10] In addition, different methods of blocking the use of the internet were addressed in the case of *Ahmet Yildirim v. Turkey* (18.12.2012). The Court saw that there were problems with foreseeability and also the blocking of Google sites produced arbitrary

---

9 Bullying has been so far acknowledged, especially in the context of sexual minorities. For e.g. in the *Smith and Grady v. the United Kingdom* case, 27.9.1999 (para. 102), the Court noted the approach to prevent racial discrimination, racial and sexual harassment and bullying in the armed forces. Similarly, in the case of *Bayev and others v. Russia*, 20.6.2017 the applicants complained about the ban on public statements concerning the identity, rights and social status of sexual minorities. The applicants were gay rights activists. They were each found guilty of the administrative offence of "public activities aimed at the promotion of homosexuality among minors". The Court considered that the ban violated the applicants' freedom of expression and it was counterproductive to the aim of preventing bullying. The Court referred to standards set out by the Committee of Ministers. In para. 82, the Court stated:

> In sensitive matters such as public discussion of sex education, where parental views, educational policies and the right of third parties to freedom of expression must be balanced, the authorities have no choice but to resort to the criteria of objectivity, pluralism, scientific accuracy and, ultimately, the usefulness of a particular type of information to the young audience. It is important to note that the applicants' messages were not inaccurate, sexually explicit or aggressive... The Court recognises that the protection of children from homophobia gives practical expression to the Committee of Ministers' Recommendation Rec(2010)5 which encourages 'safeguarding the right of children and youth to education in safe environment, free from violence, bullying, social exclusion or other forms of discriminatory and degrading treatment related to sexual orientation or gender identity' (see para. 31 of the Recommendation) as well as 'providing objective information with respect to sexual orientation and gender identity, for instance in school curricula and educational materials' (see para. 32 of the Recommendation).

> The Court went on to say (para. 83) that "Above all, by adopting such laws the authorities reinforce stigma and prejudice and encourage homophobia, which is incompatible with the notions of equality, pluralism and tolerance inherent in a democratic society." In the *Vejdeland and others v. Sweden* case, 9.2.2012, judges Spielmann and Nussberger pointed out in their dissenting opinion that certain restrictions are justified in educational settings in order to prevent bullying of those belonging to sexual minorities.

> > It should also not been forgotten that a real problem of homophobic and transphobic bullying and discrimination in educational settings may justify a restriction of freedom of expression under paragraph 2 of Article 10. Indeed, according to studies carried out across member States and supported by some government research, LGBT students suffer from bullying from both peers and teachers.

10 See *Özgur Gündem v. Turkey*, 16.3.2000, para. 43. The Court recalls the key importance of freedom of expression as one of the preconditions for a functioning democracy. Genuine, effective exercise of this freedom does not depend merely on the state's duty not to interfere, but may require positive measures of protection, even in the sphere of relations between individuals and para. 70. "The Court concludes that the respondent State has failed to take adequate protective and investigative measures to protect Özgür Gündem's exercise of its freedom of expression."

effects and could not be aimed at the offending site. The judicial review procedures were insufficient to meet the criteria for avoiding abuse, as the domestic
law did not provide any safeguards against blocking; order in respect of a specific
site is not used as a means of blocking access in general.[11] The Court noted that
blocking all access to Google sites substantially restricted the rights of internet
users and had a significant collateral effect. This is similar to views taken by the
UN Human Rights Committee (HRC) in General Comment 34, where it is
especially mentioned that generic bans are not compatible with Article 19 paragraph 3.[12] The HRC has been concerned, for example, about the Syrian situation and "allegations that the Government has blocked access to some Internet
sites used by human rights defenders or political activists (art. 19)".[13]

The protection of rights and freedoms of children and other vulnerable individuals has included positive obligations to ensure that legislation would provide
a framework for internet services that protects those groups (*K.U. v. Finland*
(2.12.2008)).[14] The Court also noted in this first internet case that the internet, because of its anonymous character, could be used for criminal purposes.[15]
Also, the new technological solutions have increased the element of data protection to the equation (*Satakunnan Markkinapörssi and Satamedia v. Finland*
(27.6.2017)[16]) including guarantees under the EU directives.

Challenges of media neutrality online and offline

The Strasbourg Court's freedom of expression case law is based on the presumption that the form of media is neutral.[17] A similar finding can be found
in the *International Covenant on Civil and Political Rights* (ICCPR), where

11 See *Ahmet Yildirim v. Turkey*, 18.12.2012, paras. 67 and 68.
12 See HRC General Comment No. 34, 12.9.2011, para. 43:

> Any restrictions on the operation of websites, blogs or any other internet-based, electronic
> or other such information dissemination system, including systems to support such com-
> munication, such as internet service providers or search engines, are only permissible to the
> extent that they are compatible with paragraph 3. Permissible restrictions generally should
> be content-specific; generic bans on the operation of certain sites and systems are not com-
> patible with paragraph 3.

13 See CCPR/CO/84/SYR, 9 August 2005.
14 See *K.U. v. Finland*, 2.12.2008, para. 49.

> Although freedom of expression and confidentiality of communications are primary con-
> siderations and users of telecommunications and Internet services must have a guarantee
> that their own privacy and freedom of expression will be respected, such guarantee cannot
> be absolute and must yield on occasion to other legitimate imperatives, such as the preven-
> tion of disorder or crime or the protection of the rights and freedoms of others.

15 See ibid., para. 48.
16 *Satakunnan Markkinapörssi Oy and Satamedia Oy v. Finland*, 27.6.2017.
17 See e.g. *Jersild v. Denmark*, 23.9.1994, § 31, Series A no. 298. *Animal Defenders v. United Kingdom*, 22.4.2013, para. 100: "This protection of Article 10 extends not only to the substance of
the ideas and information expressed but also to the form in which they are conveyed ()". See also
Sokolowski v. Poland, 29.3.2005, para. 44. "Lastly, the Court recalls that Article 10 protects not

the General Comment 34 describes that paragraph 2 (of Article 19) protects all forms of expression and the means of their dissemination. This includes all forms of electronic and internet-based modes of expression.[18] In the case of *Jersild v. Denmark* (23.9.1994), the Court noted that although principles are primarily formulated with regard to the print media, these principles without doubt also apply to the audiovisual media. The idea of media neutrality is relevant in the contemporary world. In the modern media landscape, it is typical that the same news is distributed by several different methods. In this pluralist environment, the print version is often preceded by several forms of digital media. All big news providers, whether based on newspapers (e.g. *New York Times*) or a broadcasting tradition (e.g. BBC), are delivering news via the internet. These websites often have both free content and content which requires subscription or certain parts that are not available without registration or in a particular location. News websites have written content, which traditional print media provides, and video and audio recordings and podcasts that you can play. In addition to their own websites, many news media corporations also use YouTube, Facebook and Twitter accounts.

The challenges in relation to media neutrality relate to the question of how different media that have been used to convey a message should be taken into account while considering the other issues such as duties and responsibilities also mentioned in Article 10. According to the Court, in considering the duties and responsibilities, the potential impact of a medium is an important factor and certain media types, such as audiovisual media, may have a more immediate and powerful effect than the print media. At the same time, the Court pointed out that Article 10 does not only protect the substance but also the form in which information is conveyed.[19] The censorship of print media (for example, confiscation of printed materials) is replaced by authorities using technology to block access to sites like Google and YouTube.

Thus, it is important to consider whether certain media environment related issues should be acknowledged, and whether these factors should be relevant in tailoring existing balancing tests to correspond to the demands specific to new media and the digital media environment.[20]

The EU has also considered the importance of freedom of expression in the digital media environment by drafting the EU Human Rights Guidelines on

---

only the substance of the ideas and information expressed but also the form in which they are conveyed".

18 HRC General Comment No. 34, 12.9.2011, para. 12.

19 *Jersild v. Denmark* (see supra note 17), § 31. See e.g. *Pentikäinen v. Finland*, 20.10.2015, para. 87.

20 See *Einarsson v. Iceland*, 7.11.2017, paras. 46 and 51.

The availability of the defamatory information to all Instagram users was recognised, but the judgment does not provide a tailored test. The balancing focuses on the issue of whether the Supreme Court failed to take adequate account of the important chronological link between the publication of the statement and the discontinuance of the criminal cases against the applicant.

Freedom of Expression Online and Offline (12 May 2014). According to these Guidelines:

> The Internet and digital technologies have expanded the possibilities of individuals and media to exercise the right to freedom of expression and freely access online information. Any restriction that prevents the flow of information offline or online must be in line with permissible limitations as set out in international human rights law.[21]

The Guidelines also refer to media neutrality: "Freedom of opinion and expression further includes the freedom to express and impart information and ideas of all kinds that can be transmitted to others, in whatever form, and regardless of media."[22]

Technology neutrality is also one of the key principles of the regulatory framework for communications. The concept appears in the EU telecom legislation, the EU data protection regulation, and in the Organisation for Economic Co-operation and Development (OECD) (OECD Council Recommendation on Principles for Internet Policy Making 2011) principles for internet policy. Technology neutrality should mean that the same principles apply regardless of the technology used. These principles should be adopted to diminish the traditional dualism of media regulation (print media/electronic media) and to prevent the creation of new, technology based silos (print media/electronic media/online (digital) media).

However, even though the UN, the EU and United Nations Educational, Scientific and Cultural Organization (UNESCO) do not support the special treatment of digital media, it should be noted that these statements are general in their nature and do not take into account context dependency. Thus, even though the international trends do not support the Court in developing separate balancing tests for digital media, the particularities of each digital media type should be taken into account, case by case.

An approach that would automatically separate the legislation in accordance with the media form can be problematic, especially since the form of digital media is in a constant state of change. For example, MySpace and IRC-Galleria were once mainstream digital media in Finland, but currently both have lost their significance.

It would be important to invite the Court to develop a coherent model based on the main principles established in traditional media cases (*Von Hannover II* and *Axel Springer* (7.2.2012))[23] but at the same time to elucidate rules that should be taken into account in the digital media context.

---

21 EU Guidelines on Human Freedom of Expression Online and Offline, https://eeas.europa. eu/sites/eeas/files/eu_human_rights_guidelines_on_freedom_of_expression_online_and_ offline_en.pdf (last accessed 13 February 2018), para. 16.
22 See ibid., para. 17.
23 Von Hannover v. Germany (No. 2) (Grand Chamber), 7.2.2012, and Axel Springer v. Germany, (Grand Chamber) 7.2.2012

In the case of *Satakunnan Markkinapörssi and Satamedia v. Finland*, the Court did not contribute to the media neutrality discussion by setting up clear doctrines. However, it clearly acknowledged the challenges of media neutrality by pointing out that there is increased availability related to the dissemination of information via new technologies, such as SMS services.

> Publishing the data in a newspaper, and further disseminating that data via an SMS service, rendered it accessible in a manner and to an extent not intended by the legislator.[24]

In the case of *Animal Defenders* (22.4.2013), there was a clear acknowledgment of the changes in the media environment, especially the internet and social media. This changes the synchronicity and impact of information.

> In addition, the choices inherent in the use of the internet and social media mean that the information emerging therefrom does not have the same synchronicity or impact as broadcasted information.[25]

However, it does not lead to the conclusion that special measures considered in the field of broadcast media are in the past. According to the judgment, notwithstanding therefore the significant development of the internet and social media in recent years, there is no evidence of a sufficiently serious shift in the respective influences of the new and of the broadcast media in the respondent state to undermine the need for special measures for the latter.[26] The important argument in the case of *Animal Defenders* was the lack of consensus in regulating broadcast media advertising. This lack of consensus also broadens the margin of appreciation to be accorded as regards restrictions to public interest expression.[27]

In the *Delfi* case, the internet platform and its wide readership were noted, and it was one of the biggest internet media publications in the country.[28] In the case of *Cengiz and Others v. Turkey* (1.12.2015), following the interpretation adopted in *Ahmet Yildirim*, the Court found that prior restraints (e.g. blocking websites)

> were not incompatible with the Convention as a matter of principle but had to form part of a legal framework ensuring both tight control over the scope of the ban and effective judicial review to prevent any abuses. Judicial scrutiny of such a measure, based on the weighing-up of the competing interests at stake and designed to strike a balance between them, is inconceivable without a framework establishing precise and specific rules regarding the

---

24 See *Satakunnan Markkinapörssi Oy and Satamedia Oy v. Finland* (see supra note 16), para. 190.
25 See *Animal Defenders v. the United Kingdom* (see supra note 17), para. 119.
26 See ibid., para. 119.
27 See ibid., para. 123.
28 See *Delfi AS v. Estonia* (see supra note 4), para. 117.

application of preventive restrictions on the freedom to receive and impart information and ideas.[29]

Behind this is the same consideration of the collateral effect of blocking internet sites, which made large quantities of information inaccessible in the case of *Ahmet Yildirim*.[30]

Digital media as an important platform for democratic debate and citizen media

In this book, the comparative articles provide a clear picture of new forms of digital media as essential to the democratic debate in Nordic and Baltic countries. The citizen's role in the media has become increasingly important. Citizens are actively participating in the public debate and are often contributing to democratic discourse in more ways that just traditional voting during elections. Citizens are creating their own websites, blogging or micro-blogging via Twitter to initiate new ideas. The individual blogger usually has total control over using the medium. Consequently, this means that the traditional roles in print media, like editors-in-chief, are vanishing. The case law has acknowledged different forms of media and tried to provide some essential principles on pluralism in the digital media. One of the key critical arguments towards recent cases is the categorisation of professional media and the media that does not have all the similar characteristics.

As platforms, the digital media does not have a significant place in the argumentation of new media cases. In the *Satakunnan Markkinapörssi* case, the Court was deciding the relevance of tax information for the societal discourse and at the start of its analysis made a comparative finding that there are only a few countries in Europe that provide access to individual tax information.[31] It also noted that in Finland the data could be received in a digital form.[32]

---

29 See *Cengiz and Others v. Turkey*, 1.12.2015, para. 62 and Ahmet Yildirim v. Turkey (supra note 11), para. 66.
30 See ibid., para. 64.

> [T]he authorities should have taken into consideration, among other aspects, the fact that such a measure, by rendering large quantities of information inaccessible, was bound to substantially restrict the rights of Internet users and to have a significant collateral effect.

31 See *Satakunnan Markkinapörssi Oy and Satamedia Oy v. Finland* (see supra note 16), paras. 81–82. From the information available to the Court, it would appear that, apart from Finland, only Iceland, Italy, France, Monaco, Sweden and Switzerland provide for some form of public accessibility of individual taxation information. The other 34 countries surveyed had secrecy of taxation information.
32 See ibid., para. 189. Journalists could receive taxation data in a digital format, but retrieval conditions also existed and only a certain amount of data could be retrieved. Journalists had to specify that the information was requested for journalistic purposes and that it would not be

However, the Court only briefly referred to the relevance of this version, rather than print, in terms of freedom of expression.[33]

The question of protecting whistleblowing has become more important in recent judgments. A need for its protection was recognised in the case of *Guja v. Moldova* (12.2.2008),[34] and the criteria for protecting whistleblowing were connected to the reasons behind the disclosure. According to the Court (para 77),

> it is important to establish that, in making the disclosure, the individual acted in good faith and in the belief that the information was true, that it was in the public interest to disclose it and that no other, more discreet means of remedying the wrongdoing was available to him or her.

The possibility to report irregularities was evident in the landmark case of *Medžlis Islamske Zajednice Brčko and Others v. Bosnia and Herzegovina* (27.6.2017). The Grand Chamber was divided on which kind of standard of proof should be set for media types other than traditional media. The minority was in favour of a more lenient standard.[35]

Some references to advertisement in political elections could be detected, but they are mostly in the argumentation of third parties rather than forming the core of the Court's own argumentation.[36] In the *Animal Defenders case*, the dissenting opinion of Judge Tulkens, joined by Judges Spielmann and Laffranque, stated that

> information obtained through the use of the Internet and social networks is gradually having the same impact, if not more, as broadcasted information. Their development in recent years undoubtedly signals a sufficiently serious shift in the influence of traditional broadcasting media to undermine the need to apply special measures to the latter.[37]

---

published in the form of a list (see paras. 49–51 above). Therefore, while the information relating to individuals was publicly accessible, specific rules and safeguards governed its accessibility.

33 See ibid., para. 190. "Publishing the data in a newspaper, and further disseminating that data via an SMS service, rendered it accessible in a manner and to an extent not intended by the legislator."

34 *Guja v. Moldova*, Grand Chamber, 12.2.2008, para. 77.

35 See *Medžlis Islamske Zajednice Brčko and Others v. Bosnia and Herzegovina* Grand Chamber, 27.6.2017. Joint Dissenting Opinion of Judges Sajó, Karakaş, Motoc and Mits. Against this background, we find it unjustified to assess the truthfulness of the statements contained in a private letter with the same rigour as if they were contained in an article published by the applicants in the press.

36 See e.g. *Sitaropoulos and Giakoumopoulos v. Greece*, 15.3.2012, GC, para. 61. The Court refers to the opinion of the Hellenic League for Human Rights, noting "the fact that electoral campaigns were now conducted principally via computer-based social networks (such as Facebook and Twitter)".

37 See *Animal Defenders* (see supra note 17), Dissenting Opinion of Judge Tulkens, Joined by Judges Spielmann and Laffranque, para. 11.

In the Polish case of *Remuszko v. Poland* (16.7.2013), the Court also referred to the internet as a means of disseminating information to the general public.[38]

In the case of *Editorial Board Pravoye Delo and Shtekel v. Ukraine* (5.5.2011), the role of the internet in "professional media activities" was highlighted. The Court considered that the absence of a sufficient legal framework at the domestic level, which would allow journalists to use information obtained from the internet without fear of incurring sanctions, seriously hinders the exercise of the vital function of the press as a "public watchdog".[39]

Broadening the definition of journalists

The new media continuum and the internet have challenged the traditional understanding of the concept of journalism. The definition of media actors has expanded as a result of new forms of media appearing in the digital age.[40] On the internet, even an individual blogger can have a major impact on the public. This can happen e.g. via a blog, a YouTube channel or on Twitter/Facebook/Instagram. Subscribers to the most popular YouTube Channels can exceed 10 million and followers of Twitter accounts amount to even higher numbers. The institutional definition of journalism, which emphasised the link between the journalists and media institutions or membership in the professional association of journalists, have been taken over by a functional definition, which emphasises the nature and purpose of journalistic activities.

The Court has highlighted this on a number of occasions. In the case *Társaság a Szabadságjogokért v. Hungary* (14.4.2009), the Court emphasised:

> The function of the press includes the creation of forums for public debate. More importantly, the realisation of this function is not limited to the media or professional journalists, but also includes non-governmental organizations.[41]

---

38 *Remuszko v. Poland*, 16.7.2013, para. 82. At no point was the applicant prevented from disseminating information about the book by any means he wished. Indeed, he created his own internet website, through which he informed the general public about the book, its content and its potential significance for the public debate.

39 See *Editorial Board Pravoye Delo and Shtekel v. Ukraine*, 5.5.2011, para. 64.

40 Recommendation CM/Rec(2016)4 of the Committee of Ministers to Member States on the protection of journalism and safety of journalists and other media actors, para. 4. See also Report by UN Special Rapporteur David Kaye (A/70/361, 8.9.2015), who mentions two categories which expand beyond officially recognised journalists in the sense of source confidentiality. First, there are those who most closely reflect the professional engagement in the collection and dissemination of information: members of civil society organisations, who conduct research and issue findings, and researchers—academics, independent authors, freelance writers and others—who regularly participate in gathering and sharing information publicly. Second, "citizen journalists" and bloggers and other media "non-professionals" engage in independent reporting and disseminate their findings through a wide variety of media, from print and broadcast to social media and other online platforms.

41 *Társaság a Szabadságjogokért v. Hungary*, 14.4.2009, para. 27. See also *Vides Aizsardzības Klubs v Latvia*, App no. 57829/00 (ECtHR, 27 May 2004).

Similarly, in the case of *Steel and Morris v. the United Kingdom* (15.2.2005), the Court rejected the Government's argument that the applicants were not journalists and, therefore, should not attract the high level of protection afforded to the press under Article 10. The Court stated:

> [...] in a democratic society even small and informal campaign groups, such as London Greenpeace, must be able to carry on their activities effectively and that there exists a strong public interest in enabling such groups and individuals outside the mainstream to contribute to the public debate by disseminating information and ideas on matters of general public interest such as health and the environment.[42]

According to the Court, the function of a public watchdog can be realised not only by traditional media but also by the non-governmental organisations. Therefore, the concept of media actors includes others who contribute to public debate, who perform journalistic activities or fulfil public watchdog functions.[43] For instance, bloggers and citizen journalists in certain situations can realise this function and be afforded wider protection, historically applied only to traditional media. The importance of citizen journalism was acknowledged by the Court in the case of *Cengiz and Others v. Turkey*:

> User-generated expressive activity on the Internet provides an unprecedented platform for the exercise of freedom of expression. In this connection, the Court observes that YouTube is a video-hosting website on which users can upload, view and share videos and is undoubtedly an important means of exercising the freedom to receive and impart information and ideas. In particular, as the applicants rightly noted, political content ignored by the traditional media is often shared via YouTube, thus fostering the emergence of citizen journalism.[44]

A wider understanding of the journalistic concept is also emphasised by the Court of Justice of the European Union in the case of *Tietosuojavaltuutettu v Satakunnan Markkinapörssi Oy and Satamedia Oy*:

> If the object of activities is the disclosure of information to the public, sharing opinions or ideas, they can be classified as journalistic activities irrespective of the medium which is used to transmit them.[45]

---

42 *Steel and Morris v. the United Kingdom*, 15.2.2005, para. 89.
43 Recommendation CM/Rec(2016)4 (see supra note 39), para. 4.
44 *Cengiz and Others v. Turkey* (see supra note 28), para. 52.
45 Case C-73/07 *Tietosuojavaltuutettu v Satakunnan Markkinapörssi Oy and Satamedia Oy* [2008] *I-09831*, para. 61.

Similarly, the UN HRC (Human Rights Committee) in its General Comment 34 acknowledged the changing notion of journalism by stating that:

> Journalism is a function shared by a wide range of actors, including professional full-time reporters and analysts, as well as bloggers and others who engage in forms of self-publication in print, on the internet or elsewhere, and general State systems of registration or licensing of journalists are incompatible with paragraph 3. Limited accreditation schemes are permissible only where necessary to provide journalists with privileged access to certain places and/or events. Such schemes should be applied in a manner that is nondiscriminatory and compatible with article 19 and other provisions of the Covenant, based on objective criteria and taking into account that journalism is a function shared by a wide range of actors.[46]

However, the changing media continuum and conception of journalism has left open questions, such as whether every individual active in the public debate can be considered a journalist and benefit from all journalistic privileges? While the Court has been open to applying a wider notion of journalism in cases related to access to information,[47] it has not yet decided whether a similar approach would apply to all journalistic privileges, such as the protection of sources, privileged communications and protection against seizure of journalistic material. The ambiguous nature of how to apply all journalistic privileges to other media actors is evidenced from the text of the Recommendation of the Parliamentary Assembly of the Council of Europe on the protection of journalists' sources:

> The right of journalists not to disclose their sources of information is a professional privilege, intended to encourage sources to provide journalists with important information which they would not give without a commitment to confidentiality. The same relationship of trust does not exist with regard to non-journalists, such as individuals with their own website or web blog. Therefore, non-journalists cannot benefit from the right of journalists not to reveal their sources.[48]

Lastly, the issue of corresponding duties of unconventional actors in a new media ecosystem has been left open. The Court has held that the safeguard afforded by Article 10 to journalists in relation to reporting on issues of general interest is subject to the proviso that they are acting in good faith, on an accurate factual basis, and provide "reliable and precise" information in accordance with the ethics of journalism.[49] The Court has confirmed that the same principle must

---

46 See HRC General Comment No. 34, 12.9.2011, on Article 19 of the ICCPR.
47 *Társaság a Szabadságjogokért v. Hungary* (see supra note 40).
48 Recommendation 1950 (2011) "The protection of journalists' sources", para. 15.
49 *Fressoz and Roire v. France* [GC], 21.1.1999, para. 54; *Pedersen and Baadsgaard v. Denmark*, 17.12.2004, para. 78; and *Stoll v. Switzerland* [GC], 10.12.2007, para. 103.

apply to others who engage in public debate.[50] A similar approach is taken by the Committee of Ministers of the Council of Europe:

> As regards in particular new media, codes of conduct or ethical standards for bloggers have already been accepted by at least part of the online journalism community. Nonetheless, bloggers should only be considered media if they fulfil the criteria to a sufficient degree.[51]

The chilling effect in the new media context

The "chilling effect" has been one of the key concepts applied in Strasbourg's freedom of expression case law. The Court has illustrated an awareness of the importance of freedom of expression and information. It has constantly referred to the danger of a "chilling effect" and its impact on the possibility of the press and journalists to fulfil their "public watchdog" functions in the democratic society. The Court has emphasised this concept in different regulatory frameworks.

In the context of the protection of journalistic sources, the Court in *Goodwin v. the United Kingdom* (27.3.1996) underlined:

> Having regard to the importance of the protection of journalistic sources for press freedom in a democratic society and the potentially chilling effect an order of source disclosure has on the exercise of that freedom, such a measure cannot be compatible with Article 10 (art. 10) of the Convention unless it is justified by an overriding requirement in the public interest.[52]

Furthermore, the chilling effect has been found when criminal sanctions are applied to journalists reporting on matters of public interest or when classic defamation cases have resulted in prison sentences. In *Kaperzyński v. Poland* (3.4.2012), the Court emphasised:

> (..) the Court must exercise caution when the measures taken or sanctions imposed by the national authorities are such as to dissuade the press from taking part in a discussion of matters of legitimate public concern (..). The chilling effect that the fear of criminal sanctions has on the exercise of journalistic freedom of expression is evident (..). This effect, which works to the detriment of society as a whole, is likewise a factor which goes to the proportionality, and thus the justification, of the sanctions imposed on media professionals.[53]

---

50 *Steel and Morris v. the United Kingdom* (see supra note 41), para. 90.
51 Recommendation CM/Rec(2011)7 of the Committee of Ministers to member states on a new notion of media.
52 *Goodwin v the United Kingdom*, 27.3.1996, para. 39.
53 *Kaperzyński v. Poland*, 3.4.2012, para. 70.

The Court has also underlined the chilling effect of prior restraints, for instance, Article 8 of the European Convention on Human Rights does not require states to impose a legally binding pre-notification requirement on the media, when the information published relates to the privacy of the individual.[54] Last but not least, the concept of "chilling effect" has also been highlighted by the Court in relation to actors other than the media, who contribute to the debate on matters of public interest. In the context of the protection of whistleblowers, the Court indicated that the dismissal of a civil servant for leaking two confidential letters from the public prosecutor's office to the press was in breach of Article 10 of the Convention, also referring to the serious chilling effect of the applicant's dismissal on other civil servants or employees, discouraging them from reporting any misconduct.[55]

Can these traditional rules for applying the "chilling effect" doctrine be similar in the new media environment? This issue was raised in the case of *Delfi AS v. Estonia*. The applicant complained about the chilling effect concerning the regulations that placed liability on the applicant company to take actions against private communications on the discussion forum. In the joint dissenting opinion of judges Sajó and Tsotsoria, the chilling effect of the Supreme Court's line was mentioned when the dissenting judges considered that the unforeseeable nature of the laws (vaguely worded, ambiguous, and therefore unforeseeable laws that have a chilling effect on freedom of expression) contributed to a chilling effect.

The Court has referred to the *Delfi* case cautiously in subsequent case law and seemed to clarify that higher standards of monitoring and the liability for third party comments established in the *Delfi* judgment was, in fact, limited in scope to "clearly unlawful" comments consisting of hate speech and incitement to violence. In the judgment of *Magyar Tartalomszolgáltatók Egyesülete and Index. hu Zrt v. Hungary* (2.2.2016) (MTE case), the Court acknowledged the chilling effect regarding the liability for third party comments:

> Such liability may have foreseeable negative consequences on the comment environment of an Internet portal, for example by impelling it to close the commenting space altogether. For the Court, these consequences may have, directly or indirectly, a chilling effect on the freedom of expression on the Internet. This effect could be particularly detrimental for a non-commercial website such as the first applicant.[56]

The Court seems to be aware that the consequences of holding the host liable as a co-perpetrator for anonymous comments might cause an undesired chilling effect, resulting in intermediary service providers disabling most content reported as potentially illegal in order to avoid any liability. The Court referred

---

54 *Mosley v. the United Kingdom*, 10.5.2011, para. 132.
55 *Guja v. Moldova* (see supra note 33), para. 95.
56 *Magyar Tartalomszolgáltatók Egyesülete and Index.hu Zrt v. Hungary*, 2.2.2016, para. 86.

to the MTE case to substantiate the chilling effect of the liability for third party comments on the comment-related environment of an internet portal in the subsequent case of *Pihl v. Sweden* (7.2.2017).[57] However, in the latter case the Court used very careful language by indicating that "had the comment been of a different and more severe nature, the association could have been found responsible for not removing it sooner".[58] Therefore, in what circumstances there is a chilling effect and when are the criteria established in the MTE case and later in *Pihl v. Sweden* applicable, still needs to be clarified by the Court.

The *Delfi* case identified that obligations of intermediaries for third party comments at least in cases of hate speech may require more than they are obliged to do within the traditional "notice and take down" system. However, the Court has recognised a horizontal effect of Article 10 and the positive obligations for Member States to protect the right to freedom of expression.[59] Therefore, another issue yet to be answered by the Court relates to the self-regulation practices by hosts, which have led to excessive removal of content in order to avoid liability, and the obligation of states to establish sufficient guarantees, especially from the due process perspective, to avoid the chilling effect on freedom of expression on the internet.

What is next? What should still be clarified?

The European Court of Human Rights does not take a strict stand on what should be regulated and what is left to self-regulation. However, as was pointed out in the case of *Editorial Board Pravoye Delo and Shtekel v. Ukraine*, there needs to be a sufficient legal framework at the domestic level that would not prevent the public watchdog role. The UN Human Rights Committee has stated that regulatory systems should take into account the differences between the print and broadcast sectors and the internet, while also noting the manner in which various media converge. Also, the UN Committee on the Elimination of Racial Discrimination (CERD) has pointed out that since Article 4 of the CERD is not self-executing, States parties are required by its terms to adopt legislation to combat racist hate speech that falls within its scope.[60] At the same time, the Committee also supports self-regulation by stating that States parties should encourage the public and private media to adopt codes of professional ethics and press codes that incorporate respect for the principles of the Convention and other fundamental human rights standards.[61]

The Court has introduced new tests and has tried to make references to particular aspects of the new media, one of them being its increasing importance. It has provided guidance to the national legislator in order to improve internet

57 *Pihl v Sweden*, 7.2.2017, para. 35.
58 Ibid., para. 36.
59 See for e.g. *Fuentes Bobo v. Spain*, 29.2.2000.
60 See CERD General Comment No. 35, 26.9.2013, para. 13.
61 Ibid., para. 39.

legislation and protect against abuse of power (e.g. *Cengiz and Others v. Turkey*). The same development has been observed by other human rights bodies and the EU.

> The reach of the speech including the nature of the audience and the means of transmission: whether the speech was disseminated through mainstream media or the Internet, and the frequency and extent of the communication, in particular when repetition suggests the existence of a deliberate strategy to engender hostility towards ethnic and racial groups.[62]

The UN treaty body is referring to the dangers of the new media when it comes to the dissemination of hate speech, raising concerns that repetition suggests the existence of a deliberate strategy to engender hostility towards ethnic and racial groups.

It is important to be cautious about new forms of censorship. The Strasbourg Court has decided cases concerning the blocking of certain websites in Turkey.[63] As was discussed recently via the Organization for Security and Co-operation in Europe,

> new forms of censorship do not seek to make undesired content disappear, merely to make it so improbable to find that it will have little or no impact in public debate and policy discussions. This is done mainly by private corporations, according to unclear guidelines and with no due process.[64]

With regard to internet censorship, in his recent report on Turkey the European Human Rights Commissioner, Nils Muisnieks, pointed out a series of censorship instances: increased blocking and filtering of web pages; resorting more to bandwidth throttling during times of domestic crises, making certain social media and platforms inaccessible; and full internet shutdowns that took place. In all, there was an increase in the number of prosecutions and detentions for online activities causing a great chilling effect.[65]

It is important to see that certain issues are essentially the same, despite the new media context. Instead of looking at technical details, new forms of censorship are ultimately serving the same purpose. It is also relevant to remember that media actors are often the same, even if the method of dissemination changes. New media is often part of the bigger media company, which includes print media, broadcasting and online media. The same news story is first published on a

---

62 Ibid., para. 15.
63 See *Ahmet Yildirim v. Turkey* (see supra note 11); *Cengiz and others v. Turkey* (see supra note 28).
64 Wiener Akademikerbund, Identifying and Countering New Forms of Censorship, 11 September 2017, www.osce.org/odihr/339176 (last accessed 13 February 2018).
65 See Memorandum of Nils Muiznieks on freedom of expression and media freedom in Turkey https://wcd.coe.int/com.instranet.InstraServlet?command=com.instranet.CmdBlobGet&InstranetImage=2961658&SecMode=1&DocId=2397056&Usage=2.

website and then in the print media, and print media is also available to read on the internet.[66] There are mixed results of new media and press freedom. First, the news cycle is very short, the print version has often lost its news value and, second, there is a bigger problem with the right to be forgotten (Google Spain case (13.5.2014)[67]). Previous behaviour on the internet can be easily searched and retrieved.

The Court has contributed to the freedom of expression discourse in recent decades in two major fields. One of them has been the protection of sources, which was crucial in the case of *Goodwin v. the United Kingdom* and has since been embedded in case law (e.g. *Guja v. Moldova*). The new focus on the protection of whistleblowers is confirmed even in the UN Special Rapporteur's report.[68] The Court has also introduced a comprehensive test in relation to private life and freedom of expression in the *Axel Springer/Von Hannover II* cases. Could these cases provide some of the answers we are awaiting from the Strasbourg Court in the field of new media?

In the case of *Satakunnan Markkinapörssi and Satamedia* (§ 165), the Court referred to identified criteria that included: contribution to a debate of public interest, the degree of notoriety of the person affected, the subject of the news report, the prior conduct of the person concerned, the content, form and consequences of the publication, and, where it arises, the circumstances in which photographs were taken. When it examines an application lodged under Article 10, the Court will also examine the way in which the information was obtained and its veracity, as well as the gravity of the penalty imposed on the journalists or publishers.

What seems to be rather concerning is how the contribution to a debate of public interest is weighed. In the *Satakunnan Markkinapörssi* case, the Court and domestic courts saw not just political speech, which is based on strict scrutiny. This conclusion was based on factual circumstances: the layout of the publication, its form, content and the extent of the data disclosed. It seems that the Court has introduced principles that are often heavily linked to the particular circumstances of the case. In the recent inadmissibility decision in *Pihl v. Sweden*, it was relevant for the Court's assessment that the comment was posted on a small blog run by a non-profit association.[69]

One of the key findings that has raised concern among scholars is the unpredictability of the consequences of individual judgments when there are numerous existing practices in Member States. There are also some concerns about the incoherent approach between the two European Courts—Luxembourg and

---

66 See e.g. ECtHR case *Fürst-Pfeifer v. Austria*, 17.5.2016, where the article was first published online in "meinbezirk.at" as well as in the print version of *Bezirksblatt*.

67 EUCJ, Case C-131/12 *Google Spain SL, Google Inc. v Agencia Española de Protección de Datos* (es), Mario Costeja González, 13.5.2014.

68 See A/70/361, Report by Special Rapporteur on the promotion and the protection of the right to freedom of opinion and expression, David Kaye, 8.9.2015.

69 *Pihl v. Sweden* (see supra note 56), para. 37.

Strasbourg. For the Strasbourg Court, it comes down to its role of developing general principles for the European human rights system. New media judgments are closely followed by media lawyers, so it is time to introduce an updated version of the Von Hannover principles for the new media context as well. In order to respond to the present interpretative deficit, these principles should contribute to the concepts of media neutrality, online media as a democratic platform, expansion of the definition of journalists, chilling effect and censorship in new media.

Index